Congo Colossus

Congo Colossus
The Life and Legacy of
Franco & OK Jazz

Graeme Ewens

BUKU
PRESS

First published in 1994 by BUKU Press,
4 Aylsham Rd, North Walsham, Norfolk NR28 OBH

British Library Cataloguing in Publication Data. A catalogue record
of this book is available from the British Library.

ISBN 0-9523655-0-2 (hardback)
    0-9523655-1-0 (paperback)

Typeset in London by Henderson Print and Design

Printed and bound by Page Bros, Norwich, England

Contents

Acknowledgements

First thanks must go to the musicians of OK Jazz: in particular Mose Se Fan Fan who has spent much time over a period of ten years in helping this project come to fruition. Great help, encouragement and hospitality have also been provided by Sam Mangwana, Simaro Lutumba, Gege Mangaya and the late Rondot Kasongo wa Kosongo. I would also like to thank the following for their observations and general assistance: Jerry Malekani, Michelino, Ntesa Dalienst, Malage de Lugendo, Papa Noel, Thoms Toroma Sika, the late M'Pongo Love, and two members of Franco's business staff: Malambo Ma Kizola and Nsala Manzenza. The Kinshasa perspective was further defined by meetings with Verckys Kiamuangana and Rubens Kunsita. Atafouka Mbunzi of Voix du Zaïre, Nyoka Longo Mvula, Bob Luzolo Mbemba, Gilbert Benamay, Biolo Binganzenza, Daniel Nkomi N'silu and Jean-Jean opened many doors. In Kinshasa I also met Vincent Kenis whose knowledge and assistance were greatly appreciated. Valuable insights into the pre-history and early years of OK Jazz were provided by Henri Bowane, Bill Alexandre and Manu Dibango.

Encouragement, contacts, information and inspiration have come from Emmanuel Maradas, Nono Atalaku, Carlos and Jason Mbala, Flavien Kasavubu, Barbara Bayramian, Nsimba Foggis, Mick-Djo Lusala, Aimedo Aziza, Charles Easmon, Safro Manzangi Elima, John Collins, Martin Sinnock, Anver Versi, Moussa Awaounda, Mopanzi Sango, Johannes Fabian, Stefan Werdekker, Jumbo Van Renen, Rick Glanvil, Don Bay, Robert Urbanus, Scott, Dominic, Ian, Lois, Dave, Daniel and all at Stern's.

Vital documentary and recorded material was supplied by Flemming Harev, Chris Stapleton, Gary Stewart and Richard Noblett, while Ronnie Graham provided the initial impetus. Prior to publication encouragement was given by Paul Webster, Foreign Editor of The Guardian, Maxwell Nwagboso, acting editor of West Africa, Max Jarrett of BBC World Service, Ian Anderson of Folk Roots, Jo Shinner of GLR and Lucy Duran of SOAS. The comments of Dr Kazadi wa Mukuna were highly valued

The technical assistance of Roger Burnett was crucial. Thanks also to Marika Skipp for the index and Robin Debell for process camera work. Without the stalwart support of M.G. nothing would have been possible. Special thanks to Rajan Hooper, Music Officer of the Arts Council of England whose benevolence helped bring this book to press.

Preface

This work is obviously directed to those with an interest in music or Africa, or both. Most readers will, presumably, have an aural image of OK Jazz to accompany them through the story of Franco, which is as much about Africa as about music. To know something of Franco is to know something about that great continent. He was more than a symbol of Africa. In the opinions of his peers, he was Africa personified.

This does not pretend to be the inside story of Franco, but is rather an outsider's attempt to reach an understanding of an undoubtedly important man through documenting his career and providing an English-language commentary of some of his works. He deserved more than the standard pop music hagiography, and I have tried to do him the justice of setting his story in the context of his society and his time. Franco was a complex personality and only the protruding peaks of his persona were visible.

I was fortunate enough, and honoured, to have met the man on several occasions and to have collaborated on the re-release of some of his old records, which maintained a real, if slender, working relationship. Following the publication in 1986 of a 'work-in-progress', titled *Luambo Franco & 30 Years of OK Jazz*, Franco agreed to cooperate on a full-scale biography. This depended on snatching brief conversations in various European capitals and eventually visiting him in Kinshasa. He was already ailing and the promised access to his archives was never realised. However, through contact with the Grand Maître, as he liked to be addressed, a door was opened on the world of OK Jazz.

Through tracing back Franco's works to their source I entered that fantastic, yet distantly-familiar, state of mind that is called Zaïre, but which used to be known as Congo. The renowned Africanist, historian and author Basil Davidson has said, in relation to the nation-state in Africa, that Zaïre is not so much a mystery as a myth. 'Congo', however, has a clear identity as the name of a people, an ancient kingdom and a region-state. To distinguish it from its neighbour, Congo-Brazzaville, Zaïre was once known as Congo-Kinshasa. It is a land as 'fantastic' to the European imagination as the *Concise Oxford Dictionary*'s definition of that word: 'Extravagently fanciful, capricious, eccentric, grotesque or quaint in design, excellent, extraordinary'.

The country, which really is the heart of Africa, has suffered for years from the doomful title of Joseph Conrad's story, *Heart of Darkness*, that gave the Congo such a fearful image in the minds of 'civilized', white people. To develop Conrad's metaphor, the expressions of European faces and culture are deliniated by shadows, the hidden darker corners which give their lives (and the title of Conrad's book) meaning. In the mirror, the face of Franco and his culture were expressed in highlights — flashes of expressions that are less the symptom of frivolity than a means of continually balancing the affects of sadness, repression or resignation with an insatiable thirst for, and acceptance of, life.

Like Africa, Franco was comfortably large, expansive, generous, contradictory, turbulent, mysterious, prolific and unpredictably spontaneous. Africa is a fascinating, ever-changing, yet never-changing land. Natural and man-made disasters apart, the most commonly-perceived positive image among Westerners is of spectacular landscape and exotic wildlife. But the elegance, the warmth, the creativity and the diversity of the people — and their precarious yet confident hold on life — are even more stimulating. Zaïre is the third largest, and was once the most flamboyant, country in Africa, with a population of 30 million and a capital that has the biggest population of any French-speaking city outside France. It is home to a variety of peoples speaking some 250 languages. There is a rich, vibrant cultural life which connects the modern, urban world with the pre-colonial village society that has remained virtually intact since humans domesticated themselves.

Franco was one of the best-known and most loved figures in post-war African culture — a milieu which is lively, imaginative and adaptable but which is being increasingly marginalised by the new world order, and which is often dismissed by Western commentators as trivial in comparison with the continent's great historic treasures. Part of this attitude is undoubtedly because museum pieces can be catalogued and incorporated into a system of criticism which reflects the preoccupations of Western pundits. By comparison, contemporary Africa has often been ignored. Living artists pose too many problems, while performing 'artistes' and musicians are often overlooked as being unreliable witnesses.

Even the greatest composers of popular music rarely appear in studies of African oral literature, or 'orature', long recognised as being the repository of cultural history throughout the Black Diaspora. In researching this project, I was fortunate to be able to talk directly to people who were there at the time; 'primary sources' of a kind whose recollections have sometimes been questioned by more literary researchers as being subjective and self-interested. But the same criticism could be applied to almost any sources, and among the written material that is available there are many inconsistencies of fact as well as opinion. I recognise the ease with which errors can be introduced or overlooked at every stage of the writing process and accept that I will have unwittingly perpetrated some of my own.

There is fortunately a handful of Congo-Zaïrean writers and academics, listed in the bibliography, who have published serious research and analysis of their region's major form of cultural expression. The publications of Kazadi, Bemba, Lonoh, Tshonga-Onyumbe and Mbamba Toko have been extremely useful in establishing social and musical contexts. One or two interviews by Western writers have been referred to, but the published literature in English is slim. Starting from Franco himself, the sources consulted are almost all Zaïrean or Congolese musicians, who talked freely on the record, and even more so when they knew their words would not be attributed. Observers and collaborators responded openly, and throughout my personal communications, there was a notable reluctance to embellish Franco's reputation or draw conclusions from hearsay evidence. However, the man was a focus for the widespread rumour and gossip of 'radio trottoir', and whatever his constituents believed did have a bearing on how he was perceived.

Franco was not a saint, and there are several negative aspects to his character which go to make up the composite being his friends believed to him to be — "The man with all the characteristics of the human race," as one colleague labelled him. The natural reluctance to speak badly of the dead is often waived, in Franco's case, in favour of telling it like it really was. Franco did not like secrets and he would be the last to thank anyone for papering over the cracks in his character, or smoothing the rough edges of his experience. As he himself put it: "If I see someone with torn trousers, I say they are wearing torn trousers."

Now that Franco is no longer with us, he might be taken more seriously by Western observers. His contribution was at least recognised in 1991 by the authoritative directory *Makers of Modern Africa*. He was one of only two musicians among 680 deceased public figures so honoured by the Nigerian publishers of the book. In the West the work of 'pop' musicians has been analysed and discussed with all the fervour of an investigative science. Countless theses have been presented on the pop icons of the Sixties and Seventies. Yet the role of someone as seemingly important to the Western world as, for example, Bob Dylan — for all his poetry, mysticism, prolixity and enigmatic posturing — had nowhere near the compound effect on his 'own' people. Franco, almost alone amongst African musicians, had a much more widespread and understanding audience. The rhythms, tunes, lyrics and hidden agenda — the meaning of his songs — was in effect known to virtually all his primary audience. And because his music was so familiar and his personality so strong, he could not be assimilated into anybody's system.

Franco was such a prolific composer that he and his OK Jazz averaged nearly two new songs a week for 30 years. Most songs did their job. And that is one of the factors which distinguishes African from Western music: it has a job to do. Franco created an international career, and also a secondary audience that could have kept him in comfortable stardom outside his country, among people who didn't even understand the language he sang in. That in itself was a great achievement for a humble market mammy's son; but Franco's real value came from being taken seriously. That respect was earned at home, where sometimes he was taken more seriously than the country itself. If, as Davidson maintains, Zaïre should be considered to have been a myth, so, perhaps, should its most prominent citizen. But the Franco myth was created around a very real person.

BOOK ONE: The Life

Franco, Luambo Makiadi: Grand Master of Africa's most popular music

Meetings with a Remarkable Man

THE MAJESTIC SOUNDS of OK Jazz first worked their way into my consciousness as late as 1974 when, travelling on a freighter down the west coast of Africa, the radio picked up a full spectrum of African pop. There were many features which made the different African musics stand out from the strongest Black American or Jamaican dance staples of the time, but the somewhat Latin-sounding 'Congolese' style, seemingly beamed out from every transmitter along the coast, was the obvious favourite. OK Jazz in particular — with waves of insistent, fluid rhythms, golden-toned fanfares, huge walls of vocal harmony and interacting guitars as bright as bells and sharp as needles — combined to weave a web of enchantment. This was popular, urban dance music, for sure. It was monolithic, in a grand, rather than primitive, sense; compared with the craggy, brutal constructions of rock music, the OK Jazz sound was like magnificent, palatial architecture. And behind that grandiose, ornate formality undoubtedly lay a level of content and consciousness far removed from the impoverished Western listener's experience.

Nineteen seventy four was a big year for Zaïre. It was almost like a launch party for the newly-named republic which used to be known as Belgian Congo. The country wrote its way into sporting history as winners of the African Nations football cup and participants in the World Cup, but it was the astonishing 'Rumble in the Jungle' heavyweight championship fight between Muhammad Ali and George Foreman which proved to be Zaïre's best public relations coup. The world's press descended on Kinshasa in their thousands to be met by a people revelling in a most flamboyant culture and a city that seemed almost permanently 'en fête'. Music was everywhere and, although there was a contingent of Black American musicians in town, the *ngandas,* dancing bars and clubs of Kinshasa swayed through till dawn on a steady wave of home-grown rumba.

It was the period of 'Authenticity'. President Mobutu Sese Seko had visited Mao Tse Tung in China in 1972, returning with a vision of starting his own cultural revolution to help establish a strong national identity. Franco and his Tout Puissant OK Jazz had played a big part in bringing Mobutu's message to the hundreds of disparate ethnic groups, and he was at a high point of his career. The songs pumping out over Africa and the Atlantic Ocean were some of the best in the orchestra's long, productive history. Both in and outside Zaïre, millions of Africans knew and loved Franco's music, but in 1974 OK Jazz had never played a concert outside the continent, although they had often recorded in Europe.

Paris, April 1983. By the early 1980s, thanks to several of his own business initiatives, Franco's records had become readily available in Europe, particularly in the francophone capitals of Paris, Brussels and Geneva where, by now, OK Jazz had made a few spectacular appearances. In 1983 Franco was planning to break through the anglo/francophone barrier with a tour of the USA. He was pleased to give his first interview to an English-language magazine — via an interpreter.

His reputation had gone before him. Those who knew the man obviously held him in awe, not just for the dominating force of his orchestra, or for his masterful guitar technique, but also for his acerbic tongue, the legendary control he had of the Zaïrean music business and, by extension, the power he could exercise over people. Contemporary photos showed he had the massive physique to match that reputation. He also had a formidable title, Grand Maître (Grand Master). But add

Franco in Paris: he gave a dazzling display of guitar virtuosity

the sweetness and vitality of his music, and the terrifying spectre became transformed into a big ball of fun. The rave album of 1982, *Coopération* with Sam Mangwana, had featured a wonderful cover photograph with the big man looking like a benign bear blowing a kiss and hugging his one-time protégé.

The interview had been set up by the Zaïrean guitarist Jerry Malekani, a long-time accompanist of Manu Dibango, who had joined Franco for a recent show in Paris. Also playing guitar had been Michelino (Mavatiku Visi), whose Parisian apartment was to be the meeting place. A TV set and an acoustic guitar were the only visible accoutrements. It was a hot spring day and the shaded, minimal apartment had an atmosphere reminiscent of an African hotel room. Franco arrived late, as befits a legend, and filled the room with his voluminous wax-print boubou, big brusque voice and keenly probing eyes set in an almost cherubic, and very chubby, face. He was in magnanimous mood.

A recently released collaboration with his long-time rival Tabu Ley Rochereau, titled *Choc Choc Choc*, was as much a creative achievement as a commercial or public relations success. In addition to the Mangwana disc, there was also *Missile*, the dance-favourite, double album with Josky, and a solo project for Michelino. By the end of the year there would be eleven new OK Jazz albums on the market. And most were instant classics. The purpose of the meeting was to get a first sight and understanding of the man whose name had become synonymous with one of the world's greatest musics. As there was no reason to ask provocative questions about his supposed exile from Zaïre, his much rumoured involvement with sorcery or the iron hand with which he was said to rule the band, Franco was polite and accommodating. He was also fascinated by the possibility of playing in London.

With the linguistic assistance of his business manager, Malambo Ma Kizola, Franco filled in his biographical details and gave a short history of OK Jazz and the development of Congo-Zaïrean music. He was expressive of hand and face, showing concern, wit and a few belly laughs as he ran through the story. But it was scarcely two months since the death of Kabasele, the Grand Kalle, whose African Jazz were the original pioneers of Congolese music, and Franco was anxious to give his mentor all due credit. He explained that Kalle was the father of Congo-Zaïrean music and that he himself came 'after', not just chronologically, he implied, but in importance. Franco could never be accused of false modesty.

Following an entertaining and educational interview, the Grand Master posed for some photos. The acoustic guitar looked like an obvious prop, yet no sooner had he gripped it than his big fingers were rippling over the strings in a dazzling show of virtuosity. Using thumb and forefinger he made the instrument sound like a 12-string. Those few minutes gave an insight into the wealth of technique and cultural background which is literally at his fingertips. The audience of one stood transfixed, and the seed of an obsession which was planted out on the ocean in 1974 began to sprout.

London, April 1984. On the rebound from their debut American tour, Franco and OK Jazz finally made it to Britain, but not without an expensive false start and a nerve-wracking haul through the immigration gauntlet. This time, in an hotel and ambience which were depressingly British, a privileged group of journalists waited for an audience with the Master, who held court on a rumpled single bed, spicing his replies with guffaws of laughter, hand slaps and asides in Lingala. Throughout the day he had been carrying around an A4 pad of notepaper, on which he would frequently make notes: "Composing a song," he had confided. Following the informal press conference, he produced and signed gift copies of the Josky CHOC album, before giving his characteristic observation on the British capital. It had been pleasing enough but being a Sunday afternoon he'd had trouble finding a restaurant open. When he did find a cafe, and his meal was delivered he could not believe the size of it and waited for more food to be served before realising he'd have to order another complete meal, just to stave off hunger. "Don't these people eat?" wondered the big man, who was carrying about 130 kilos (290 pounds) at the time.

The poster read, 'The Greatest African. . .' something or other. The one word which stood out from the list of names beneath was 'Franco'. The godfather of Zaïrumba was making his first visit to London for an independent promotion at London's Hammersmith Palais. As expected, Franco's band, the legendary TP OK Jazz, proved to be a tightly orchestrated and superbly disciplined big band. They took the stage in matching white band jackets, dancing up the front line like a soul revue. While the music was strictly Lingala rumba, the presentation seemed to owe a lot to James Brown — it was heavy riffing dance music which never faltered as it built up excitement on the dance floor. Those familiar with any OK Jazz music over the last twenty years would have found what they wanted in the two-and-a-half hour show. Apart from a late start and a 2am curfew it could not be faulted.

When the Grand Master appeared at the side of the stage wearing a suit jacket with his guitar clasped to his considerable stomach, it was like a visitation for many in the audience. The man had a commanding presence over band and audience. And there he was in person injecting those familiar clipped guitar licks into the swaying rumba riffs, and singing with oratorial elegance in the gruff, conversational tones which imply personal experience behind every song, whether singing about love, tragedy, personal anecdote, public morality or even commercial promotion. An overwhelming wave of swing engulfed the crowd as the rumba whirled into the up-tempo *sebene* section, where the band run away with Zaïrean rhythms like the *odemba* or *cavacha*, validating Franco's claim to make music for all generations. The most insistent rhythms from bass and drums underpinned the multi-layered interwoven guitar sounds, punctuated by the highly-charged horn section. There was solo improvisation within the relentless rolling arrangements; there was some intensely rich vocal harmonising; there were three energetic dancing girls who flashed off stage as fast as they appeared; and over everything there was Franco's presence — at once distant yet compassionate, severe at times but ultimately honest. It was plain to see why the man was a legend. And the name is no overstatement either — the TP in TP OK Jazz means Tout Puissant (Almighty). And every aspect of the content and presentation was underlined by the power, of the band certainly, but especially the power of Franco.

Three months later in midsummer in Paris, the Cirque

d'Hiver was due to host a Grand Ball with Franco et Le
Tout Puissant OK Jazz, Champions d'Afrique. It was
scheduled to start at 10pm on a Friday night, but by
midnight the ornate, circular circus hall was still empty.
Musicians gradually began arriving and plugging in their
instruments. By 1am there was the beginning of an
audience and OK Jazz were running through their rumba
warm-up. In the dressing room, Franco sat with his back
to the doorway, watching over his shoulder through a tall
mirror. The room had the high smell of the African bush;
a caged tunnel along one wall was the run-in for the
circus's performing lions. Franco was lightly applying eau
de toilette and beaming at the string of well-wishers. In
the middle of an anecdote about his recent Ugandan tour,
Franco broke off to call one musician. With hand gesture
to match he hummed the first few notes of the classic
Cuban rumba, *El Manicero* (The Peanut Vendor). The
musician left and moments later OK Jazz segued out of
the song they were playing into *El Manicero*. Franco was
ready. The hall was full; the show was about to start.

Brussels, January 1987. Franco was back in Europe
and had been tracked down to his Belgian headquarters.
Each year he had been billed to appear in Britain but one
thing or another had got in the way. Now there was
business to be done and a rendezvous was arranged at the
African Sun Music office near the Belgian royal palace. A
newly published booklet on 30 Years of OK Jazz (a work in
progress) was to be shown for his approval, and there was
the re-release of some old OK Jazz 78s to discuss.
Manzenza, Franco's right-hand man, came round to the
hotel as an escort. The ASM offices were spacious, and
completely empty, except for a hi-fi system and expansive
wooden desks, also empty. There was no phone and no
telex. The numbers on the letterheaded stationery had
long been disconnected.
The Grand Maître arrived in a fashionably cut trench-

coat, carrying a broom, new, with the clean bristles held up in front of him. (A rare cultural report from Zaïre on BBC World Service had recently looked at a traditional rural culture where brooms were carried as symbols of authority: probably just coincidence.) He was pleased to be greeted in a few faltering words of Lingala, and when it came to the business he studied the proposals keenly but not too strenuously. A deal was amicably agreed. Franco signed a copy of the booklet, and the contract. About three months later he sent a formal, signed and rubber-stamped letter announcing the release of his latest disc, *Attention na Sida* (Beware of Aids). On Good Friday OK Jazz played an all-night dance for the Zaïrean community in Brussels. Simaro, Josky, Madilu and all the band were there. The new song they were launching was Josky's *Mata Kita Bloqué*. A bulky Franco looked as if he was carrying top weight, accentuated by the loud checked suit he was wearing, but he had plenty of bounce.

Kinshasa, July 1988. The dry season in Zaïre falls right on cue for the college and school holidays, and for the European summer. The temperature is mild, the streets dusty but dry, and the bars and clubs do the best business of the year, although Franco's club, the Un-Deux-Trois, had been quiet for some time. The once impressive three-storey building, on the first corner of the Avenue Gambela, was half gutted and, even when the musicians gathered there to receive their salaries, it had the feeling of a haunted house. OK Jazz were playing weekends at Le Faubourg, an attractive, tree-studded, open-air club in a middle-class area close to Matonge. Franco had been performing up till the end of June, mostly cameo guitar solos but not much singing. By the week of his 50th birthday in early July he was resting at his mansion in Limete. The word was the big man was sick, and he had certainly lost kilos in the space of a year.

The OK Jazz vice-president Simaro Lutumba's new,

Relaxing at home in the chalet-style mansion in Limete, Kinshasa

black, top-of-the-range BMW dropped the visitor off outside the Franco mansion on 12th Street, just off the Boulevard Lumumba. A large tree provides shade for those waiting outside the Grand Maître's electrically-operated garage gates. The three-storey, chalet-style mansion is crammed, with its maze of extensions, into a high-walled compound, outside which is a strip of pavement going nowhere but illuminated with European-style street lights. At the far end stood the OK Jazz equipment truck.

The sentinel showed the visitor up some breeze block steps to a long office with a boardroom table, French repro antique chairs and a portrait of President Mobutu at the far end. After talking into his 'Motorola' two-way radio he led the way back down into the residential section of the built-up compound, into an area like an outdoor sitting room with a set of swinging sun loungers and two large tables permanently laid out for dinner with a full set of gilt-trimmed glasses, cutlery and crockery. Two trees grew up through the tiled floor and out through the corrugated roof. There were miniature street lamps and a large TV set in the corner. Around the uncovered area another five or six sun loungers waited like armchairs for a party of giants. Faces of the staff flickered past the decorative gaps in the breeze block walls. Then a phone rang somewhere and one of the many retainers led the way into the salon. It looked like the high kitsch section of a big money department store, fairly standard for a major celebrity anywhere from Dallas to Manila. Acres of gilt 'Louis XIV'-type furniture, upholstered in a rich red.

Franco sat on one such gold-trimmed couch, wearing a dressing gown and watching a giant TV. He motioned toward the empty seat beside him. He had lost a lot of weight and explained that he was sick, and under doctor's orders to reduce his prodigious bulk. He talked about possible heart problems, kidney failure and diabetes, but his condition was proving hard to diagnose. He seemed to be in good enough humour, but his expression and bonhomie were subdued. The booming laugh was muted and the hand gestures strangely inhibited. He was pleasantly surprised to receive a pile of press cuttings from around the world — Europe, America, Asia as well as Africa. He put on his spectacles to study one photo showing him at his top weight of 140 kilos, and asked wistfully when that was taken. Small talk and business chatter took up most of the meeting, but he was keen to learn the visitor's response to Matonge, the music quarter of Kinshasa, which had been his constituency for more than 30 years. Franco compared it favourably with Harlem or parts of Paris, but he acknowledged its unique ambience and the freedom from many of the dangers found in Western fun spots. Because of his health, he would not be playing again for a while, he said, but OK Jazz would always be there. It was a moving experience to see Franco so subdued. Although slimmer, he still looked reasonably

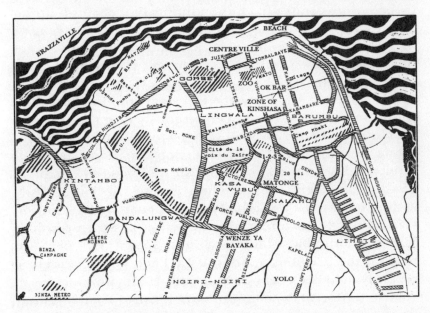

Plan of Kinshasa showing Matonge, which is usually not marked on maps

fit, but the great man's personal aura appeared to be fading the same way as his flesh. It would not have been appropriate to photograph him in that condition. We shook hands and parted company.

Kinshasa, October 7, 1989. One of the last passengers to board the Air Zaïre flight from Kinshasa's Ndjili airport bound for Paris was Sam Mangwana, the 'Pigeon Voyager', and erstwhile vocalist with both OK Jazz and Zaïre's other great cultural institution, Afrisa. Mangwana is one of Zaïre's brightest musical exports and was returning from a rare visit to his homeland. Somewhere over the Sahara in the middle of the night his attention was drawn to the listings column of an outdated English newspaper which had been left on the plane. Franco and OK Jazz were supposed to have played in London the previous week. Mangwana smiled. His current record releases were two albums jointly credited to himself and Franco. For the last three months songs from the albums had been pumping out of Voix du Zaïre radio and from the countless *ngandas*, or open-air terrace bars, of Kinshasa like aural street furniture. Franco was back on form, with Sam. Things couldn't be too bad.

Only those who knew the full story could tell how bad things were. Franco had been seriously ill for well over a year and was known to be in Europe for medical attention. While he was away OK Jazz's problems had been well publicised, with the Zaïrean music tabloids full of stories of dissension and further ruptures to the band. Only within the past few weeks had that great national institution started up again under the direction of vice-president Simaro Lutumba. Mangwana had seen them perform himself the previous Sunday at Le Faubourg. Even more recently he'd been reminiscing with Henri Bowane, a still robust figure of a man who was Franco's early guitar master and his first and only professional boss. There hadn't been any news of the Grand Maître for a while.

The Air Zaïre flight landed in Europe on Sunday, October 8. Back in London the first news was that Franco had not, in fact, appeared the previous week. The OK Jazz 'away' team, led by Dizzy Mandjeku, had turned up and were well into their stride when it was announced that the Grand Maître would not be playing. The power was cut, the band scattered and hundreds tried to claim refunds on their tickets.

Even worse, Franco had been in town a few weeks before the show to give press interviews and convince the punters that he would perform this time, following a disastrous no-show the previous March. The British press met a frail man, formally dressed but unable to rise from his bed to be photographed, and seemingly creased with bitterness towards the Western music 'establishment', which he believed had never acknowledged his own, or even Africa's, continuing contribution. How mistaken he was. Of course, he had countless unequivocal admirers outside Africa.

Friday, October 13. BBC2 television had scheduled an episode of their series *Under African Skies*, about the music of Kinshasa, which would show Franco in his prime and then, sadly, in those last weeks of his life. Early that same morning, BBC World Service radio news announced that Franco Luambo Makiadi had died the previous day, on October 12, in a Belgian hospital.

The news of Franco's death came as a hard blow. To the people of Zaïre it was a national tragedy; the main pillar of their country's culture had crumbled, leaving a huge void. He had provided virtually the only line of continuity and consolation through three of the most turbulent decades any country has had to endure. Although his death was not a surprise, it took some adjustment to realise that the Grand Maître was indeed a mortal human being. It seemed to many people as if he had transcended that state some time ago, but if creative output can bestow immortality, Luambo Makiadi will certainly live forever.

The big man turning in a power performance in Belgium in 1987

CHAPTER ONE

The Luambo Legend

"Franco was unique. Like Shakespeare or Mozart, combined with Pele or Muhammad Ali. He was irreplaceable. The sort of man who appears once every 100 years. He left his mark on his own time."

Sam Mangwana

FRANCO, WHOSE FULL NAME was L'Okanga La Ndju Pene Luambo Makiadi, was one of those rare characters who could be fairly described as larger than life, whichever way his career is assessed. For over 30 years the man stood like a Colossus over Africa. He loomed particularly large over the francophone music scene, which he dominated so much it might have been named after him, but he also had huge followings in other parts of the continent where he helped to make Congo-Zaïrean music the ubiquitous sound of Africa. When, in the 1980s, the music of his continent began to break down European misconceptions Franco was quickly recognised in the West as the prime mover. At home he had been a star before independence, before even the first generation of Congolese politicians had the vote, and he survived most of them. He outlived all the practising artistes of the 1950s, with whom he forged the beginnings of Congo-Zaïrean music, and outshone them at their own trade as well. But he gave the people of Africa more than music. He gave them a legendary hero of mythical status, whose reputation was often distorted, though never diminished, by controversy and rumour.

Ultimately it was his music which spoke for him, and through which he is immortalised, but the music was a direct expression of Franco himself. Outwardly he was a cheerful, confident character, as comfortable sitting with presidents as with the 'ordinary' people of Kinshasa who comprised his primary audience. His charisma and bonhomie could transcend cultural barriers, but he was also sensitive enough to recognise suffering, and hard enough to overcome sentimentality. He was an uncompromising character who grew used to having things his own way and he was not ashamed to flaunt his power. From a penniless, half-educated street kid, he achieved considerable power and wealth, but he was not an empire builder. Although he inevitably moved with politicians and businessmen, he ironically and regularly referred to himself as a 'bandit' or street urchin.

In a posthumous tribute, the Zaïrean ambassador to Washington, Tatanene Manatane, described him as a "prototype of the self-made man". He disregarded rules and broke taboos, and the sheer volume of Franco's contribution to Zaïrean culture even won over the Catholic church, which recognised and ultimately appeared to condone his "mission to disrupt, provoke and tell the truth". A man of contradictions, Franco epitomised a new breed of African hero who found his own way, and succeeded, in the complex modern world without losing contact with his African identity. He was a role model for millions.

Franco was above all an artist. As a composer, guitarist and vocalist he was sensitive, observant, and compassionate. He was also a great entertainer, a passionate performing artiste who loved to excite a crowd, and who was never happier than when making people dance. Throughout Africa the crowds reciprocated, and wherever he went there were lines of people struggling just to touch his hand, in some cases even dying in the crush to get close to their hero. The awe with which his public perceived Franco affected even the more cynical commentators. One East African political journalist, waiting to interview him for the first time in London, claimed to have been more nervous meeting Franco than having an audience with a president. When his photograph was taken with the Grand Master, the journalist claimed his people back home would never believe it was genuine.

To understand the man behind the myth, some of the statistics about Franco help to put the Grand Master in context. Although he was not tall, Franco looked like a giant, weighing some 140 kilos (300 lb) at his peak. His career spanned 40 years, although he was only 51 when he died, during which time he claimed to have released well over 150 albums and to have composed some 1,000 titles, recorded on equipment which spanned the technological gulf between fragile, pre-electric 78rpm records and digitally recorded compact discs. His band, TP OK Jazz, generally included more than 40 musicians and, at the time of his death, it was calculated that over 100 families were directly dependent on Franco. He had at least eighteen children. To complete the picture of a 'typiquement' African character, he loved football, and stayed loyal to his favourite Vita Club from when he was a small child to becoming their president and donor of several trophies, and inspiring them to their first Zaïrean cup victory in 1972. He was a confirmed Roman Catholic, who later converted to Islam, but reconverted and was buried as a Catholic.

He had many names, being christened François Luambo Makiadi, later indigenised to L'Okanga La Ndju Pene Luambo Makiadi, and again Islamicised as Aboubakar Sidiki. His nicknames, sobriquets and titles included: Le Fou (the Crazy Kid), Franco de Mi Amor (Franco My Love), the Sorcerer of the Guitar, Officer of the National Order of the Leopard, Grand Maître of Zaïrean Music, the Balzac of African Music. His musical associates called him Grand Maître or Yorgho (Godfather). He called them Le Tout Puissant ('The Almighty') OK Jazz.

His appeal was pan-African. With OK Jazz, Franco played in some twenty African states including: Angola, Benin, Cameroon, CAR, Chad, Congo, Côte d'Ivoire,

Gabon, Gambia, Ghana, Guinea, Kenya, Nigeria, Rwanda, Senegal, Sudan, Tanzania, Togo, Uganda and Zambia as well as Zaïre — while the records were danced to, and the name recognised, in over a score of other countries. The band also performed in Paris, Brussels, London, Geneva, Amsterdam, New York and Washington DC.

Among the rumours and gossip which inevitably arose around such a fascinating character were the obvious day-to-day accusations which would be aimed at almost any public figure in Africa: Franco was one of the richest men in Africa (no). He ruled the band with an iron hand (yes). He was cruel and heartless (no). He underpaid his musicians (sometimes). He tried to block the careers of his rivals (often). He was President Mobutu's right-hand man and/or his most feared critic (both). He was a prodigious womaniser (yes). He trafficked in marijuana (denied). He was a sorcerer who used sorcery to eliminate his rivals (doubtful). He died of Aids (possible).

A man of substance

So how did the big man measure up to his image? Physically he worked hard at becoming a big man. He once said the size of his stomach reflected well-being and contentment, rather than symbolising power. He obviously enjoyed eating, although his diet sometimes appeared like force feeding. According to one of his musicians Franco could eat 25 *kwanga* (slabs of cassava dough) at a sitting, with a whole chicken for himself, plus sausages, *kamundele* (kebabs) and *pondu* (green vegetable). These feasts, which often took place with his equally voracious friend, Madiata, (a conservatory trained opera singer as bulky as Franco but much taller) were, no doubt, expressions of 'well-being and contentment' but there were also less attractive episodes when power was certainly on the menu, such as the time he attempted to eat a whole goat while his hungry musicians watched enviously.

A more predictable indicator of power is wealth.

Franco undoubtedly became a rich man by normal standards, but nowhere near the multi-millionaire class of Western pop stars, African politicians or businessmen. Seen in the context of the ownership of wealth in Zaïre, Franco was not in the major league. As a citizen of a country whose leader, President Mobutu Sese Seko, was in the mid-1980s rated as the fourth richest person in the world, Franco knew the difference. "A truly rich person is one who does not work, assured of lasting the rest of his life with the fortune he has", he told *Zaïre Digest* in 1987. "Now with me, the fans have seen me perform with my guitar for many years. One can say that money is indispensible to making a decent life, paying one's staff, bringing up a family, organising for the future. That is just as true for an artist as the rest of the world." He also said, on another occasion, that he needed to play not only for personal satisfaction but also to feed and educate his eighteen children. Franco obviously had business interests, although most were directly related to his musical commitments, such as record labels and a nightclub. There were also interests in hotel and plantation projects, including a cattle ranch at Mont Ngafula just outside the Zaïrean capital, and he owned several properties for rent and for family homes in Kinshasa, Brussels and Paris. He could accumulate wealth, usually in cash or kind, directly from his music, but he was not a ruthless capitalist. In business he was firm, but reasonable, and usually very straight. After discussions a price would be agreed, handshake, finish. Once the deal had been done both parties were expected to stand by it.

Since his country's independence, Franco had been in personal control of his own recording, publishing and record pressing, and he followed every franc and zaïre carefully. He later took over the distribution of his own products — a necessary expedient in such a wide open business where a popular album could sell well over 100,000 copies. As with many African musicians, Franco had seen too much disappear. Because of the rampant piracy in some parts of Africa and the West, Franco preferred a policy of frequent releases, so he was always one jump ahead of the bootleggers. Franco did not trust promoters too well, either. Travelling with over 40 musicians is very costly and all expenses had to be paid up front, as did his fee. Again this was not greed, but expediency. In 1984 he toured Uganda, where OK Jazz played for several weeks. The band was escorted everywhere by armed soldiers (for their own protection) which Franco said made him feel uneasy. His fears were realised when, at the end of the tour, the soldiers escorted them straight to the airport, leaving Franco with empty pockets. He had been 'protected' from collecting his fee.

A good measure of Franco's power is the loyalty he inspired in both his musicians and his public. "None of the musicians is tied to OK Jazz by contract", he said in 1987. "Each is free to stay, to leave or to return. The organisation in OK Jazz is flexible on this point. When someone looks to poach my musicians I find that normal. Only they know that, for my part, I will be able to pay them. Keeping a wife is not a trivial business. If you think of seducing your neighbour's wife you will not be safe from a reversal of fate. Everything is paid back."

This flexible, extended family policy of OK Jazz is confirmed by the small number of musicians to have left OK Jazz permanently. Once a member, always a member. For example, the singer Wuta Mayi, who went solo in the early 1980s, was interviewed on Zaïrean radio in 1989; although it was eight years since he last worked with the band, he said he had never left them. This was born out by his fellow vocalist Ntesa Dalienst, who also quit in 1984 after some six years, yet would return for several recording projects and, towards the end of Franco's days, for live performances. "OK Jazz, was at that time, an enterprise where the door was always open," remembered Dalienst. "You could leave and return when you wanted. That's why

Franco used to call it Onatra [after the Zaïrean river ferry company]. As Franco used to say, all the musicians in OK Jazz had eternal membership." Franco did, occasionally, reverse this policy and declare the door was closed but, for those who could express their genuine desire to return, he usually relented.

Franco's loyalty to his musicians was as strong as he expected theirs to be. "He was not hard to work with, if you understood him," recalled the saxophonist Rondot, who played with Franco for twenty years and became his personal aide, "but musicians who made problems would find it hard. If you needed some help with money or family problems and you asked him politely, he would listen. But if you approached him aggressively he would be hard. If you understood him things worked out fine." He often took personal charge of bad debts and collective responsibility for musicians' misdemeanours. Once, on the band's return from Brazzaville in 1966, a musician was arrested for carrying a stolen amplifier; as president of the band, Franco stood by his man and spent some time in the cells with the other musicians while the problem was sorted out.

Since the founding of OK Jazz in Belgian colonial times there had been a formal constitution for the band, which was re-verified under the subsequent admini- strations, later becoming a limited company. Power, and finances, were supposedly shared on an equitable basis with a sliding scale of percentage payments from the band leader (or president) down. Only when times were good did band members receive salaries. In effect, Franco kept tight control over the finances, but power was always an issue for debate. According to the rules of the band the president's decisions could be challenged by any member, in which case a meeting would be called to discuss the matter. Franco's decisions to suspend or sack musicians were debated passionately and often overturned. Arriving late for a show was, however, inexcusable. Disciplinary hearings often led to violent arguments, but money problems caused the most frequent rows. In the Sixties and Seventies there was no shortage of argumentative musicians ready to stand up to Franco. During one such dispute the boss was called a 'carnivore' by one of the protagonists. It was a word Franco did not know. He called for a dictionary and, on finding the definition, his ebony complexion reportedly turned red, then blue, then green with anger.

In creative matters, Franco did eventually come to exercise ultimate control over his musicians, although he gave them plenty of opportunity to show their talents, within the framework of OK Jazz. Sam Mangwana, who spent three important years with OK Jazz, and even as a solo artiste retained close contact with Franco, explained the working method. "There was no arranger in OK Jazz. If you compose a certain thing, and as everybody has a certain sensibility, you have to reach agreement together. If you are not in agreement, it is the chef d'orchèstre who decides, who will say 'look this thing is good but the other does not fit the style of OK Jazz. We think you should try this or that'. It is the chef d'orchèstre who has the last word. When you had something technical to sort out, there was a committee. You had Simaro, Brazzos and the other elders who would discuss and make suggestions. Really, OK Jazz was the most democratic of orchestras, where you could speak as you felt. You had no inhibitions." Mangwana, and countless other musicians, doubtless found great job satisfaction with OK Jazz, but the democracy he goes on to describe sounds more like a form of benign paternalism. "Franco himself left the decisions to us and once we had decided we would give him the cassette and he would listen to it in his car and he would tell you the next day what his decision was. He made the final decision. We would give him the best songs and he would pick, 'that, that and that'. But he would give the chance to everybody.

Supervising an OK Jazz rehearsal: 'Franco respected people with talent'

OK Jazz had a very good atmosphere, the feeling in the band was very good."

During the heyday of OK Jazz, when the band were not touring, they expected to play every day. Fridays and Saturdays, and eventually Sundays, were reserved for the residency at their current 'siege' or base, while any musicians were free to make bookings for the band on the weekdays. The climate in Kinshasa, however, is dominated for much of the year by heavy rainfall and, as most of the dancefloors are in the open air, the programme was prone to change. As a general rule, if it had rained during the day and stopped by evening, the show would go on. If it was raining heavily at dusk when people were making their way home from work, the rain would be set for the night and there would probably be no performance. During the late 1960s, shows were nominally scheduled to finish by midnight, although they gradually became later and would sometimes last until dawn. Franco himself could be guaranteed to play for at least an hour and a half. Even if the audience was small, he would deliver, unlike other band leaders who would just leave their musicians to get on with it. If he was particularly well charged he could dominate the stage all night.

Once he had become a superstar, Franco's methods of recruiting musicians were sometimes unconventional. If he was interested in a new musician he would usually send his bodyguard, Jean-Jean, to bring him to his house. At other times he would send a woman. The young aspiring musician would be invited by one of the women members of the OK Jazz fan club to enjoy a meal and a drink. The candidate's whole demeanour would thus be discreetly checked out and the results passed on to Franco. If the musician was called to join the band he would probably never see the woman again.

Singers could afford to be more independent in their careers than the instrumentalists. In common with practice throughout Africa, all instruments and equipment were, and still are, owned by the band. If a musician decided to quit he would leave his instrument behind for the replacement. They could only afford to move to a guaranteed place in another band and most preferred to remain with OK Jazz, even if it meant waiting all night like a football substitute to be called to play accompaniment on only one song. Another common practice has been that payment for live work be split, with 50 per cent going to the leader and the remainder divided up on merit, from the chef d'orchèstre and soloists down to the apprentice band boys. Musicians fortunate enough to have their compositions recorded would often receive a cash payment, or if shown real favour, a substantial gift such as a car. When the Soneca copyright agency was set up in 1969, Franco invited all the musicians to contribute songs, and even accepted one from the road manager, Petit Jean, appropriately titled *Naboyi Publicité* (I Scorn Publicity).

Sometimes the arbitrary system of paying royalties did not satisfy the recipients. For instance, during the 1970s, the guitarist Fan Fan was given a new Triumph 2000 car in lieu of royalties. On this occasion he had no quarrel with Franco but, believing his work had been undervalued, he took his protest to the Soneca office where he threatened to douse the car with petrol and set fire to it. Another member of OK Jazz was once given a new car by Franco. Sitting in traffic the musician was hailed by a well-known dignatory. "How do you like the cars?" he asked. "What cars? This one is great." — "Oh, you only got one, but I gave Franco two cars to give to you." Such is one face of the endemic corruption in Zaïre which has been well documented over the years. Values have at times become so distorted that, on one occasion, all the OK Jazz musicians were given new cars, when their band salaries were not enough to buy petrol or food for their families. Against this background Franco's erratic patronage alternating with apparent cruelty does not appear so strange. He was, after all, only playing the system, which was being invented and circumvented daily.

By the timing of his birth, Franco's career was fated to run parallel with the country's liberation from colonial oppression and the struggle to build a new nation. He reached the age of majority the year before Congo achieved independence, by which time he was already an acknowledged star, and his unofficial co-option into the new 'establishment' was inevitable. Growing up during the last years of Belgian rule, Franco had been seen by the authorities as a delinquent and a rebel. He ran foul of the colonial censors in 1957, when they banned a song which he composed in jail while serving time for a motoring offence. From 1945 to 1960, Lonoh Bokelenge has observed, "Music took an active, though clandestine part in the struggle for independence, the common struggle which engaged all oppressed people." Franco was one of the few musicans to maintain the criticism after independence, and under President Mobutu's autocratic rule he continued to suffer from censorship, and was detained at least twice for singing out of turn.

Although claiming to have always remained apolitical, Franco was often closely associated with President Mobutu, who took control of the country in 1965. In fact, if Franco had any political leaning it was probably towards Joseph Kasavubu, the federalist spokesman of the Bakongo people who was independent Congo's first president, until Mobutu replaced him. But the President is the President, and it was inevitable that Franco would be called to play at his command. As one Zaïrean musician from a younger generation explained, "A musician is like a wife to the President. If the President goes, the new President would 'inherit' the widow" (as happens in many African societies). Most of the public realise the musician has little choice in the matter.

OK Jazz was never a state band in the manner of Bembeya Jazz from Guinea, but Zaïrean musicians travel on service passports and when the party calls, they play.

This is common in many one-party states in Africa. The state is not only the best client but also one which it would be foolish to antagonise. On at least one occasion Franco preferred not to answer the call and was briefly locked up for his impertinence. At other times he incurred the collective wrath of the state by recording songs with pointed moral criticisms of the regime and its administrators. He was balanced delicately on a political tightrope and occasionally fell on the wrong side. More than once he opted for voluntary exile.

Franco was a turbulent character, described by an ex-colleague as "sometimes good/bad, sometimes bad/good". Despite being a pillar of society he was never wholly 'respectable'. In 1976 he was made an Officer of the country's highest honour, the National Order of the Leopard; two years later he had to return the medal when he received his longest prison sentence, for singing songs considered so obscene they can still shock his friends as well as the moral majority. But while Franco was always his own man, he was inseparable from the birth of the new Zaïre and, in a country where the Presidential slogan was for many years 'One Father, One Mother, One People, One Party, One Chief', Franco maintained the thread with 'One Music'.

Another of the apocryphal windows on Franco's character set him in the frame as a 'drug trafficker'. The rumours putting the secret of his financial success down to exporting local marijuana, *nzumbel* or *diamba*, to Europe, proved so fascinating a provocation he responded in song, flatly denying the accusation in *Kinshasa Mboka Ya Makambo* (Kinshasa Town of Problems) performed live on Voice of Zaïre television in 1982; and he denied it again a few years later on French radio.

In 1986, during a local Paris radio transmission hosted by Tonton Ngoy, Franco took phone-in calls from listeners. Early on in the show, he was asked straight out by a listener if the rumours were true that he was a 'drug trafficker'. Franco replied that the person was ill-informed. Further into the programme, after more music and discussion about it, another listener prodded the Grand Maître once again: "Why did you avoid the subject of drugs?" — "It is not the object of my visit to this music programme, but what do you want to know?" — "Franco you are African, don't you know that on your continent grass is good to smoke? Do you take drugs or any other intoxicants?" Franco laughed, "Yes, I drink alcohol, that is a drug. In fact, I prefer pastis." Tonton Ngoy used that anecdote to good effect in an article marking 30 years of OK Jazz, in the francophone magazine *Afrique Elite*.

In common with his peers, Franco smoked the herb as a young man and, although he preferred not to let the senior musicians see, in later life he was known to like a taste before going on stage. There was no evidence to implicate him in smuggling, but suspicions were aroused and the rumour stuck; it could never be proved or disproved. However, the accumulation of malicious gossip directed against Franco never plumbed the depths of human (mis)understanding as much as the belief that one of his musical rivals regularly exported human body organs, blood and even heads, to customers in Europe.

One of the perceived public images of Franco was more clear cut. As a womaniser, his reputation was prodigious; for a virile African, and a popular star from the age of fifteen, an active sex life would have been obligatory. Contrary to President Mobutu's publicly declared complaint that Zaïreans knew more about the love life of Mozart than of their own great artists, the names of Franco's mistresses were common currency in Kinshasa. Franco himself admitted how much he liked women. At the time when he had eighteen children, only one of whom was a boy, he said that having so many daughters was the price he must pay for having many girlfriends, although he always took one wife at a time.

Following his death Franco's mother reflected on the problems of his serial polygamy. Disunity between her grandchildren was inevitable, she said, considering they were born of fourteen different mothers and each had their own way of seeing things. According to several ex-members of OK Jazz, and 'common knowledge' in Kinshasa, he retained his sexual appetite into later life. Whether it was also the cause of Franco's decline and premature demise at the age of 51 is something he rarely discussed, except to provide alternative diagnoses.

Evidence of Franco's alleged involvement with sorcery is harder to find. Such allegations that have been made come mostly from the gossip of ill-informed, illiterate Kinois who thrive on rumours, the more sensational the better. It should be said that, in Zaïre, such rumours attach themselves to many successful musicians, public figures and even businessmen who make themselves a good deal. Success, the street people and market women say, depends on sorcery. The biggest stars are known to have the strongest 'fetish' or juju. However, Franco always had an ambiguous public relationship with sorcery. He has sung about it often, usually in a patient, critical fashion, but he has also played the part of so many sorcerers in his songs that he has given the character a certain credibility.

His primary audience obviously believes in sorcery and fetishism: both witches, *bandoki*, and the more benign psychic practioners of traditional medicine sometimes known as 'witchdoctors', or *banganga*, and Franco accepts them as characters in the reality of his compositions. In the song *Suite Lettre 2* he answers a listener's letter by saying that he knows about such subjects because he was initiated in his youth. This is a normal part of African culture. It is also not abnormal for those who retain their animist inclinations, and even converted Christians or Muslims, to visit 'fetishers' for help or guidance in their affairs. In 1987 Franco put the secret of his success down to "work, perserverance, discipline and silence". Referring to the rumour-mongers, he added, "I let the dogs bark while the OK Jazz caravan passes on its way."

A year or two later, when Franco's illness had taken hold, it was widely reported in Kinshasa that he had publicly renounced sorcery and re-embraced the Catholic faith. He apparently threw away the gris-gris and fetish charms which he was known to have worn for protection. Responding to the allegation that Franco himself was a sorcerer, his aide, Rondot, insisted that he never saw anything in Franco's house, or in his behaviour, to associate him with the practice of sorcery. But, when asked in a television interview about the role of sorcery in the success of any African band, Franco was revealingly evasive, seeming to suggest that sorcery was something everyone was doing. "Why do you ask me that?" he bristled. "Why, even the Cameroon football team took sixteen doctors to the World Cup. Don't you think there were some sorcerers among them? And their manager was a white." Whatever his personal belief system, however, the title Sorcerer of the Guitar is one he never relinquished.

Hearing is believing

In measuring the Legend of Luambo, it is virtually impossible to separate the person from the band. In many African countries a photo of Franco alone will be greeted with the recognition 'OK Jazz'. Even on those hit records on which he did not appear, or when the band were playing without him on stage, Franco's presence was always there. His legacy is OK Jazz, and their repertoire. Franco has been credited with the round figure of 1,000 compositions. This compares realistically with the documented 400 for Kabasele and Tabu Ley's claim also of 1,000. One long-serving band member, the saxophonist Isaac Musekiwa, estimated in 1986 that the total OK Jazz repertoire was closer to 3,000 songs. On record, Franco's compositions account for some 40-50 per cent of the band's output. On some albums all songs were composed by other band members, yet each retains the unmistakable sound of Franco.

With up to 40 musicians available at a time, the line-up of OK Jazz was always flexible. There were sometimes two OK Jazz bands existing at the same time in different places. On tour, Franco might take seven singers and seven or eight horn players, although in the West three or four of each was more usual. There were frequent defections from the band, with personnel turning over constantly. But there was never any shortage of new talent waiting to fill the gaps. The reasons underlying these changes may have been personality clashes, the creative expansion of highly talented musicians, deteriorating social conditions which caused them to look outside the country, or specific money problems with Franco. Payment of salaries was sometimes erratic in OK Jazz.

While no one would deny a musician the right to make a decent living, it was always a great honour for any young musician to play with OK Jazz and, as many of his past associates have proved, it can be a stepping stone to stardom. Jean-Serge Essous, Vicky Longomba, Papa Noel Nedule, Verckys Kiamuangana, Simaro Lutumba, Sam Mangwana, Youlou Mabiala, Mose Se Fan Fan, Wuta Mayi, Ndombe Opetum, Michelino, Mayaula Mayoni, Ntesa Dalienst, Josky Kiambukuta, Malage de Lugendo and Madilu System are just some of the graduates of TP OK Jazz who achieved personal stardom in Franco's lifetime, often outside Zaïre. The influence of Luambo Makiadi is at least as big as his reputation.

Many people have called Franco a genius, although several colleagues consider that, despite his prodigious output, his talents were never fully developed. As his one-time lead guitarist, Fan Fan, believes: "The tragedy of Franco is that his genius died with him. He left the legacy of his music, but the genius has gone. And the genius of Franco was unrealised." Fan Fan's theory is that Franco actually held back from experimentation and, in the interests of musical continuity and the collective nature of the band, he did not consciously try to influence its musical direction. As if tapping into an ever-flowing musical continuum, OK Jazz relied on a formula of rhythm, melodic structure and guitar solo which was rarely modified throughout his career. As the music evolved Franco actually minimalised the role of solo guitar. Compared with a brief experimental period in the years either side of Congolese independence, when he introduced small virtuoso flourishes and jazzy runs on the guitar fretboard, Franco's mature work had an inevitability about it, which some 'progessivists' found tedious. For the most part, however, his audience just wanted Franco to be Franco.

Tabu Ley Rochereau, in a tribute to his life-long competitor, said that, although Franco was a monument, an all-round phenomenon and a 'human god', he had so much potential that if he had been educated he would either have been super extraordinary or he would have gone mad. Franco did not go mad, and trying to rate his contribution is a pointless task, but the comparisons which come to mind are names which are associated with 'genius'. When asked to sum up the Grand Master's contribution to African culture, Sam Mangwana had a ready epithet: "Franco was unique. Like Shakespeare, or Mozart, combined with Pele or Muhammad Ali. He was irreplaceable. The sort of man who appears maybe once every 100 years. He had great value and he left his mark on his own time."

Over the years, Mangwana had many opportunities to get a clear view of the man behind the 'living legend'. As the singer observed: "Franco did not like things to be hidden. He preferred for everything to be out in the open. He was someone who did not like people to be secretive or withdrawn. He believed that if you were beautiful, you should not stay home and hide your beauty, you should go out and share it in public. When you are rich you should share your wealth. Even those who don't profit directly can testify to your generosity. I believe that when people say Franco's manner was too brutal, too crude, it was just that. He did not like secrets. He created Editions Populaires, which means a lot. It shows that Franco wanted to popularise things. OK Jazz was an orchestra of the people. The other side, with Rochereau and African Jazz, was more intellectual.

"But he also had his snob side. He was fond of luxury. He liked to enjoy his riches, probably because of his humble beginnings. When he wanted to be like anybody else he would go out wearing shorts. People would gossip, 'O, Franco shouldn't be walking about like that,' but it didn't bother him. He was not anti-intellectual, but his manner of speaking was more direct. He spoke for the people who did not have the benefit of education. In any public you have a minority of intellectuals and a majority who are not so well educated. His style was always simple. Franco was someone who had humour. He was also very generous. Someone who liked to give, who did not like to see people suffer. He had pity for people, but he could not tolerate being pitied himself. He respected people with talent or determination but he had no time for people who had nothing to contribute."

*Franco at an age when he was already being taken seriously as a musician.
The style of dress was fashionable among many non-Muslims in the 1950s*

CHAPTER TWO

Franco My Love

"Eyes the colour of fire, sometimes laughing,
sometimes dreaming."   Jean-Jacques Kande

FRANÇOIS LUAMBO MAKIADI first exercised his vocal
cords on July 6, 1938 at a Catholic maternity clinic in Sona
Bata, in the Bas-Zaïre region (then Lower Congo). It was
then a small village near Mbanza Ngungu, the strategic
halfway town on the road and rail route between the port
of Matadi and Kinshasa (then Leopoldville), some 78km
from the capital. His parents were Joseph Emongo, a
railroad worker from the Equatorial region, and his fifteen-
year-old bride, Mbonga Makiesse, a local girl whose hand
in marriage had been requested by Emongo's father.

Mbonga Makiesse had returned to her maternal home
in Sona Bata specifically to give birth to her first child,
and her own mother was on hand to assist at the clinic,
which had the best medical facilities in the area. As the
first son in the family, tradition dictated that the boy be
named after his paternal grandfather, François Luambo,
while Makiadi was a name bestowed by his mother. It is a
Kikongo word meaning a 'subscriber to misfortune', or
one who is born to suffer, and referred to the sickly state
of the child. This is a frequent custom amongst the Bakongo
people, whose word for suffering *mpasi* is often bestowed
on similarly unfortunate boys or girls. The nun who
delivered François apparently pulled a sad face, and few
people gave the young boy more than six months to live.
According to his mother he suffered all the possible
diseases which take such a high toll of African chidren,
and as Mama Makiesse once reflected, he had the annoying
habit of regularly 'dying'. In her maternal heart, she

claimed, only she believed he would survive.

Shortly after the birth of their son, Emongo was arrested by the colonial authorities for a minor infringement and imprisoned. Mama Makiesse returned to Bas-Zaïre, where she had borne a second child by another man before Emongo was released. They moved back to Kinshasa where, thanks to a combination of dedication and medication, the once sickly François grew into a skinny but energetic 'petit', or small boy, scuffling around the streets chasing a rag football and never dodging a fight. Emongo and Makiesse had two other children together, a son, Tshongo Bavon Marie-Marie, born in 1944, followed soon after by a daughter, Marie-Louise.

By then the young François was enrolled at the Saint Georges school. He attended class reluctantly and he had only a limited command of French, and it was soon apparent that his main interests were not academic. His real passion was football, at which he liked to play in goal, but when the bigger boys took the pitch he would animate the sideline, playing music with first a harmonica and then a home-made guitar, and giving his natural talent somewhere to shine. He soon became an ardent supporter of Vita Club, an allegiance he would maintain throughout his life. By the age of seven he had constructed his first guitar from a tin can, and his ebullient character and ability to entertain had earned him his second nickname, 'Le Fou', the Crazy Kid.

Emongo was a hard working railwayman, toiling for Le Chemin de Fer du Congo (Congo Railways), one of the better employers in the Belgian colony, which at that time, just after World War Two, could claim the highest per capita income in Africa. Emongo had ambitions for his son to pursue a career, perhaps as a *kalaki* (clerk) with the colonial administration, or as a teacher. Education was available to elementary level but the Belgian colonial system restricted entry to management and the professions to whites only. The army provided another possible livelihood and, by the age of ten, Franco believed he would soon be signing up for a military career that might have lasted 30 years.

The thought of the boy becoming a musician would have horrified his father. Emongo, like most people, enjoyed listening to music during his short leisure time. He could even play guitar, but his preference was for the accordion music of players like Feruzi, who was among the first generation of Congolese artistes to be recorded. However, he would never have considered music to have career possibilities. There were very few professional musicians at the time and, as in many parts of Africa, there was an ambivalent attitude towards entertainers, whose lifestyle was generally disapproved of, even by the people who enjoyed their music. Traditionally, music was considered a magical force through which deities could be summoned and received into the body as well as the human spirit, and in some cultures music was accepted as the divine source of human creation. As such it belonged to the people, and for music to be requisitioned by any individual for personal gain was an alien concept. Music was neither considered as a profession nor way of life; it is a communal experience, the purpose of which has been likened to a kind of game which people play to find their place in society. And the young Franco was playing it to the full.

The carefree days of childhood came to an abrupt end, however, one day in his eleventh year when Franco returned home from playing football to find his mother distraught. His father was dead. Emongo's death, from viral hepatitis in 1949, had a traumatic effect on the child. As Franco later recalled: "It was simply unacceptable for me. In those days children were not allowed to see a dead person, and people were trying to remove me from my father's body. I kicked so many shins, I bit so many hands that they let me approach the deathbed. I don't remember crying much. I could not get over that this hideous thing called death had struck my father, who represented for me life, health and strength. And really I could not imagine living without my Papa." Death was to become something of an obsession for Franco; a subject which weighed heavily on his mind and about which he was later to compose several expressive songs. He hated attending funerals, which are great social occasions in Africa, and he claimed to look away whenever he saw a hearse or funeral parlour. He never came to terms with death, always finding it 'unacceptable'.

Ironically, if Emongo had not died at that stage of his childhood, Franco would probably not have been allowed to become a musician. As he remarked later in his life, "Out of bad things, good sometimes comes." Any thoughts of a future career were now postponed in the face of the short-term need to survive. Although Emongo's family offered to take care of the children, Mama Makiesse remained alone to bring up François, Marie-Louise and Bavon Marie-Marie in a house she rented at Ngiringiri. With no regular income she resorted to making *mikate* or beignets (local doughnuts) for sale at the nearby Wenze ya Bayaka market, and François increasingly took time off his studies to assist her.

Wenze ya Bayaka, which is still a thriving market for hardware, household goods and furnishings, is named after the Bayaka people, the most visible of whom are the short, stocky, dark-skinned boys who hustle their *pousse-pousse* carts around town delivering from the markets to the clients. In the early 1950s, Wenze ya Bayaka was one of the most animated quarters of Kinshasa, known in street talk as the 'Quartier Far West', after the craze for American culture picked up from Western movies. Here gathered the youth cults of 'Yankees', who affected the 1940s gangster fashions of pegged trousers and crisp shirts, and the exuberant 'Bills' (after Buffalo Bill), or 'Hindu-Bills' (combining the influence of cowboys and indians and popular Asian movies) who posed around on their mopeds and scooters, riding recklessly and pulling all kinds of tricks. There were rougher elements who enjoyed a fight, but the Yankees were not a particularly wild or dangerous cult, rather an early expression of teenage culture and Zaïreans' love of style and fashion.

The more sartorially conscious young men made a habit of posing in the market and other public places, copying attitudes from international magazines. These 'still picture fashion shows' were sometimes organised as competitions between rival elegance clubs with a jury of connoisseurs and complex rules which took into account the price of the European and American clothes, the way they were worn, the harmony of the colours, etc. One such club was known as La Pause (from the word to 'pose'). Those early fashion victims were the direct forerunners of the 'sapeurs' (members of the Society of Ambiencers and Persons of Elegeance) who burgeoned in the 1980s under the inspiration of Papa Wemba and a handful of wealthy underworld clan leaders. The Yankee poseurs of the 1950s also presaged the cult of voguing which 30 years later became a popular pastime with African-American exhibitionists from the spiritual home of the Yankees in New York. In Leopoldville most of the Yankees would have been quite poor and these ostentatious displays can be seen as a way of seeking attention and status among their peers. Western clothes denoted a worldly sophistication and established the wearers as city people separated from the lowly villagers who came, wide-eyed and gullible, to the metropolis.

One of the most popular characters in the market was Mbelekete, a unicycle rider, whose tricks drew huge crowds and earned him a kind of immortality. Mbelekete was renowned as the 'No 1 Kinois', a real free spirit who could not only pull extraordinary stunts but would also behave as anarchically and provocatively as he liked. An ex-soldier with the 'Force Publique' (colonial army),

Mbelekete was seemingly immune to, or protected from, the strictures of colonial regulations. He would openly defy the curfew and the law against smoking marijuana, which he consumed constantly under the noses of the police. He would take charge of traffic control at major road junctions, sometimes accompanied by a 'totally crazy' friend who played exquisite flute, often completely naked. His bike riding made him legendary; swooping through the traffic, standing up on the pedals with his arms outstretched, circling cars and criss-crossing junctions to a barrage of motor horns expressing encouragement or outrage. When Mbelekete came to see a band there would be a guaranteed full house. He eventually lost his life in an accident with a truck soon after Congolese independence.

This was the lively environment in which Franco grew up, and with which he remained closely identified throughout his career. Hanging out alongside his mother's steaming cauldron as she dipped the dough balls into the boiling oil, the boy attracted customers by playing *kebo* party music on his homemade guitar, based on a tin can and strung with wire from stripped electrical cable which he plucked with two hands like a harp.

Rumba roots

There was, and still is, a huge variety of traditional music in Zaïre, a country with some 250 languages and diverse ethnic groups. And there are probably more types of instruments than in any part of Africa. To outsiders this musical heritage is immediately obvious. The accounts of the earliest Western travellers (the Portuguese navigators) on the music of the Congo, published in John Payne's *A System of Geography* in 1794, noted: "The chief pastimes of the Congo blacks are dancing and singing. They sing love songs and play upon an instrument of a very extraordinary shape; the body and neck resemble those of a lute, but the belly part is not made of wood but of a skin as thin as a bladder. The strings are hairs of an elephant's tail, or threads of palm-tree reaching from the bottom of the instrument to the top of the neck, and tied to several rings placed some higher and others lower. At these rings hang thin plates of iron and silver, of different sizes and tones. When the strings are struck, the rings shake, which moving the plates, the latter yield to a confused jingle. Those who play on this instrument tune the strings and strike them with their fingers like a harp very skilfully, so that they make a sound agreeable enough." That was probably the *kokolo*, just one of the plethora of stringed instruments including the *njenje* or *libebe*, which were played throughout the Congo region.

In most cases these instruments and their musics have remained the exclusive province of a particular people but in the inter-ethnic social music which developed in the early twentieth century among migrant workers, traders and the growing urban population, several traditional elements survived. Notable was the *likembe*, a ubiquitous African instrument otherwise known as 'sanza', or thumb piano, which was played for entertainment, often accompanied by *patenge* frame drums and a bottle struck with a nail for ringing percussion. The *patenge*, also found throughout much of Africa, is a drum made by stretching a skin over a square frame. The larger bass versions are held between the legs, with the heel being used to vary the pitch by putting pressure on the drumskin.

The European 'box' guitar, *lindanda*, had become familiar in the west coast regions following the appearance of the Portuguese and had been re-introduced via the eastern mining communities during the early years of the twentieth century. The Portuguese had also introduced the accordion (which confusingly shared the name *lindanda*) into the western regions and these instruments apparently became so popular that traders would present them as gifts to local chiefs, who often passed them on to their women-folk who used them to accompany their recreational singing.

For each instrument there was a repertoire of rhythms and dances. Early in the twentieth century, when the settlements of Kintambo and Kinshasa were merging into the new metropolis, popular dances included the hot-stepping *agbwaya* and its slower cousin the *nzambele*, along with the *ebongo*, *patenge* and *maringa*. The *maringa*, which remained popular for years, was danced to the local variety of 'palm wine' music. It was a subtle dance involving the smooth shift of body weight from hip to hip, and was the root of the cool 'rumba' step which Zaïreans seem set to dance into the 21st century. In the cultural melting pot of post-war Leopoldville these dances were matched with the fusion of local rhythms with 'imported' ingredients, eventually giving rise to the *rumba-sukuma*, *rumba-kara*, *rumba-boucher*, *rumba-odemba*, and the *rumba-sukusu*, which became *soukous*, the term adopted in Europe as the generic name for Congo-Zaïrean guitar dance music.

In 'Leo la Belle' the people spoke Lingala, a non-tribal trading language, which evolved out of Lobobangi, the language of a riverine people from the Equatorial region, mixed with words from Kikongo of Lower Zaïre and others taken from Swahili, Portuguese, French and even English. Lingala was spoken by the military, the church and bureaucrats as well as traders. Its use in the city further diminished the ethnic identity of much of the music, and Lingala became a vital ingredient in the development of a homogenised urban popular music.

As the country's capital and major inland port, Leopoldville had always been a cosmopolitan city where musicians were exposed to many new influences, from the interior by way of the Congo river, and from the west coast and Europe, via the sea port of Matadi. There had long been a community of West Africans, known as 'Coastmen', 'Ghanamen' or 'Doualamen', working in the Congo who had brought their highlife dance music with them. Highlife, which fused American jazz, European and Caribbean dance styles with the folk music of the West

Africa region, was the first successful blending of African and Western ingredients into a popular dance music. Franco once cited early highlife as a strong influence on Congolese dance music. The West African immigrants, attracted to the Congo by good employment prospects and the highest standard of living in Africa, brought their own musical entertainment and founded the first dance orchestra in Leopoldville to be known by name: it was called Excelsior, after a pioneering highlife band from Ghana. Most 'Coastmen' were too busy working and rarely played at organised functions, however, and their music remained social.

There were also any number of itinerant guitarists arriving in the city from the west coast. One name that Franco remembered hearing in his childhood was Dondo Daniel, a sailor who had travelled the coast of West Africa as far as Senegal, and who had returned to Leopoldville before World War Two with an extensive repertoire of guitar picking techniques. At the same time a stream of individual stylists descended on the capital from the up-river ports deep in the interior of the Congo. The accordionist Feruzi disembarked from the Kisangani (Stanleyville) steamer, while from Bolobo came the guitarist and troubador Antoine Wendo, whose recording of *Marie Louise* for the Ngoma label in 1949 was one of the first studio recordings by a Congolese musician.

Also fresh off a river boat came the guitarist Paul Ebengo 'Dewayon', who rented a room in Mama Makiesse's compound, and whose presence was to establish Franco's future as a musician. As Franco recalled: "When my father died we rented a plot at Ngiringiri; rue Bosenge, no 100. That is where I met citizen Ebengo Dewayon. He had a guitar he had made himself. He worked at Tisaco [a textile factory]. At Tisaco, sometimes you had to work nights, sometimes days. When he worked at night I used to pinch his guitar. That's when I started to discover some sounds." Finally the young François' secret activities were discovered by Dewayon when he came home from work unexpectedly. Far from punishing the child he began showing him his own dynamic finger picking technique, and eventually persuaded Mama Makiesse that if the boy's talent was allowed to develop he could possibly make a living as a musician. "But that was not all," continued Franco. "In that area was a citizen called Luampasi (ex-Albert) who had sung the song *Cherie Mabanza*. He had loads of acoustic guitars at his place. He lived nearby at Lokolenge. Because of his guitars we used to go round to his place sometimes to practise. From then on, Luampasi thought of us as his children. We went out with his guitars and played at *matangas* in the area."

A *matanga* is a wake held for the dead after a suitable period of mourning has passed and the spirits are believed to have arrived safely back in the realm of the ancestors. Because these celebrations are family affairs the entertainment often includes a strong traditional element through which the revellers can link up with their forebears, although there is often space for modern popular music as well. Music and refreshments are provided free to the family members and, although the guests invariably contribute to a collection, *matangas* are big occasions which are expensive to run. People might need to save for months, even years, before they can afford to give their deceased kinfolk a good send off.

According to Sam Mangwana, who grew up in the same neighbourhood, "Dewayon was, at the time, part delinquent, part artist. He took the music of the village and turned it into a kind of rock-and-roll music for the young people. It was the music of the 'street' people of Kinshasa and, because of the influence of the Western films, the musicians became known as bandits." Dewayon's style was recognised as the rhythm of the 'Hindu-Bills'. Franco naturally started playing with Dewayon's group which was based in his own compound, and fronted by a singer called Bikunda. Another inhabitant of the

Franco's early mentors Dewayon (left) and Bowane recorded for Loningisa

compound, who hung out with Franco from those early days until the very end, was his inseparable friend Jean-Jean, with whom he shared a room, living, playing and fighting together. Jean-Jean's allegiance to Franco was fanatical; he even lost an eye in a fight while protecting his hero, and thereafter became his bodyguard, personal assistant and 'bad messenger', who knew Franco's most intimate secrets and carried out many clandestine assignments on his behalf.

The mid-1950s really saw the birth of Congolese music as a vital entity. African music had been introduced on to Radio Congolia (later Radio Congo Belge) as late as 1942-43, and after World War Two it was also played on Radio Brazzaville, a powerful, 30Kw station, set up as a long-range propaganda medium by the French government-in-exile which had its base there during the war. The dance music proved popular not only with Africans but also with European listeners. There is plenty of anecdotal evidence to show that the Belgian colonists not only tolerated, but actually enjoyed African music to an extent which never occurred in other colonies. This was no doubt due to the undeniable charm and sensitivity of the music, as much as any quirk of European culture. African musicians would be invited into the white neighbourhoods to play at European dances; many years later, when reminiscing on the early days, Franco reprised the popular Victorian waltz, *After the Ball*, as an example of the kind of melodies they had been expected to play for the whites.

A recording studio, Olympia, had opened during the war, but the first commercial outlet for Congolese musicians came in 1949 when a Greek businessman, Mr Jeronimidis, started up the Ngoma (Drum) studios. The following year Loningisa (Shake it Up) studio was opened in the quartier Kimbangu by two Greek brothers, A & B Papadimitriou, followed soon after by the Benatar brothers' Opika label, then CEFA in 1953 and later Esengo. These concerns were all run by Greek traders who imported and distributed goods from Europe, including domestic equipment, fashion items and imported records. As a purely commercial indicator the sudden interest in domestic record production showed that popular Congolese music was growing up.

In 1950, at the age of twelve, Franco was invited to make his professional debut in Dewayon's reconstructed group now known as Watam. The name was taken from the Lingala word, *watama*, used by colonial authorities and Africans alike to identify 'delinquents' or the unemployed. By now Franco, who had started performing on maracas and vocal animation, had a 'proper' acoustic guitar of his own, and was really cutting a dash: "When I was small, everybody was astounded at how I played the guitar. People asked how such a small person could play such a big guitar." The instrument had been given to him by Abbe Cornil, a priest from the Père Blancs who had taken an interest in the boy's upbringing following his father's death. Cornil was a great enthusiast for cultural development; he would give weekly film shows in the neighbourhood and even made his own documentaries. He also took a paternal interest in Joseph-Desiré Mobutu, a corporal in the army pay corps, who was eight years older than Franco. In 1950 the country's future leader began his journalistic career contributing to the Père Blancs' magazine, *La Révolution*.

In Watam Franco carried his new guitar alongside Dewayon and his brother Johnny Bokelo, backed by a rhythm section using *patenge* frame drums. Dewayon's local version of rock-and-roll, which he called *yembele*, was a progressive fusion of available technology with traditional folklore rhythms such as the powerful *agbwaya* and, while his lyrics had a mature, philosophical edge, the beat had particular appeal to the rebellious young 'bandits'. Originally playing for private parties, weddings and *matangas*, Watam quickly made a name around Kinshasa, and found a regular spot at the Bolingo Bar in Ngiringiri, where the young François attracted as much attention as the group's leader. Music was a haphazard occupation in those early days, however, and no musicians were fully professional. Dewayon himself had arrived in town as a fisherman but by now he was earning most of his living as a carpenter working on the construction of Kinshasa's Ndjili airport. His young sidekick, François, was found a job as a builder's labourer and he spent many months working in Dewayon's construction gang during the day, and playing music together at night.

Franco left temporarily in May 1953, when his old teacher Luampasi called him to play accompaniment at a wedding celebration in Kwilu-Ngongo (then Moerbeke), near his birthplace, where they stayed for three and a half months. "While I had been to play at Moerbeke with Luampasi, Dewayon went to record at Loningisa. He told Papadimitriou: 'I've got a guitarist who is travelling in Bas Zaïre; as soon as he gets back I'll introduce him to you.' That was in 1953," recalled Franco.

One fine day

On August 3, Franco entered a recording studio for the first time. "One fine day Dewayon takes me to the studio. At the time I was skinny, just a kid who played guitar which we called *libaku ya nguma* [a hollow-bodied electrified guitar known as a 'lucky break'] and the guitar was bigger than me. I arrived at the studio and played. All the Europeans were there. And they were amazed." The first song he played guitar on was probably *Esengo ya Mokili*, (The Pleasures of Life), in which Dewayon sings; 'Let the priest, Dewayon, Franco and the others sing the rumba. The pleasure of life is to be famous.' Franco had just passed his fifteenth birthday.

Papadimitriou was so impressed by the young guitarist's performance that, at the end of the first day's recording, he presented Franco with the guitar he had been using, and signed him to a ten-year exclusive contract at a starting salary of 900 francs per month. In effect, this meant becoming a session guitarist in the studio band, a loose collection of musicians known as Bana Loningisa (The Loningisa Boys), who backed up the many solo singers being recorded for the label. The instrumentation included guitars, sax or clarinet, accordion, percussion and double bass, an innovation which had been introduced that year as a replacement for the tuba used previously to maintain a bass line. There was also a primitive organ called the Solovox, played on some tracks by a Greek musician, Carlos Sarti. The early stars of Loningisa included Dewayon, Henri Liengo, Adikwa, Tino Mab, Pierre Kalima and the first female Congolese recording artiste, Pauline Lisanga, who was employed as an announcer on Radio Congo Belge. One of the biggest stars, and leader of the house band, Bana Loningisa, was the guitarist Henri Bowane. It was he who started calling the young wizard Franco.

Bowane, a robust, jovial character who came to Kinshasa from the Equatorial region to the north east of the capital, brought his own style which was based on the folklore of the Mongo people (known for their *zebola* rhythm), but which also included a Latin-American influence. He incorporated elements of rumba and beguine, having picked up tricks from several celebrated Latin bands which had visited Leopoldville in the early 1950s, such as Sam Kasande, Orchèstre Aragon and some Puerto Rican bands. Their music was so popular that even those who had their own unique style would be obliged to add some Latin colour to modernise the music for the popular market. As the music developed, Bowane later recalled, "everyone was looking for a certain modernism". Bowane was also astute enough to see that the new music being forged in the Congo had commercial potential, and when he started to hassle for payment that reflected the sales of his records, he was briefly imprisoned. He turned this to his advantage, boasting about it in one of his early hit songs, *Kotiya Zolo Te* (Don't Stick Your Nose in Our Business). Bowane made his point, and while he was with Loningisa he became the country's wealthiest performer and one of the first Congolese to cruise the capital in a Cadillac.

Among other guitarists making an impression on the fifteen-year-old Franco were 'Jhimmy' Zacharie Elenga, who played 'Hawaiian' guitar style with plenty of vibrato, and Adou Elenga, who in 1953 had amplified his guitar using a microphone, on a number called *Mokili Ekobaluka* (The World is Going to Change), a 'utopian' song, looking forward to a post-colonial society, which caused him to be locked up by the Belgian authorities. For Franco, however, the doyen of local guitarists was Balozi, aka Tino Baroza, who used vibrato to create an ornate guitar sound and who developed into a virtuoso soloist alongside locally-based European jazz musicians.

A less predictable influence was the Belgian instrumentalist Bill Alexandre, one of several Europeans recruited by the studio proprietors to play in the colony during the early 1950s. In addition to Sarti, there was another keyboard player, Gilbert Warnant, saxophonist Fudd Candrikx and a bassist, Freddy Dupre, scattered among the various studios. But Alexandre's influence was much the most pervasive, as he was the first person to introduce the electric guitar, which transformed Congolese rumba into a contemporary dance music that has evolved in a steady linear growth ever since. An all-round musician with knowledge of bebop jazz and Latin music, Alexandre's mastery of the fretboard was a revelation to many Congolese who more often strummed their instruments than picked out notes.

Bill Alexandre arrived in Leopoldville in 1953 with a commission to set up and run the CEFA recording operation for a European-based owner. With him he brought two Gibson Les Paul guitars, two amplifiers, one double bass, an Ampeg tape recorder and one ElectroVoice microphone. He also brought steel-wound strings for acoustic guitars and the first plectrum to be seen in the land where guitarists picked with finger and thumb. Alexandre had maintained a thriving career in Europe either side of World War Two. He led the first Belgian bebop band, which had been well reviewed in the British *Melody Maker* in 1947, and he was a good friend of Django Reinhardt, whose band he often sat in with. In the early 1950s, the European jazz scene had begun to slump and Alexandre turned overnight to his other love, the Latin-American rumba. The introduction of juke boxes and a dancefloor tax in Belgium in 1952 inspired him to take up the offer of working in the Belgian Congo. Once there he ran the studio single-handed, and recruited a house band which included the singer Vicky Longomba, bassist Roitelet Munganya, guitar accompanist Antoine Brazzos (all soon to join up with Franco) and the percussionist Roger Izeidi.

Arriving in the Congo at the age of 33, Alexandre claims, like many Europeans, to have fallen in love with

Bill Alexandre with the CEFA recording artistes (l-r) Vicky Longomba, Roger Izeidi, Roitelet Munganya, Armando Brazzos and friends

Africa immediately, and fallen for the charms of the people, and their music. As a trained musician, however, he considered the level of guitar playing needed improvement. "Guitarists could only play in one position on the keyboard. So what happened was, instead of the guitarist following the singer, the singer had to follow the guitar, which was contradictory. So I began by showing them the different positions, how to play the different chords, place the fingers." Alexandre illustrated his personal theory about the Congolese limitations by referring to their preference for using a 'capo d'astre' to modify the tuning — although he did concede that the musicians may have deliberately chosen to use the device to gain an additional resonance from keeping their strings open. Vocalists, he believed were trapped in a high register by the guitarists' inability to play the full length of the fretboard. He was unaware that high-register alto and falsetto male voices were common in the traditional music of the region, but as Alexandre pointed out, he was there to make commercial Congolese rumba, not folklore music.

After two or three months' rehearsal he had coached some musicians sufficiently to make the first CEFA recordings. The tapes were sent to Germany for pressing into 78rpm discs, which were then played over a loudspeaker fitted to the American station wagon which Alexandre paraded through town as part of his one-man operation. Although he would have fitted the 'cowboy' part, Alexandre was pleased to have been known to his musician friends as 'Indian' — indicating they thought he had a certain natural wisdom.

Bill Alexandre's name is remembered fondly by several generations of Kinshasa guitarists, even those too young to have heard him play, and his method of playing runs of 'sixths' has become the trademark of the Congolese guitar style. Records in those days would only last for a dozen or so plays before deteriorating, and Alexandre's would have been worn out by ambitious guitarists, if no one else. One youngster who later played guitar alongside Franco was Mose Se Fan Fan, who recalled how in those days, "Every guitarist would be judged on whether they played like Bill. 'No, no,' they would say, 'not like that — this is how Bill does it.' You had to play like Bill. His influence was very important in creating our modern music." Alexandre left the Congo just as independence was dawning and he laid down his guitar and changed his career. Thirty-five years later, his memories were faint but, he recalled, "Brazzos was one of the best guitarists at that time." The young Franco he remembers as being "a little bit better than the others."

With the growing demand for fresh original music it was not that easy for a young musician to develop his craft. Youngsters who had the ambition to perform had to integrate themselves into the musical community and search out the 'grand' musicians who really knew their instruments. The young guitarists, for example, would hang out with the masters to learn the chords and study how they used their fingers to handle the strings and pluck. By that time gramophones and radios were quite common and people were familiar with the music; before independence there were even public radios set up at strategic points in the cité indigène (African quarters) of Leopoldville. But in order to study the music it was necessary to see the musicians at work to understand their techniques.

As Sam Mangwana remembers: "Often in public the old guitarists would play with a handkerchief covering their guitar so young rivals could not see what they were doing with their hands, how they plucked the chords and how they placed their fingers. When they played they would take a handkerchief or the wrapper from a woman's head to cover their hands. Many musicians did this, from Tino Baroza onwards. Most guitarists would do this. Which meant that if you wanted to learn their techniques you had to become like a disciple." The youngster would respectfully ask his chosen master to be able to sit and study his technique. This involved a process of ingratiation, because if they knew people were just coming to copy their style the masters would clam up. "Sometimes," says Mangwana, "a guitarist would be sitting in a band, playing for a dance quite normally and as soon as another guitarist came in, he would pull out the handkerchief."

The way Franco attacked his instrument was something no one had heard before. It was almost brutally exciting for its time, and radical enough to attract the post-war generation of teenagers who, like their Western counterparts, adopted a rebel as their musical hero. By the end of 1953, Franco had recorded the first of his own compositions, *Bolingo Na Ngai Na Beatrice* (My Love for Beatrice), *Marie Catho* and *Lilima*, juvenile love songs on which Franco played solo guitar accompanied by the Solovox organ. These records were the first of many hits for Loningisa, and their instant popularity laid a solid foundation for Franco's career. But 1953 was a trebly important year in the history of Zaïrean music as, in addition to the arrival of Alexandre and the debut of Franco, it also saw the formation of Joseph Kabasele's African Jazz, a band which both recorded and performed at formal dances, and which was to provide the greatest commercial and artistic competition for much of Franco's early career. It was a challenge which Franco found stimulating.

Although Franco had a technical interest in what other guitarists were doing, Joseph Kabasele Tshamala, aka the Grand Kalle, provided the greatest inspiration. "Kalle, was without doubt, one of the pillars of Zaïrean popular music," Franco later recalled. "For some time we both lived in the rue Kongolo in the zone of Kinshasa. He was about eight years older than me and I was one of his regular admirers at the Astra cinema where he sang with Georges Doula's band, before he founded African Jazz. Of all the young musicians I followed, he was the model for me, although I never knew that I myself would also become a great artist and founder of a school. Kalle was really great. He was the father of our music. It was he who introduced the tam tam and electric guitar into our music. He was also important because he defended our profession at a time when it enjoyed little consideration. Kalle was from a good family and had received a sound education for those times. That such a guy could follow a musical career, brought some credibility. He also struggled on our behalf for composer's royalties and he was always ready to help other musicians to develop their own careers."

Kalle, who was signed to the Opika label, played a popular fusion of imported and local music with a deliberate Latin flavour. He was a noted arranger and interpreter of other people's material as well as a composer in his own right. He was the lead vocalist of African Jazz and among his musicians were the solo guitarist Tino Baroza, and two brothers who picked up much of their technique from him, the accompanist Dechaud and eventual guitar star 'Docteur' Nico Kasanda, who carried the 'Hawaiian' style of Jhimmy to new heights.

Kalle and his musicians were the darlings of the progressive-thinking class of self-titled 'intellectuals'. He was educated to secondary level, as was his most famous protégé, Tabu Ley Rochereau, while Nico Kasanda had attended technical school. The difference in social class was evident in the way they spoke the colonial language of French. Kalle, Nico and Rochereau clearly had command of the langauge, while Franco had a limited vocabulary of some 30 French words when he left school, and he always spoke the European language with a heavy accent.

Franco had the greatest respect for Kalle but he had already noticed that the limelight was shared by the vocalist/bandleader and the lead guitarist. In Congolese music the role of singer and instrumentalist have always been kept separate — singers sing, guitarists play guitar. There was surely an opening for one artiste who could combine the roles. Although almost all the popular music at the time was based on adaptations of Latin rhythms, Franco's had stronger connections with indigenous folklore styles which he would have to develop if he was to provide a competitive alternative to the African Jazz formula. And the young Franco was certainly ambitious.

A year after his recording debut Franco was a local celebrity with at least four hit singles to his name, but nobody had yet seen him play his own music at a dance because he was under contract to Loningisa and the only equipment available was for exclusive use at the studio. However, in October, 1954 Franco and some of his colleagues decided to smuggle the equipment out of the studio on a Saturday night using Papadimitriou's truck, and for the best part of a year they played around town, packing out the bars they visited, and returning the equipment before morning.

There were reportedly more than 150 bars in Leopoldville at the time, the most popular of which were in the present-day zone of Kinshasa. They included Quist, Yaka Awa, Siluvangi, Kongo Bar, Nzao Bar, Amouzou, Mbuma Elengi, Mingiedi, Nzizi, Air France and Macaulay, all within a few blocks of each other. By the mid-1950s the more salubrious establishments had brick walls built around them in place of the older fences, while the glow of electric light bulbs hanging in the warm night air attracted people on to the purpose-built cement dance floors. The Yaka Awa was the haunt of the young Patrice Lumumba, who later became the country's first post-independence prime minister. Lumumba worked as a publicist for the Bracongo brewery, promoting their Polar beer, in competition with the more popular Primus brew. This job kept him in the bars for much of the time and he was a great success at it, with Polar soon outselling the rival brewery. As an outsider, the man from Stanleyville (Kisangani) quickly learned his way around the capital and in a short time became widely known and liked, not least because he was able and willing to dispense free beer. Later, as his political career developed, the Yaka Awa bar became the 'siege' or base for his followers.

Franco played at most of the bars which featured live music, at first for the fun and the experience of working with older professional musicians. For a while he and Dewayon worked at the Air France bar in Bowane's outfit, but Dewayon was first to split away. Then, in 1955 Bowane wanted to take the musicians on tour to Angola but Franco and the singer, Rossignol, refused to go, preferring to enjoy their local success, and their studio salaries. They all went their separate ways. A band called Negro Jazz took their place at Air France and when Franco and Rossignol proposed a collaboration, the band's leader, Jean-Serge Essous, agreed.

Now, as a hit recording artiste and member of the hottest dance band, Franco was in demand everywhere.

One of François Luambo's earliest hit records, recorded in 1953

His music was proving particularly attractive to the new generation of socially and financially liberated young women of Kinshasa, who organised themselves into *moziki* societies, which combined social meetings with a cooperative savings club. Each society had its own favourite rhythm, and the *odemba* which Franco later made his own, was originally associated with *moziki* members of Bana Amida (Friends of Daring football club). Among the societies which fanatically supported Franco and his colleagues some had evocative names, like La Beauté, L'Elegance, Bana Ages (Contemporaries), Bana Mode (Fashion People), even Bana 15 Ans (15-year-olds). The young women signalled their devotion by coining the Latin-style nickname 'Franco de mi Amor' (Franco My Love), a name which he would proudly stick on his first solid body electric guitar.

But performers cannot survive on an adoring public without material support, whether donated by a patron or 'borrowed'. In November 1955, a year after the musicians took out their unofficial loan on his equipment, Papadimitriou discovered their trickery and confiscated everything. He told the musicians he did not mind them playing together in their own time but he could not allow them to use his equipment. This possessive, patronistic attitude was not really surprising. The producers were commercial people, traders with a colonial mentality, and music was just another aspect of their business. Musicians were retained as long as their popularity lasted; they were not indispensible. But according to Sam Mangwana, the early contracted musicians did have some security. "When the local record companies began to support the music, they started to provide a structure. Musicians were taken on as author/composers or studio musicians with a salary payable every month. Later the studios with the hits would provide the musicians with a house, and a car, or Vespa scooter. It was then that the professionalism really started." Papadimitriou's Loningisa records were selling well, with many of the 78rpms being shipped deep into the interior, together with wind-up gramophones, to be exchanged alongside sewing machines and hurricane lamps on the barter market. The gramophone was considered an ideal status symbol which could be kept secure in the house while being played loud enough to let the neighbours know about your wealth. Papadimitriou presumably did not see any potential in helping promote his artistes' live performances to publicise his products. But at this stage another businessman with more imagination stepped into the picture and left his mark indelibly on the cultural map of Africa, even if he never fully capitalised on his vision.

'On entre OK'

Omar Kashama was owner of the OK Bar (also called Chez Cassien) on Rue Itaga in the zone of Kinshasa close to the Avenue Rwakadingi, the boundary which kept people curfewed inside the African quarters of the 'cité' after 7pm, and which also prohibited whites from enjoying the night-time ambience. Kashama invited the young musicians to play for him and he provided guitars for Franco, Daniel Loubelo (De la Lune) and a bass for Roitelet. In the absence of Western drum kits or shop-bought instruments, the drummers Pandy, LiBerlin and La Monta made their own. Bosuma Dessouin, until then a rhythm guitarist, was encouraged to take up conga drums, a role in which he accompanied Franco throughout his career. Landot Philipe 'Rossignol' (The Nightingale) was the lead vocalist and they were joined by flautists/sax players Lievre and Jean-Serge Essous. Most of the musicians were from Bana Loningisa, but Essous brought a fresh touch and useful experience. Essous was a clarinettist and saxophonist from Brazzaville with a clear-toned jazzy style and a penchant for merengues, beguines and mazourkas, who had been playing in Leopoldville for a few months with Negro Jazz before Papadimitriou recruited him into Bana Loningisa. Essous was a prime mover in getting the band out of the studio and on to the dance floor.

Encouraged by Kashama, who recognised the public demand for an organised dance band, seven of the members, excluding La Monta and Lievre, came together for a Sunday matinee at the Hommes des Mulatres dance hall, close to the OK Bar on the Boulevard Prince Baudouin (now Avenue Kasavubu), the road which winds its way through most of the more animated quarters of Kinshasa. This was the debut performance of OK Jazz. In seeking to promote his business, Kashama had originally suggested the name OK Boys, but 'jazz' was a common generic term for popular dance music, and 'jazz' was in the name of the top band in town. The OK could mean Orchèstre Kinois (Kinshasa band) as well as Omar Kashama. The name also had a nice tough, Yankee feel. The date was June 6, 1956, one month from Franco's eighteenth birthday. The senior men, De la Lune and Essous, were both 22 years old.

The group had the advantage of playing together

almost every day at the studio, which was now in the 7ème Rue, Limete, directly opposite the house of Kabasele which was owned by rival producers, the Benatar brothers, who ran the Opika label. Just down the road was the Ecodis pressing plant, later Mazadis, which pressed for all the studios in Kinshasa. Enveloped in the security of Papadimitriou's patronage, the Loningisa house band could play as a tight, confident unit even with different permutations of musicians. But having a name gave OK Jazz cohesion, even though that name did not appear on the record labels for some time.

There was another singer recording for Loningisa who did not join the band immediately but who was soon to become a crucial member of OK Jazz. Vicky Longomba, originally signed to Alexandre's rival CEFA label, was about a year older than Franco. They first appeared in company on the Loningisa records *Wapi Yo?* (Where are You?) and *Tango Ekoki* (Time Enough), for which the artistes' credits read: Franco, Vicky, Rossignol. This was to become the front line of OK Jazz but the band's eventual sound had still not completely gelled. The high-register voices, almost pre-pubescent, were to remain a characteristic of the band's early days; Franco's clipped, syncopated guitar style was already evident and the rhythm section was hotter than any wind-up gramophone could communicate. A strange and, in retrospect, charming feature of those discs was the use of the Solovox organ. This instrument was unable to play chords and its single note style probably sounded too quaint even then, however much zeal the uncredited player (presumably Carlos Sarti) attacked it with. As the new band evolved out of Bana Loningisa, the organ was abandoned and the sound of a keyboard instrument disappeared from the aural spectrum of OK Jazz for the next 35 years.

The system in those days for labelling and selling records was to release them under the name of the singer(s). The composer's name followed the song title in brackets and beneath it the accompanists were listed. Some of the instrumentalists, such as De la Lune and the bassist Roitelet, had recorded under their own names, as had Franco, Vicky and Rossignol. The first allusion to the name OK Jazz on a record was in the title of *La Rumba OK*, by Franco. The full introduction, however, came with *On Entre OK, On Sort KO* (You Enter OK, You Leave Knocked Out), a rumba written by Franco, sung by Franco, Vicky and Rossignol, accompanied by Franco and De la Lune. In the song they introduce Essous, Franco, Vicky, Rossignol, De la Lune and Dessouin, and a squeaky-voiced Franco calls out 'OK Jazz en form'. It is a gem of an introduction, very much formula music which had to fit into the three-minute limit of a 78rpm record, but full of vitality and controlled virtuosity. Appropriately the title was retained as the band's slogan. The first record to actually have the band's name printed on the label, was *Etali Yo* (It's Your Problem) backed by *Colette*, credited to Franco and Essous, accompanied by OK Jazz.

During 1957 OK Jazz released more than a dozen records for Loningisa. One of the biggest hits was *Passi ya Boloko* (Suffering in Prison) composed by Pandy, the drummer from Brazzaville who spoke from personal experience after being locked up by the Belgian authorities on the wrong side of the Congo river for non-payment of tax. Despite the label's reputation as a producer of folklore, rather than commercial pop music, the predominant style was the rumba, a generic term for various Afro-Cuban musics which had become popular throughout the continent, particularly through imported records such as the GV series of Cuban recordings, re-released by the English EMI company and distributed from Europe to many African countries. The music touched a familiar chord everywhere, so that a song like *El Manicero* (The Peanut Vendor) is known, and still played, by almost every dance band in Africa. Merengues, boleros, cha cha chas, charangas, pachangas, tangos and beguines were also popular. These Afro-Caribbean rhythms have remained the basis for Congo-Zaïrean music through to the 1990s, and while there is no doubt that some music did come directly to Congo from Cuba, it is apparent that such Afro-Cuban music was simply coming home to where it had originated many generations before the slave trade.

Franco himself would later get quite agitated with people asking why Zaïrean music sounded so Latin, meaning Afro-Cuban. "Some people think they hear a 'Latin' sound in our music," he once said. "It only comes from the instrumentation, trumpets and so on. Maybe they are thinking of the horns. But the horns only play the vocal parts in our natural singing style. The melody follows the tonality of Lingala, the guitar parts are African and so is the rumba rhythm. Where is the Latin? Zaïrean music does not copy Cuban music. Some Cubans say it does, but we say their music follows ours. You know, our people [the slaves] went from Congo to Cuba long before we ever heard their music."

Thanks largely to the OK Jazz stream of music, the Congo-Zaïrean rumba has evolved into a very different form from the Cuban version, but in the 1950s the public taste was for 'imported' music and the rumba was not alone. Franco had a practical reason for preferring it, however. "When we started everyone wanted bolero and the cha cha cha, then they switched to rumba. For us it was better. If you play the cha cha cha people only dance in twos. With the rumba everyone joins in." Explaining its significance to the British writer Chris Stapleton, Franco drew an analogy. "The rumba is like jazz. You have reggae, rock, twist, soul. But jazz is the mother, it's always there. It's the same with Zaïrean music. You've got the *boucher*, the *cavacha*, the *yeke yeke*, but rumba is the root."

By 1956 African Jazz had a head start in the popularity race on both sides of the Congo river and, by the time OK Jazz was launched, Kabasele had fully developed his distinctive blend of Congolese dance music. Although in the early years the OK Jazz style was very similar, there was one important difference. Kalle interpreted and even copied popular imported rumbas, cha cha chas and European variety songs, creating a Congolese equivalent of the 'highlife' atmosphere with its good living, sophisticated and international (i.e. Western) connotations. OK Jazz were even then appealing to the less well-off, less intellectual or pretentious sector of the population.

The folkloric core of the music was the guitar of Franco, which was the strongest feature of the band. This can be heard to great effect on a record from the 1957 sessions, entitled *Merengue*, on which Franco uses the popular Dominican rhythm as a springboard for one of the most stunning guitar solos of his early career. It introduces the grinding, almost metallic sound which reproduces the resonance of a traditional harp zither and which became his trademark. On the guitar, his greatest competitor was 'Docteur' Nico Kasanda, the soloist with African Jazz, who had an altogether different style based on Baluba xylophone playing. Although he was less able than Franco to sustain a melody, Nico pleased his own fans with his softer tone, florid runs and tremolo technique. Nico and his brother Dechaud were both tutored by Kabasele's original soloist, Tino Baroza and, as his regular accompanist, Dechaud's presence was crucial to Nico's development. The music's main function was to make people dance, and both the star guitarists played as if each note they plucked was reaching out to drag listeners on to the dance floor. They both played direct to the spinal cord, but while Nico's music affected the lower spine and pelvis, Franco's fingers often seemed to be picking at the brain itself.

After half a dozen releases with Vicky and Rossignol as lead vocalists, the two singers fell out for ego/artistic reasons, and one of the first OK Jazz power struggles ensued. Both singers wanted to take the lead vocal part.

The small, excitable Rossignol, who reportedly revelled in argument, lost the battle and quit the band. Vicky, who had the stronger voice anyway, was joined by another singer, Edo Nganga, and there was a shake up in the horn section. Essous' fellow countryman and sax player, Nino Malapet, sat in for a time, joining the trumpter Willy Mbembe, and soon after the Rhodesia (Zimbabwe)-born saxophonist Isaac Musekiwa arrived. Musekiwa had been brought to Kinshasa from the Copperbelt region to play on records for the Opika label and when he transferred to OK Jazz in 1957, it was his last career move. Along with the conga player Dessouin, Isaac, who was some three years older than Franco, was to accompany the bandleader until the very end, becoming one of his closest cronies. Essous quit around the same time and linked up with Rossignol, Pandy, Malapet and others to form a Latin-style band, Orchèstre Rock-a-Mambo. Essous later founded two other influential orchestras, Les Bantous, which became a national institution on the Brazzaville side of the river, and Ry-Co Jazz.

As the main vocalist and administrator of the band, Vicky was billed as the leader of OK Jazz when, in 1957, they took the ferry across the silvery waters of the Malebo pool to Brazzaville. In the capital of the French Congo they set out their stall at the Macedo bar for several months. Newcomers who joined the band during that period were another vocalist who doubled on maracas, Kouka Celestin, the young clarinettist Edo Lutula and rhythm guitarist Armando Antoine 'Brazzos'. Several of the musicians in that line-up remained with Franco throughout, others left and returned some time later, but the band already had the basic structure which it was to maintain for three decades.

Largely due to technical developments, which allowed for longer songs and increased the range of musical effects and instruments, the band's sound developed rapidly, but many of the elements contained in those early 78rpm recordings can be found in the most majestic of OK Jazz's later productions, particularly the product of Franco's fingers which, as one commentator remarked, "attack the strings like talons".

On returning home to Kinshasa in 1958, Franco discovered that although he was a local celebrity he was not beyond the reach of the law. As his near-contemporary, Sam Mangwana, recalled, "I was at school at that time, 1957-58, at the Salvation Army school on Avenue Kabinda. When Franco was working at the studio you would see him pass by there every day on the Vespa which Papadimitriou had given him. Very well dressed. At the time I believe he used to wear Portuguese shoes, because there was a shop which sold Portuguese shoes, and Franco was used to promote those shoes. Each time new shoes would arrive they would give them to Franco. And as Loningisa also had shops selling clothes to women, all the *moziki* women fans of OK Jazz used to buy their clothes at Loningisa. The fans of African Jazz, who were with Opika, would buy their clothes from Benatar who also had a shop. That was the way it was done then. And as Franco was so elegant, every time new cloth came from England, they would make him a costume to promote the goods. Everyone would see him wearing it on his Vespa. He was young, good-looking and already a star. People wanted to use him as a model."

The journalist Jean-Jacques Kande, writing at the time, was obviously not attracted by Franco's physical charms, but he did notice the young man's charisma: "Not a pretty boy," he wrote, "Slightly taller than average. Eyes the colour of fire, sometimes laughing, sometimes dreaming. Hair cut any which way to give his physiognomy a very combative air. Very dark black skin. Thus appears the current number-one guitarist of the town of Leopoldville, the electric guitarist who makes the hearts of women spin. For them his name is Franco, from his real name François Luambo. He wears plaid shirts and narrow pants cut cowboy style."

That 'combative air', and Franco's tendency to show off on his Vespa, caught him out. The commissioner of traffic police had Franco arrested because of his fast riding. He had already been cautioned several times by the colonial officers for driving without a licence but as he continued to re-offend he was arrested and imprisoned for ten days. It is interesting to note that while a licence was required to drive in the Belgian Congo, the Belgians themselves did not introduce a driving test at home until the 1960s. This was Franco's first time inside, but the deterrent effect did not work. Following his release from jail, he could not keep off the Vespa and when he was inevitably caught again he was sentenced to two months. At the centrally located Ndolo prison he was being visited by so many well-wishers that he was moved out of town to Luzumu. While inside he composed a song, *Mukoko*, based on the story of Willy Mbembe, the OK Jazz trumpeter, who was also in prison at the time. The song involved Franco entering the jail to ask a life sentence inmate, named Mukoko, when Willy would be released. For the refrain he sang about liberation. The personal perspective was seen as a cloak to obscure the real subject of the song, which was the expectation of political independence and the coming liberation from the Belgians. Mukoko, aka the 'Congolese Al Capone' was considered a subversive by the colonial authorities. The song was released but withdrawn on orders of the Belgian authorities after only a few days.

The Sorcerer proclaimed

By the time Franco was discharged from prison the band had travelled to Mbandaka (then Coquilhatville) in the Equatorial region, up-river from the capital. He followed after them by river steamer. Under Vicky's leadership, OK Jazz had been able to consolidate their reputation, but everyone agreed they were lacking that vital guitar ingredient. When the errant 21-year-old turned up at Mbandaka he wowed the crowds with a new song,

Masumbuku, dedicated to the captain of the steamer on which he had travelled. In fact, it was the same song, *Mukoko*, with a new, less contentious lyric, but it ensured Masumbuku's fame as the legendary 'king' of the riverboat captains. Franco's return to the capital from Mbandaka was more propitious than his previous homecoming. This time he received a hero's welcome.

A celebration show was arranged in the zoological gardens at the Parc de Boeck, now Parc de la Revolution, a few hundred metres from the OK Bar. When Franco launched into his latest hit composition, the crowds went wild with delight. *Masumbuku* was a dance number with a passage of syncopation that lifted it out of the ordinary. Franco's guitar solo was actually very similar in structure to what Nico was playing in African Jazz, but even when playing the same sequence of notes, Franco's fingers were telling a different story. During a previous event at the Parc, Nico had earned himself the title 'Docteur'. This night the promoter made a speech to the public praising Franco and bestowing an honorary title on the young guitarist which stayed with him throughout his career. The impresario, disc jockey and virtuoso dancer, Maître Taureaux Ngombe Baseko, proclaimed: "In our villages there exist those we call sorcerers. They have a power which we don't understand but which works. In music, here we have the Sorcerer of the Guitar. Someone whose sound can penetrate us and make us dance even if we don't want to."

Franco's head was not turned by his booming popularity. He was now a mature, well-paid young man, full of self-confidence. But he retained a high regard for his elders, always respectfully calling them 'vieux' (elder), and his attitude to the band was organised and professional. Whenever OK Jazz played a gig it was always Franco who arranged the equipment and by the time the older musicians arrived they would find everything in place. Although he was certainly a ladies' man, Franco was not a great drinker like some of his colleagues and he was always serious about his work. Many of his contemporaries expected big things of him. Mangwana's observation is not unique: "I think from that young age he already had a sense of organisation. I believe it was not for nothing that he became leader of OK Jazz."

During this period Franco was at probably the most experimental stage of his musical career. The formula for Congo-Zaïrean music was by now well established but there was still plenty of room for personal expression. Some of his virtuoso solos in the years either side of Congo's independence showed the young maestro's latent talent, even though he later maintained an almost rigid restraint on his own contributions. The young Franco was interested in jazz, to the extent that he would inject short complicated flourishes, and on the 1958 song *Ah Bolingo Pasi* (Oh the Pain of Love) there is an extremely rare trumpet solo. The trumpet and saxophone players were Senegalese guests from the band M'Bengwe et son Cha Cha Cha Boys de Dakar, who had visited Congo that year. The two horn players had been asked to stay behind to do some sessions for Loningisa. Unfortunately other examples of this 'jazzy' face of OK Jazz are hard to find on record.

The late 1950s was a period of social upheaval and political unrest in the Belgian Congo and across the river on the French side. Demonstrations in 1956 had prompted the Belgians to introduce reforms the following year, giving Africans limited representation in city and local government for the first time. Political organisations included Abako, founded to safeguard the Bakongo people's interests and led by Joseph Kasavubu; Conakat, the party of Moise Tshombe in Katanga and, in 1958, Patrice Lumumba founded the MNC, a national, non-tribal grouping with pan-African aspirations which hastened demands for an early independence. The Belgians were unsympathetic, however, and trouble broke out, with riots in Lubumbashi (then Elizabethville) in late 1958 influencing events in the capital.

In January 1959, the first disturbances hit the streets of Leopoldville, when the colonial police broke up a meeting called by Kasavubu and attended by Lumumba at the Vis-à-Vis club in the Matonge district. The subsequent riot, in which dozens of people were shot by police and one officer was killed, led to a hurried announcement by the Belgians that Round Table talks would be convened the following year in Brussels, setting the programme that would lead to full independence in June, 1960. Franco made his contribution to the debate with the song *Kodi Yaya*, a party political number for the Abako party. It was one of several songs in which Franco alluded to the subject of independence, usually commissioned by one of the new political parties. Although confusion reigned, and traumatic times were soon to follow, there was a euphoric mood in the cité of Leopoldville at the end of the decade. Independence, *lipanda*, was just around the corner. The 1960s would be a new era.

'Franco de mi amor' was already a national hero by the age of 21: he came of age at the time of the Belgian Congo's independence

CHAPTER THREE

First Flush of Independence

"Zaïre (Congo) at that time was running on politics and music. Everything was negotiated in bars. The stars were an integral part of public life. This country was the exception in Africa."

Manu Dibango, *Trois Kilos du Café*

THE MOVEMENT FOR INDEPENDENCE and self-government had begun to spread across Africa, following Ghana's independence in 1957, and no people deserved the deliveration it promised more than the Congolese. They had endured generations of suffering and exploitation, first at the hands of slave traders who penetrated from both coasts of Africa, and later under the brutal rule of King Leopold II of Belgium, who acquired this vast country, absurdly named the Congo Free State, as his own personal property in the mid-1880s. By comparison with the huge wealth of ivory, rubber and minerals to be plundered, human (African) life had little value. Under Leopold's instructions the Europeans behaved ruthlessly and barbarically. News of the worst atrocities, including forced labour, punitive mutilation and genocide, led to an international outcry and Leopold was eventually obliged to hand over control to the Belgian government. The territory became a colony in 1908.

However, the Belgians' paternalistic colonial system brought little real change. The Belgian Congo was still run as a massive business enterprise, with large private companies given monopolies on the exploitation of the country's resources. The government and the economy of the colony were so welded together that the American journalist John Gunter, who visited there in 1954, said, "it probably represents the highest level of state capitalism ever attained". The Belgians used some of their profits to buy the Africans' goodwill by providing social and health services and a high standard of living. But they showed no interest in helping the intellectual development of the Congolese. There was no citizenship; neither Africans nor Europeans had political rights, and a strange form of apartheid applied, whereby Europeans were discouraged from settling and Africans were practically banned from visiting Europe.

Bill Alexandre recalled the difficulties of making his first visit to establish the CEFA recording studio in 1953: "In Belgium people knew little about the Congo because it was 'out of bounds'. It was really hard to get there, unless you were hired by a company that paid your return ticket and made a deposit of at least 50,000 Belgian francs to cover eventual repatriation expenses." From the other perspective, as Gunter reported, Congolese sailors who jumped ship in Europe were forbidden from returning home in case they generated a consuming envy in their countrymen by describing all the wonders they had seen.

Restrictions were also placed on travel at home, with residence permits, employment certificates and curfews, and Africans were not allowed to drink anything stronger than beer, or to own firearms. Musicians, in demand by white patrons and studio bosses, could usually obtain a 'laissez passer' and had much greater liberty than the average Congolese. There were no state schools, although mission facilities were heavily subsidised. Even the University of Louvanium, opened in Leopoldville in October, 1954 as a subsidiary of Louvain University in Belgium, was a Catholic institution. It offered courses in medicine, agriculture and general education, but none in engineering or law. Academic achievement was not greatly encouraged by the Belgians who viewed the prospect of African intellectualism with trepidation. Instead they created a prosperous middle class by recruiting and rewarding skilled craftsmen, junior administration workers and clerks, *kalaki*. Those who acquired sufficient education and property could aspire to achieving 'European status' as 'évolués' (literally evolved, or civilised people). However, in 1955 there were only about 1,000 members of this elite, and by the end of the decade there were reportedly fewer than twenty university graduates.

Leopoldville became a thriving commercial centre with tall buildings and a road system of wide boulevards and roundabouts, linking the downtown, European area with the many zones of the 'cité populaire' or 'cité indigène', which already accounted for more than half of the capital. Grid pattern street development had begun during the 1940s and there were several progressive housing developments. Many attractive 'deco'-style bungalows of that period still survive in the present day zones of Kinshasa, Kasavubu and Kalamu. Water supplies and electrity were also fed to the cité and, in the late 1950s, mosquito-infested areas were regularly sprayed with insecticide by helicopters. Transport was adequate; there were trolley buses running through Matonge as far as the FrancoBel bakery at the Bongolo junction around the corner from Loningisa's first studio. These electric vehicles were recharged from terminals mounted high on roadside pylons which still stand as archeological relics of one benign aspect of colonialism.

Life was sweet. There was plenty of work, money in people's pockets, good health services, food to eat, beer in the bars, music on the radio, and even radio loudspeakers in the streets for those who did not have sets at home. As permits were required for outsiders to live in the city, the population was controlled. 'Public order' was maintained by rounding up the *watama*, layabouts and the unemployed to be sent back to their villages. By the late 1950s, the whole city had a total population of only 200,000, yet a 70,000-capacity sports stadium had been opened near the Victoire roundabout. What more could the people want? Kabasele knew the answer: *Independence Cha Cha Cha*.

In January, 1960, Grand Kalle's African Jazz became the first Congolese musicians to visit Europe, accompanying the delegates to the Round Table conference on independence convened in Brussels. Kalle had been invited by the brothers Kanza, of whom Thomas was the first Congolese to graduate from university and who was to become a minister in the first independent government. This close association between music and politics was then, and remains, a characteristic peculiar to Zaïrean life. The praise-singing function of music is common to most African cultures, but Manu Dibango, the celebrated Cameroonian saxophonist who joined up with Kalle's band in Belgium and spent the next two years with them in Kinshasa, was surprised to find that music was such an important part of public life. As he recalled in his memoirs, *Trois Kilos du Café*: "Zaïre (Congo) at that time was running on politics and music. Everything was negotiated in the bars. The stars were an integral part of public life. This country was the exception in Africa. Elsewhere musicians were no more nor less than beggars: 'Amuse yourselves, but keep your place'." In many cases Congolese musicians were on familiar terms with the first-generation politicians with whom they had grown up.

Kalle was one of the country's leading figures and it was appropriate that he should have been invited to Brussels. Accompanied by Nico Kasanda, he also took with him three members of OK Jazz: the clarinettist Edo Lutula, rhythm guitarist Brazzos and, most crucially, Vicky Longomba who thereby abdicated as nominal leader of OK Jazz. In Belgium, African Jazz recorded *Independence Cha Cha Cha*, the song which was to become an anthem for the period which is still remembered as 'la Belle Epoque'. The record was the first Congolese release on the new 7-inch, 45rpm format, and it signified the end of a technological as well as colonial era.

Dibango had been recruited by Kalle to play keyboards, and in the first series of sessions they recorded

40 songs in a few days. While the 45rpms were pressed up in Belgium, Kalle took the tapes back to Leopoldville for pressing into 78rpm discs for the home market. When he returned to Brussels a few months later he was accompanied by Franco. Dibango met a "shy and gifted" young man, lacking the confidence needed to negotiate with Europeans. He recognised, however, that OK Jazz were "less sophisticated, but more popular than African Jazz" at home, and he believed that Kalle had decided to co-opt the one musician who posed a commercial threat.

Whether or not he was aware of possible exploitation by Kalle, Franco gladly seized the chance to further his career, and always acknowledged his debt. "Kabasele Tshamala and I were friends," said Franco years later, "not rivals. He was the father of Zaïrean music and I always followed behind him. He was the first Zaïrean producer in Europe. With his help OK Jazz made our first international release for his label Surboum African Jazz. When he and his band accompanied the politicians to the Round Table conference and he had the possibility to press some records, he invited me to contribute. With the money which came from those records sold on the Surboum label, Kalle provided me with the first set of equipment for the group. And I can tell you, for me it was a lot."

Following the Round Table discussions, independence formalities were rushed through hastily and, on June 30, 1960 the Democratic Republic of the Congo was born. The President was Joseph Kasavubu, and Patrice Lumumba, who had been released from prison by the Belgian colonists to attend the conference, became the country's first elected Prime Minister. Franco was quick to endorse the new Premier in the song *Lumumba Heros National*. The era of the First Republic began explosively, however. The Belgians had provided a constitution which virtually left nobody in control. There were six provincial governments, each with more or less the same powers as the central government. Only days after the birth of this new, and potentially great, nation Moise Tshombe announced the secession of Katanga (later Shaba), the mineral-rich state in the south-east of the country. The administration and the army were still largely in the hands of the Belgians who began to play off the various regional and international interests against each other. A bloody revolt by Congolese soldiers against their white officers led to a panic exodus by Europeans and the Belgian army sent in 'occupation' troops to the new country.

Lumumba, who appealed for both UN and Russian help to repel the Belgian 'invaders', became the fall guy in the ensuing political chaos, whipped up by the super-powers over this wealthy and strategically important territory. The CIA, fearing another stand-off with the Eastern bloc to compound their problems with Cuba, wanted Lumumba out of the way, and he was dismissed by Kasavubu with the support of the powerful military commander, Colonel Joseph-Desiré Mobutu, who had previously been Lumumba's personal secretary. The ex-premier was eventually caught in a road block, handed over to his enemy, Tshombe, and killed in January 1961. This was the first coup and the first political assassination in post-colonial Africa.

According to the Zaïrean music historian Lonoh Bokelenge, most musicians stifled the urge to take sides in the conflict, concentrating instead on the need for unity. But Franco could not resist speaking out against what he saw as 'irresponsible' members of the first government in the song entitled *Ba Deputés Botika Mbilinga Mbilinga* (Parliamentary Deputies Stop the Confusion). OK Jazz had recorded two commentaries in the early days of the Katanga affair, *Docteur Moise Tshombe* and *Governement Ya Katanga Oriental* (Government of Eastern Katanga). Some musicians were commissioned by politicians to sing praise/ propaganda songs, but when Lumumba was assassinated a grieving Franco expressed his own sadness with the heartfelt bolero lament *Liwa Ya Lumumba* (The Death of

Lumumba). There followed more rebellions in several other regions of the country and civil war was almost continuous until Mobutu took over the presidency in a coup in 1965.

The 'Belle Epoque'

Despite the political machinations, the post-independence period is still remembered as a golden age for the music. Most of the military action, the bloodiest uprisings, brutal retaliation, atrocities, assassinations and horror, took place far away from Kinshasa. In the capital, the flow of goods and money continued, with diplomatic observers, UN soldiers, advisers and the world's media boosting the local, short-term economy. Manu Dibango, who arrived in July 1961, when the European TV screens were full of black and white images of blue-helmeted UN troops preparing for civil war, found an "African paradise"; the downtown 'ville' had a beauty like "New York in miniature", while in the cité indigène, illuminated by candles and kerosene lamps, he found the "surging multitude warm and communicative". Dibango might have had stars in his eyes, but the period is also remembered affectionately by many of the Kinois who lived through it. As Sam Mangwana reflected, during a war there is no unemployment; and people have an even greater need for the simple pleasures of life.

A mood of optimism prevailed. European-based record companies were paying advances in the form of band equipment, while at home, the breweries and some well-established foreign companies would sponsor the bands, giving handsome payments in cash or kind for musical promotion. Although the country's economic stability was to take a battering, this system continued into the 1990s, with Kinshasa's two breweries underwriting the country's top bands. In the early days of independence there was also considerable support to be gained from the political parties who were always in need of musical propaganda. As Mangwana confirmed, in those days the musicians didn't go short of anything.

Ironically, the newly acquired independence meant that the music business was now centred in Europe. Kalle was contracted to Sofrason, the local associate of Decca, with whom he also negotiated the contracts for OK Jazz. But, as both Franco and Dibango were to find out, the first payment would usually be the last. African Jazz was making big money but the 'intellectual' Kalle gained a reputation for meanness that was to prove the eventual ruin of his band. As one contemporary observed, "Kalle had money problems with everyone. No one would argue with him because he was strong and was hard to confront. Only Tino Barosa had the mettle to stand up to Kalle and once the money started to flow past his pocket he left the band." When the Benetar brothers quit Leopoldville at independence, everything in the Opika studio had been inherited by Kalle and Roger Izeidi, increasing their financial base. The music business, however, was funded by a variety of means; Dibango had already observed that Congolese musicians were financing their enterprise with diamonds, which they smuggled into Europe with ease.

Franco evidently did well enough out of his first visit to Europe, as he returned to Kinshasa with a new American car, a status symbol already flaunted by Bowane and Kalle. Having progressed from 'Franco the pedestrian' to 'Franco the cyclist' then 'Franco the Vespa', he was now 'Franco the motor'. He quickly became familiar around town, by sight and even by sound, as he roared through the night leaving a trail of broken and battered dogs. At certain times the sound of a big V-8 motor being gunned, followed by a dull thud and a sharp howl, marked Franco's progress. He apparently hated dogs and would swerve across the road to run them down. This may have been more than a personal expression of a common African attitude to these 'unclean' beasts. In some parts of West Africa drivers believe that killing dogs ensures survival and brings

*The popular Kongo Bar in Leopoldville: Social facilities and fashion
awareness were well developed in the capital years before independence*

financial gain, and a high strike rate is part of the toll
demanded by the gods who rule the road. Franco might
well have shared that belief, as he reportedly sacrificed
dozens of the luckless animals.

Without Vicky, who was still performing with Kalle,
Franco was obliged to take most of the vocal leads himself,
although he also recruited Mulamba Joseph 'Mujos', a
singer with a similar alto voice to Vicky who helped
maintain the band's vocal identity. 'Simaro' Lutumba
Ndomamueno, rhythm guitarist with Orchèstre Micra,
joined up for the recording sessions in Brussels. Leon
Bolhen, another solo, or lead, guitarist had also come
aboard after Brazzos had left. Simaro, who was a few
months older than Franco, quit OK Jazz for a while after
the recording trip, but he was soon to return to the band
where he made his reputation as a composer, and later
became vice-president of the group. As a counterpoint to
the up-tempo cha cha cha which Kalle had launched,
Franco resorted to the slower bolero rhythm with a song

called *Majos*, inspired by a woman named Marie-Josephine, with whom he reportedly maintained a long, romantic relationship. With its modern, rock ballad feel, the record became a big success.

But holding a band together in those times was difficult. The fact that independence had also arrived across the river in the French Congo encouraged many Brazzavillois to return home. Sovereignty was formally handed over by the French in August, 1960. On the Brazzaville side of the Congo river, political involvement had come at a more orderly pace. A moderate African Prime Minister, Fulbert Youlou, had been appointed two years before independence and he became the first President. But even before the coup which aligned Congo-Brazzaville with the Eastern bloc, there was little ideological agreement between the two newly-independent countries. Following the support offered from Brazzaville to the Katanga secessionists, relations became cool. At this time a great wedge was cut out of OK Jazz as many Congolese members quit to return home. Among those who left the band were De la Lune, Edo Nganga and Celestin Kouka, who joined up in Brazzaville with Malapet, Tino Baroza, Papa Noel and Essous to form Les Bantous. This group, which has survived intermittently with the help of Congolese state sponsorship, was to become the standard bearer for Congo-Brazzaville music, developing a parallel but separate form of the Congo-Zaïrean rumba. The two bands were to share many members over the years. The relationship between OK Jazz and Orchèstre Bantous was recognised a few years later with the release of the perennially popular compilation album, *Pont sur le Congo* (Bridge over the Congo) which featured one side of songs from each band.

Independence had brought a new awareness of the commercial possibilities of music and, following the obvious success of organised orchestras, the scene in Kinshasa changed completely. Many of the early solo stars faded from view. Bowane re-formed Ry-Co Jazz as a quartet with his fellow Mongo guitarist, Jerry Malekani, and travelled with them as manager to West Africa, where he stayed for twenty years; Wendo dropped back into semi-retirement; Tino Baroza handed over the solo role in the Bantous to Papa Noel and travelled to Cameroon, where tragically he was murdered. The European studio musicians and most of the producers had quit the country around the time of independence, while many of the local solo artistes just drifted into obscurity.

Franco's old boss Dewayon, however, could see the way music was developing and the Watam group, which included his brother Johnny Bokelo, was expanded into a fully-fledged orchestra called Conga Jazz. It later evolved into Orchèstre Cobantous before Bokelo set up Conga Succès on his own behalf. The old partners still collaborated with each other and Franco played some sessions for Dewayon. Having learned from the same teacher, Bokelo and Franco had similar playing styles and they also sometimes took part in each other's recording projects. Many of Bokelo's own compositions sounded uncannily like Franco's, and he often continued the themes or replied to Franco's subject matter.

The sudden slump faced by OK Jazz after losing so many of the Congolese musicians was short lived, even though many fans had already begun to write them off. Recruiting musicians has never been a problem in Kinshasa and the group was soon back up to strength. Piccolo Tshiamala replaced De la Lune on bass, and the saxophonist 'Verckys' Kiamuangana Mateta brought new energy to the band. The singer Kwamy Munsi took the place of Mujos, who had crossed the river Congo to join Les Bantous, although he would reappear a few years later.

In February, 1962 OK Jazz set out on their first foreign tour, accompanying delegates to a political convention in Nigeria, and at the same time inaugurating the new airline service between Leopoldville and Lagos. In Nigeria the band was joined by a local saxophonist, Dele Pedro, already a fan of OK Jazz, who had renamed himself 'Isaac' after the tenor sax player Isaac Musekiwa. The two Isaacs had met up in Lagos where they became friends and collaborators, and when OK Jazz returned home, the young Nigerian went with them. Dele Pedro settled into the 'family', marrying Cheri Zozo and becoming a long-serving stalwart of the band. His position was consolidated when he composed the comic song *Tu Bois Beaucoup* (You Drink a Lot) which was a big hit throughout West Africa in the mid-1960s. In the song, an anglophone narrator explains, in broken French, that he does not speak French or Lingala, and he cannot understand what is going on around him, except that his friend drinks too much. Dele Pedro further tapped the anglophone West Africa connection with *Congo/Nigeria* and *Meet the OK Jazz*.

The fluid nature of OK Jazz as a pool of eligible musicians had been established, and already several ex-members had found their way back. At the time, the 24-year-old Franco was at one of his most creative and open-minded periods, and virtually all the band members had star rating. The band was now formally registered as a business with the Chamber of Commerce and the OK Jazz revival was announced with the hit songs, *Amida Asukisi Molato* (Amida Dresses Best) and *Cherie Zozo*, composed in honour of a great fan of the band. In 1962 De la Lune and Vicky Longomba returned to join what many consider one of the strongest line-ups OK Jazz ever boasted. The next year Edo Nganga and Simaro reappeared and the singer Lola Checain joined the vocal line, the latter two settling in for lifetime careers with the band. OK Jazz had now acquired the prefix TP (Tout Puissant), taken from the name of a top football team, TP Engelbert, and intended, among other things, to eclipse the rank of 'Seigneur', the mock religious title which Rochereau affected.

In the euphoric, post-independence mood, the new breed of record producers in Leopoldville were optimistic. The new 45rpm singles format stimulated the distribution and penetration of records, which now gave better value in terms of running time, sound quality and durability. Following the first OK Jazz 45s, released on the Surboum OK Jazz label and distributed by Decca in the early 1960s, Roger Izeidi negotiated a deal for Franco and OK Jazz to record in Paris for the CEFA label. Singles were also released on Epanza Makita, the umbrella label for overseas sales of OK Jazz product, and Likembe for Franco's own compositions, as well as Zebi, Ngoma and Boma Bango. East Africa had already been introduced to the early hits of OK Jazz when the Loningisa catalogue was licensed to ASL, of Nairobi, in 1959. From 1962 there was also a string of international releases available in West Africa on the Pathé-Marconi label, the French subsidiary of EMI. These recordings were cut at Studio Boulogne in Paris and later pressed up in Ghana, Nigeria and other countries. Pathé also distributed another label, called simply OK Jazz which, following a short run of the band's compositions, released a series of non-rumba, variety and soft jazz music by other artistes like singer Frank Lassan (brother of Checain), Leon Bolhen, and the Orchestra Hi-Fives. In the early 1970s Franco launched Editions Populaires, the first of his 'own brand' labels for the output of OK Jazz.

The reason for all these labels was to feed the market for dance music which reached its peak during the 1960s. Dance has always been at the core of Congo-Zaïrean music, so much so that Zaïrean audiences for top bands like OK Jazz do not bother to applaud, but show their appreciation by taking to the dance floor. The craze, not just for dancing but for re-inventing the dance every few months, began with the first Congo-Zaïrean social music. The rumba was not just a rhythm, but a dance, developed from the *maringa*, an early fusion of Congolese folklore styles, which had been hugely popular in the Congolese bars during the late 1940s and early 1950s. This was danced without a partner and involved a simple sideways alternating movement from the hip. The rumba proved the basis for a series of popular dance crazes throughout the 1960s, which included the *kara kara* (from the word meaning to avoid, in this case stepping back from your partner), the *boucher*, the *soukous*, the *kiri kiri*, *mombetta*, *apollo* and *cavacha*. The *boucher*, both a dance and a new rhythm introduced around 1965 by the Bantous, was quickly taken up by the Kinshasa youth who exaggerated the hip movements. The new rhythm was smoother than the more excitable rumba, and OK Jazz adapted it to become the *rumba-boucher*. Franco later revived the *odemba* rhythm, named after the strong liquor obtained from a hardwood tree with symbolic, aphrodisiac and medicinal value, and he synthesised the *rumba-odemba*.

Unleashing the *sebene*

During the early 1960s, the new affluence not only generated custom for the musicians but also gave them access to the Western technology and instruments with which to take the music forward another stage. Solid body guitars and electric basses were now available, along with Western or 'jazz' drum kits, which had not previously been in use, better amplifiers and effects pedals to alter the sound of the guitars. The increased length of a record side, from 3min 30sec to approximately 5min, allowed musicians to squeeze on to disc some of the stunning improvisation which, when played live, provided the motivation for dancing. Discs can only give a condensed version, but during a live performance numbers would be extended freely as the musicians improvised in a kind of open-ended reverie, known as the *sebene*.

The *sebene* has proved to be one of the master strokes which has made Congo-Zaïrean music so popular throughout Africa and the rest of the world. Its introduction has been credited to Bill Alexandre, who probably first used the term (from the English 'seven') back in 1953, although the form has been a feature of Congo-Zaïrean popular music since the earliest days. Possibly dazzled by Franco's power playing, the widely-experienced musician Ray Lema has overstated the case for Franco's influence, but his mastery of the form has never been in doubt. "Franco didn't study music at all," said Lema. "But one day he just grabbed a guitar and he invented (sic) what we call in Zaïre the *sebene*. The *sebene* is the starting point of what we call today *soukous*. You take a phrase and you repeat the phrase until it becomes hypnotic, till you get dizzy."

The Zaïrean musicologist Pierre Kazadi, writing in *African Music*, describes this two-part structure which has changed little during the music's evolutionary phases. In the first part, the melody, which is dictated by the poetic construction of the lyric, follows a pattern of alternating lines of question and answer established in the first verse. This is repeated once, ending on a different cadence, before a slightly varied instrumental interlude, which is followed by a repeat of the second section. The second part of the song includes a choral refrain in the responsorial singing style, followed by the *sebene,* an improvisational episode which Kazadi describes as a groove. Here the band members lock into a mesh of short, repeated rumba phrases out of which the solo guitarist breaks, playing with a restrained intensity which can mesmerise the dancers as the groove builds towards euphoria.

One element central to the *sebene* is a third guitar to play between the rhythm and the soloist, known as the medium guitar, or *mi-solo*, which fills the middle ground between the unchanging part of the rhythm guitar and the free-ranging role of the soloist. The three guitar section became the basic line-up of a typical Congo-Zaïrean band, which now featured a vocal front line of two or three singers, supported by a horn section, and the whole would be driven by a rhythm section of bass, drums and percussion.

The *sebene* had to await the appropriate technology before the outside world could appreciate its irresistible charms on record. A tactic introduced in the 1960s was to spread one number over two sides of a 45rpm disc, with the song on the A-side and the B-side reserved for the dance-inspiring *sebene*. For the first time, emphasis had begun to shift from the singers as the centre of public attention to the role of the guitarists. The country's top two guitarists were both masters of the *sebene* but Dr Nico, playing in African Jazz, was confined to a more formally structured music, with Euro/American-style arrangements. Nico had earned the sobriquet 'God of the Guitar' but in developing the music it was Franco, the 'Sorcerer', who was to make the biggest impression.

In 1963 Dr Nico, who had accompanied Kabasele since the first days of African Jazz, along with his brother Dechaud, broke away to form African Fiesta with Kalle's singing protégé, Rochereau. Franco's greatest commercial competitor had suffered a serious split up which eventually resulted in the formation of two new groups to give OK Jazz a run for its money. As Rochereau reminisced to *Bingo* magazine some fifteen years later: "At the start of 1963, I joined Dr Nico and African Fiesta. It was a difficult period since competition was fierce. We were two leaders, Franco Luambo Makiadi of TP OK Jazz, and me with African Fiesta. In order to beat the opposition, I used the weapons of my opponent against him. I built my success by modelling our songs on Franco's, arranging them in our own style and in such a manner that the author did not recognise them." African Fiesta was a great success, but within a short time the guitarist and the singer had also clashed, leading to the formation of two bands, Rochereau's African Fiesta National and Nico's Africa Fiesta Sukisa. Some contemporaries believe the split was engineered on behalf of their record company, the African label, which was now represented by Roger Izeidi, the original maracas player who picked up many tricks of the trade alongside Bill Alexandre and later Kabasele.

The rapidly expanding music scene in Leopoldville was supported in 1963 by the appearance of the first local music magazine, *Congo Disque*, which regularly published the lyrics of popular songs. The publication was joined later by *Likembe*, and soon after another title, *Ye!*, hit the street; editor-in-chief Luambo Makiadi. Franco had set up the small format magazine as a platform to defend himself from attack by gossip column, and to promote the works of OK Jazz. As he put it at the time: "The robber doesn't like to be robbed himself." The fortnightly publication boasted a print run of 10,000 copies until eventually a national paper shortage put paid to *Ye!*

A family affair

While many eyes and ears were expectantly turned in Nico's direction, OK Jazz eventually wore off the opposition and consolidated its position as the top orchestra with a line-up expanded to match the extra competition. The extended family system of OK Jazz allowed the prodigal sons to return home if they liked. In 1963 Simaro had reappeared after his venture with Congo Jazz, which had disintegrated during a tour of Kassai, and a year later Vicky Longomba had been joined by another fine vocalist, Michel Boyibanda from Brazzaville. Applied to OK Jazz the family analogy is appropriate. There were now about twenty musicians in the band and several were lodging at the house Franco had bought for his mother on Rue Gemena, in the zone Kasavubu. Most of the others were now living close to each other in the district of Yolo. But even in the closest families there are rows and serious disputes. Franco's relations with his musicians sometimes became very strained and over the next decade he was to become embroiled in some quite serious feuds. The popular press, then as now, were always ready to help these incidents on their way.

In the early 1960s, Franco was also living in Yolo in Rue Mokariya with his companion Paulina, a local woman who bore at least one of his many children. Paulina was a well connected 'fashion' woman, who moved with rich friends and was a founder of *moziki ya la mode*, the offical fan club, and also a member of the OK Jazz committee. She was a big, strong young woman of the Mbudja tribe from the Equatorial region, who would fight or frighten off challengers to her right to be Franco's woman. And she faced plenty of competition from *bandumba*, the 'free women' who flocked around Franco in the bars and public places where he used to hang out. His reputation for womanising was something he himself admitted to, and he already had several children. The older offspring, borne by a variety of mothers before he settled with his eventual wife, Annie, lived with Franco's mother at the house on Rue Gemena.

Paulina was considered to be a good match for Franco, able to equal him in spirit and vigour — and in singlemindedness. Some friends go so far as to say that Paulina made Franco what he was, by both encouraging and provoking him. Together they started to put on weight, gaining the importance of *nzoto kilo* (a big body). They used to fight frequently, neither pulling their punches but exhibiting what friends have described as a kind of 'loving brutality'.

During the civil turmoil of the first five years of independence the music business had not suffered unduly. In fact it was one obviously profitable sector which had attracted many of the newly-liberated Congolese businessmen, to whom easy credit and bank loans were now available. Record sales were booming, particularly with distributors in West and East Africa anxious to retail the hot sounds of Congolese music. But it was the major international record companies who were now behind the local studios and producers. Loningisa had closed down at independence but some studios, like Ngoma, were still run by their original management. After independence the Belgian-owned Ecodis studio was opened in Limete and Franco began to record there. They also had a pressing plant which later became known as Mazadis.

For a while in 1964, however, OK Jazz was practically crippled by debt, and Franco reportedly had to hide the band's instruments from the bailiffs. But after lifting themselves out of the financial slump, OK Jazz made a spectacular return to popularity with a song which Zaïrean commentators still regard as a milestone, considered to be the first successful synthesis of popular music with folklore not to be based on the rumba or one of its 'Latin' relatives. *Ngai Marie Nzoto Ebeba*, (I, Marie Whose Body is Crumbling) was a satire on modern morality, sung on the part of a woman (Marie) who lives by her charms and is being besieged by some of the married women whose husbands support her. Musically, the song marked a more mature OK Jazz style, with a new bass line and a dance to accompany it called the *Ye-Ye*. The *sebene* was stretched out longer, an element of swing was incorporated and Franco attacked his guitar with added passion.

In Leopoldville, the bars with live music were now allowed to stay open till around midnight, an improvement on pre-independence times, when dancing was usually an afternoon activity. Later in 1964, however, rebellion spread across the country and the war did come to the capital. A security clampdown followed a campaign of bombing which targeted many bars in the zone of Kinshasa, and the curfew was re-introduced, meaning that bands could only play from about 5pm until 7pm. When the state of emergency was rescinded the bands came back, playing later and longer than before.

In 1965, following the Simba rebellion in the north-east of the country, Colonel Mobutu took control of the nation in a coup, after mounting a military offensive against the various rebel forces in which some 200,000 Africans and several hundred whites were killed. All musicians were obliged to pay homage to the new President, and Franco's song *Au Commandement* (To Authority), likening him to a reincarnation of Lumumba, was well rewarded. Not being deaf to the propaganda value of music, Mobutu ensured that practically all the top groups now received sponsorship from the state and OK Jazz was not alone as the official state band. When there was a presidential function musicians from all regions were brought together, including one of the newer bands which had quickly become popular in the capital, Vox Africa (which later gave birth to Festival des Maquisards and Grand Maquisards, virtual nursery bands for OK Jazz, African Jazz and African Fiesta). Founded in 1963, Vox Africa had a big hit in 1965 called *Jeanine*, sung by the up-and-coming vocal discovery, Sam Mangwana.

In 1965 Mobutu had promised to hold power for a limited period only, while a democratic system was 'restored' to the country, but the omens for the immediate future were not good. Shortly after taking power, the new president's will was imposed on the people, particularly the citizens of Leopoldville, in one horrifying gesture, with the execution of five dissident politicians and intellectuals at a public hanging at the Pont Kasavubu, an open space close to Matonge, considered sacred to the memories of the independence movement. The psychological shock suffered by the huge crowd of witnesses was immense, and many of those who saw the executions believe the event transfixed the Zaïrean people into a state of submission. It was the gruesome inauguration of the Second Republic, a totalitarian regime in which Mobutu treated the country as his personal fiefdom, seeming to replace the Belgian King Leopold with the Leopard which was his personal symbol. The Second Republic was to last until the president grudgingly admitted the inevitablity of democracy in 1990. During that period human rights were ignored or abused, free speech was unthinkable and free thoughts unspeakable. The most important social rule was 'Article 15', the final, unpublished rider to the Zaïrean constitution which said 'look after your own'. The mood in Leopoldville was sombre; the pleasures of the 'Belle Epoque' had come to a brutal, if temporary, halt.

Franco, however, was by now well established as a national hero, and the aura of controversy which surrounded his personal and business affairs only boosted his standing with the 'common people'. Many of his early fans had matured into important or influential figures themselves but, although Franco's popularity transcended the newly-erected class barriers, he was by no means immune from political interference. The sweet music of OK Jazz went down easily, but the sugar coating often disguised a bitter pill of social criticism which was harder to swallow.

Like most citizens of Matonge, he had witnessed the public executions of the Kimba group of alleged coup plotters at the Pont Kasavubu, and following the events of 1965, Franco had his first serious run-in with the new regime, although it was not the first time one of his records had been censored. His song *Luvumbu Ndoki* (Luvumbu the Sorcerer), believed to be a commentary on the executions, was banned as soon as it hit the streets, and all copies of the record were hunted down on the morning of its release, not only in Kinshasa but also by agents of the regime in Europe. The song was a Kikongo folklore number frequently heard at family palavers when it was used as a vehicle of accusation. Literally, Luvumbu was a mythical chief who sacrificed members of his clan for his own benefit, but the name was used to represent any treacherous person, and everyone who understood the lyric would also know who the accusation was aimed at. Although Kikongo is not one of President Mobutu's languages his secret police understood the message and

Franco was briefly detained for questioning.

On his release, Franco fled to Brazzaville with the band, where they stayed for about six months. But no president could risk completely silencing Franco, who stretched to the maximum the traditional African concept of immunity for 'griots' who comment on society. He returned to sing another day, bringing back new recruits, including the fresh, plaintive-voiced singer, Youlou Mabiala and bassist Celi Bitchoumanou 'Bitchou'. The band made its comeback at the new premises of the Vis-à-Vis club in Matonge.

The Congolese music business was at its most prolific during the mid-1960s with new bands being encouraged to form throughout the rapidly expanding metropolis of Kinshasa, many as spin-offs from OK Jazz and the African Jazz clan. By 1966 there were reportedly 30 professional dance orchestras in the city. Kabasele had disbanded his group and was temporarily out of action. Both Rochereau's and Dr Nico's African Fiesta bands maintained the 'international' populist style of the African Jazz 'clan' against OK Jazz's more rootsy music. They provided the main competition, followed by Vox Africa, Orchèstre Manta, Los Angel, Révolution, Vedettes, Orphée Jazz, etc. Many of the new bands, lacking either an identity of their own or the imagination to recognise it, came up with derivative or imitation names which, like their music, echoed one or more of their heroes, the most transparent being OK Succès. There was also a band recording for Ngoma called OD Jazz.

One of the more interesting outfits was the Jazz Barons, sponsored by a businessman called Baron Manoka — not so much because of its influence on a 'school' of music or its famous hit records, but because it was the basis for a continuing jam session, which virtually everyone joined in. Musicians throughout Kinshasa knew that after their own performance, the Jazz Barons would still be

For ten years African Jazz provided Franco's main opposition. On the left: Manu Dibango, Tabu Ley and Dr Nico. On the right: Kalle and Izeidi

playing and as the other clubs closed they would gather at the Barons' current 'siege' to jam into the morning. Although only half a dozen records were released under the name, the Jazz Barons made many reputations and no doubt saw some crumble. Among those who regularly participated in the jam sessions were Franco's brother Bavon Marie-Marie, Mose Se Fan Fan, Michelino and sax player Modero Mekanisi, who later became Rochereau's bandleader.

The music business was based exclusively in Kinshasa, and musicians from the regions were obliged to head for the capital. There were several successful bands in the interior of the country but they had no possibility of recording and little chance of travelling to the city. Notable among those who did break through were the Baba Gaston band from Lubumbashi, Rocken Band from Kisangani and Comet Mambo from Matadi. Across the Congo river in Brazzaville, the top orchestras included the Bantous, Succès-Bantou and Cercuil Jazz. Because of the growing number of groups and the tightening competition, several musicians moved away from the Congo to try their chances farther afield. Baba Gaston became a big man in Kenya while, in 1967, OC Jazz was set up in Zambia by Ghaby Mumba who a decade later went on to form the Real Sounds of Zimbabwe, a band which gained a strong following by mixing original compositions with cover versions (or 'copyrights') of OK Jazz songs.

Some observers believe the proliferation of groups in Kinshasa, and the ease with which they could record, did not help the quality of the music which, in their ears, was becoming debased by commercial considerations. The urge for musicians to break out of virtual servitude and lead their own orchestras led to a constant swapping and changing of personnel, often to the detriment of the music's development. This scramble for success became more desperate in 1966, when career opportunities multiplied with the inauguration of a television station in Kinshasa, followed a year later by the extension of national radio broadcasting to a full 24-hour service.

During the mid-1960s the general awareness of the strengths of indigenous culture, as opposed to colonially enforced values, was being raised throughout Africa as independence spread like a bush fire. Kalle's *Independence Cha Cha Cha*, the accompaniment to many countries' celebrations, was a light, dance party number with a catchphrase that would never wear out, but it was also a song of the world, celebrating the bright lights of 'civilisation' and linking the fledgling free peoples of Africa with the rest of the planet. On Mobutu's taking power, the song was banned, not because of its internationalism, but because most of the names praised by Kalle were now unmentionable. The music of OK Jazz,

however, was more acceptable to the new head of state —
and it came indisputably from the heart of Africa.

Using the same ingredients and technology as Kalle,
Franco aimed his music at a different audience, the
'ordinary' people of Leopoldville, whose preoccupations
were hardly international. The main subject of Franco's
compositions was, for a long time, how to deal with, and
understand, 'civilized' concepts like money, property,
individualism, ambition and citizenship, which confused
many of those who came, and still come, into the city fresh
from a village existence where every aspect of life is a
communal experience.

Several generations of city in-comers have been
guided, or at least accompanied, virtually from childhood
to maturity by Franco. The advice was conveyed in the
most generally accessible form, as parables or fables usually
based on simple episodes from common experience, such
as a love affair, which Franco frequently used as a metaphor
for life. This close contact with his community was
something Franco would always preserve in his music and
in his personal life. It was the foundation on which he
built such a great career. Although Mobutu eventually
claimed the title of 'Guide' for himself, it is a name that
would have better suited Franco, and would have sat well
alongside the many credits and honorary titles he acquired.

Although Franco was now a pan-African superstar, power struggles, feuds and personal tragedy marked the second decade of OK Jazz

CHAPTER FOUR

Treachery and Tragedy

"God created Judas. But Judas stabbed him in the back."
Franco, *Course au Pouvoir*

THE FIRST FORMAL RECOGNITION of Franco's cultural contribution came in 1966, when OK Jazz were invited to represent their country at the World Festival of Black Arts, held in Dakar, Senegal. The same year, as President Mobutu's first exercise in reaffirming the country's African-ness, the capital city, Leopoldville, was renamed Kinshasa, the name of the original village on the spot where H.M. Stanley, aka Mbula Matari (Breaker of Rocks) settled when 'developing' the territory for the King of the Belgians. Franco returned home from Senegal via Brussels, where he stopped off to buy equipment, leaving the saxophonist Verckys Kiamuangana in charge of the Kinshasa squad. Franco was becoming a regular visitor to Europe, although at the time the band had not begun playing shows there. On this occasion without OK Jazz, Franco had cut some records in Studio Boulogne in Paris with a group of students including Flavien Kasavubu, the son of the first president, whose composition and contribution to OK Jazz remained anonymous. The songs were released under the name Orchestra Franco.

Behind his back, however, there was treachery afoot. On his return to Kinshasa, Franco discovered that no fewer than nine OK Jazz musicians had defected. Taking advantage of Franco's absence, Kwamy, the singer who had left his side the year before, had enticed them to join the aptly named Orchèstre Révolution. Those involved in the breakaway secession included the bassist Piccolo, rhythm guitarist Brazzos and the singer Mujos, who had only returned to the band a few months earlier and contributed the 1965 smash hit, *Pesa Ngai Dix Makuta* (Give Me Ten Cents). The accompanying vocalists Djeskin and Jojo also quit.

Kwamy, who was about the same age as Franco, was a valuable member of OK Jazz but, according to the guitarist Fan Fan, who was already a member of Révolution, "Kwamy wanted to be like Franco. He wanted everything he had, but he didn't work like Franco." Rondot Kasongo, the saxophonist who later became Franco's personal assistant and confidant, concurred: "He always had problems. When he was ill, Franco had to support him. When he had debts, Franco helped him. When he had nowhere to live, Franco had to help. And if he didn't have a car Franco had to buy him one. If Franco criticised him for anything he would become troublesome. Although Franco did everything for Kwamy, he was never happy."

Outraged at the nine-man mutiny, and personally insulted at the deception by his old colleague, Franco handled the problem of a musicians' coup with musical weapons; he attacked Kwamy in song. Franco recorded *Chicotte* (The Whip) referring to an instrument of colonial oppression with which offenders were regularly punished. It was obvious who Franco wanted to whip and, although Kwamy's name was not mentioned, the song was a virtual declaration of cold war against the 'brother' who had criticised and deceived him. 'Am I, Franco your enemy,' he sang. 'You joined me in OK Jazz and I made you what you are. Now I am your enemy because I refused to buy you a truck to carry wood to market.' This open criticism upset Kwamy who responded with the song entitled *Faux Millionnaire* (False Millionaire), in which he satirised the habits of the nouveau riche, specifically Franco. Bemoaning the fact that he was broke, Kwamy sang, 'If you hear I've been arrested don't be surprised. I've got so many debts. There's no money left in the bank.'

Franco concluded the dialogue with *Course au Pouvoir*

(Race to Power) in which he replies: 'You are running me down everywhere, my brother, but I take it as a joke. You have invaded my private life. What jealousy. It hurts you to hear that Franco has done this or that. . . You wish Franco's name would disappear for ever. God created Judas, but Judas stabbed him in the back.' The dialogue finished there, with the end of the song's *sebene* turning into a note-for-note conversation between the guitar of Franco and Verckys' sax. The fans of Kwamy gave lyrics to some of the instrumental phrases, suggesting that Franco was calling the singer back to the fold. But that was wishful thinking on their part.

The feud with Kwamy was just one of many Franco was to have with musicians and collaborators. The love/hate element of Franco's relationships with his colleagues and rivals became more exaggerated the more famous he became. At times there were almost continuous intrigues and power struggles going on within the band, and jealousy was rife inside and outside OK Jazz. But Franco was loyal to the group; as long as musicians chose to stay with him, he would stand by them. Early in 1967, at a time when OK Jazz were working steadily, a trip to Brazzaville resulted in an embarrassing clash with authority which only enforced Franco's standing as a team leader. On disembarking from the river ferry shuttle after playing in the Congolese capital, OK Jazz's equipment was checked by port officials, who discovered an amplifier which had been reported stolen. Although not personally implicated, Franco spoke up on behalf of his musicians, and along with the rest of the band he was locked up until the affair was sorted out.

The leader's loyalty was not always reciprocated, however. While Franco was again absent in Europe another coup was attempted, leading to the formation of a new orchestra which went on to give OK Jazz a serious run for its money. This time the leader was 'Verckys' Kiamuangana Mateta. Remembered by a schoolfriend as a rough-and-tumble 'young hooligan', Verckys had been recruited into OK Jazz in 1962 from a fanfare band attached to the Kimbanguist church (followers of the Congolese prophet Simon Kimbangu), and became a close confidant and lieutenant of Franco. He was six years younger than Franco, with a wild, raucous saxophone sound which drew on contemporary American soul and rhythm and blues music as well as Congolese folklore, without much reference to the mellow-toned rumba delivery of his predecessors. His ability to improvise suited Franco, who liked to hear a saxophone voice reply to his guitar solos.

Verckys was also a 'homeboy' from Franco's region, while the other two sax players, Isaac and Pedro, were both from anglophone countries. During the latter days of his spell with OK Jazz, Verckys introduced a passionate, driving energy to the *sebenes* with his powerful arrangements for the horn section, which often sounded like a reworking of religious fanfares. He was a great showman who liked to clown and play up to the crowd. In the late 1960s he affected the current American hippie fashions, with flared jumpsuits, Afro haircut and sideburns. The frenzied horns had brought a new power to the band and provided Franco with the additional momentum to crank up his guitar solos another gear. The whirlwind effect on songs like *Marcelina* identifies one of OK Jazz's most magical phases, as if they were playing with a whole line up of sorcerers. Verckys had spent six years alongside Franco, but he was ambitious.

Late in 1967, while Franco was once again away in Europe buying equipment, Verckys called some of the OK Jazz musicians to record a series of songs, to be released under his own name on the Ecodis label. Among those he invited were Simaro, Bitchou, Checain and Youlou, along with the young guitarist from Révolution, Mose Se Fan Fan. After the recording, Verckys himself travelled to Europe with the master tape in order to press the discs. In the meantime, however, Franco returned to Kinshasa with his first Dynacord amplifiers and, as he was in a position to pay salaries, the musicians who had defected were encouraged to rejoin OK Jazz. The coup was, therefore, pre-empted.

Also invited into OK Jazz was Fan Fan, who had grown up listening to the Sorcerer's guitar, and who could match his style so closely that they developed a technique of playing joint solos. Franco would utilise the 'capo' on his instrument to keep it tuned in a high register, while Fan Fan would double up on the solo parts, playing the low notes on an open-stringed guitar. The two solo guitars would be supported by a 'mi-solo' player and anything up to three rhythm guitarists. For a while Franco also called on two bass guitarists. Combined with the Verckys-inspired whirlwind horns, the band was creating a glorious frenzy of sound.

Verckys, however, did not see the best chance to further his career in OK Jazz. As one of the other horn players observed, "Verckys had been in a hurry to learn everything, so he could become a big 'patron'. Since he joined OK Jazz he had it in his head to become a big boss to compare himself with Franco. He did everything he thought necessary to achieve that." After a public disagreement with his chief, Verckys quit to set up Orchèstre Vévé, which maintained the wilder, less restrained approach, and for several years was one of the country's most popular bands. Verckys' departure from OK Jazz revealed another conflict between Franco and one of his top musicians, which would simmer away for several years to come.

The gap in the horn section was filled by Rondot Kasongo wa Kasongo, who had been playing sax in Negro Succès with Franco's brother Bavon Marie-Marie. "Whenever Franco went to visit his mother he would meet Bavon and myself, because we were close friends and always together, and he would give his advice on what was best for Negro Succès," Rondot remembered. "When

Verckys left OK Jazz, Franco told his brother he needed a new saxophonist. So I went to Franco's house at Limete, and he received me warmly. He asked the other musicians of OK Jazz for their comments and they agreed. I was engaged straight away and given some records to take home and learn, and a saxophone to rehearse the songs with. Afterwards I became very close to Franco. Apart from the music, I became his personal assistant, learning a lot about his private business, and I stayed with him until the end."

A musical event of international significance took place in 1969 when James Brown, the American 'Godfather of Soul' and pioneer of funk, came to Kinshasa amid a storm of publicity. His show at the 20 May football stadium was attended by some 100,000 people and, more importantly, seen by many thousands more in the Kinshasa region through the newly-introduced medium of television. Brown's repetitive, riffing music, which punched home a hard dance rhythm and emphasised it with full-blown horn lines and a big band delivery, had a profound effect on popular music throughout the world, notably on the early Afrobeat of Nigeria's Fela Kuti. Brown's influence was no less significant in Zaïre, although Franco, for one, claimed not to be impressed. He went to the show to witness the American phenomenon but, despite his earlier predilection for the 'Yankee' lifestyle, Franco never had much time for Western 'pop' music. He found the funky music tedious, and Brown's jerky style of dancing undignified. As some of the OK Jazz musicians recalled, Franco remarked that James Brown "danced like a monkey". Furthermore, Franco was reportedly offended that Brown had arrived back at the source of Black music, without giving sufficient acknowledgement to his musical roots, or making social contact with Congolese musicians. However, OK Jazz played a farewell show for Brown, who seemed equally unmoved by their rumba. Towards the

end of the set OK Jazz was joined by a local singer/
guitarist of pop material, named Lolo, who performed a
James Brown number which the funkster joined in on. But
the two godfathers did not share the stage.

Brown left his mark on the scene, however, and OK
Jazz and Verckys' Orchèstre Vévé, in particular, picked up
on his dynamic new sound. Later, groups like Trio Madjesi
and Bobongo Stars would fall more wholeheartedly under
the spell of funk, but its early incorporation into Congo-
Zaïrean music can be heard to good effect in two OK Jazz
songs: *Minoko* (The Mouth), with its quirky English-spoken
incitement to 'change the stakes' and a *sebene* which is
totally soul, and *Edo Aboyi Ngai* (Edo Rejects Me) which
culminates in a rousing dose of Afro-funk, and some
Brown-inspired grunts and shouts of 'come on' in which
Franco gives a rare, but recognisable, impression of the
English language. This was a kind of personal jive talk, or
nonsense scat singing, which no one could understand
and which came to be known in OK Jazz circles as
'Francophonie'.

Turbulent times

At the end of the 1960s Congo-Zaïrean music was cresting
a commercial peak, and OK Jazz had become a big money
spinner, particularly for international distributors. Since
independence, OK Jazz had been releasing records for
the CEFA and Epanza Makita labels. Most of the early
recordings came out during the subsequent decade on the
African label, successor to Decca's Surboum label set up
for Kalle. Franco retained strict control of composers'
rights and the band's cash flow. Vicky, who is considered
to have been one of Franco's few close friends and was
joint leader for much of the band's early days, was believed
to be receiving a smaller cut of the total earnings, ostensibly
because Franco was doing most of the administration
work. It is most likely that financial differences were
behind the eventual split between these two colleagues,

although some observers have claimed it was naked ambition which caused Franco to jettison his old friend. Just as Nico deserted Kabasele, they claim, Franco elbowed Vicky out of the limelight, and the credit. Others say it was only Franco's generosity which allowed Vicky such a prominent role, because he believed his friend deserved to be more than just a sideman. When Vicky had returned to OK Jazz after his adventures in the early 1960s, he had walked straight back into his role as co-president, even though the band had by then been recreated in the image of Franco, and there had always been a tension between the two leaders. By the end of the 1960s they were even recording for different labels: Franco was now to be found on Boma Bango, while Vicky had set up Viclong for his own OK Jazz productions. According to Rondot: "Franco worked hard at everything for the success of OK Jazz, but Vicky did not want to make the same effort."

Matters came to a head in 1970 when Kwamy started making attempts to rejoin the band. Vicky was set firmly against the return of his troublemaking vocal rival but the vice-president, Simaro, prevailed on Franco to take the singer back. On his return, OK Jazz gave a welcome-home party for Kwamy, but not many people came and the glory of the singer's return was tarnished. Reverting to his old ways, Kwamy demanded a car from Franco, which he quickly crashed. As Fan Fan recalled, "He immediately demanded another car, which he also crashed."

The arguments raging over Kwamy's return raised a barrier of distrust between the two co-presidents of OK Jazz which finally split them apart. Tired of supporting his old colleague, in 1970 Franco had the final showdown with Vicky Longomba, in which he accused him of not making any effort for the success of the group. "If that's the way it is," Franco reportedly told his co-president, "we should separate. You go your way and I will continue with OK Jazz." Vicky did eventually go his own way, first with Conga Succès and later as founder of Orchèstre Lovy, by which time, one of his musicians remembers, "He was so angry, he wanted to smash Franco. He was looking for a sorcerer to destroy, if necessary even kill, Franco." Disgusted, that particular musician quit the inappropriately named Orchèstre Lovy. Vicky never regained the heights of popularity he had enjoyed with OK Jazz.

Kwamy stayed on for a couple of years but by now, as another colleague recalled, "He had become bitter and vengeful, and his career gradually slipped away." Some of his fans ascribed this to Franco's behaviour, but insiders claim that Kwamy brought on his own problems. He briefly joined African Fiesta but could not recoup the lost ground. Dejected, he descended into a downward spiral of drinking, wandering the streets and sleeping rough. He eventually lost his home and his friends before fading from the scene. He died in 1974. Kwamy had not been rejected personally, however. While staying at Franco's house, he had fathered a child by one of Franco's relatives, which the big man took care of, and eventually adopted.

Franco now had a reputation for feuding and quarrelling with his colleagues and friends, which added another dimension to his public image. Amongst followers of Kwamy, Verckys and Vicky he had made many enemies and, with his growing status, he was to become a ready-made target for gossip and rumour. Power seemed more important than dancehall popularity, which he must by now have taken for granted. In 1970 Franco, Roger Izeidi, Roitelet and other respected senior musicians called a meeting at the Vis-à-Vis club to organise a new musicians union. The performing rights society, Soneca, had been established a year or so earlier with Kalle as president and Vicky as his deputy. Most orchestras had suffered serious splits between members and many artistes were anxious to recoup royalties and defend their rights against businessmen, bureaucrats — and their own collaborators. Franco was installed as president of the musicians' union, Umuza.

He also had an international reputation to develop.

The band was touring abroad more frequently now, both under the auspices of the state and for commercial promoters. The diary for 1970 shows a demand for OK Jazz in West and East Africa. First they travelled to Benin (then Dahomey) and Togo, where Franco was astounded to meet up with his old mentor Bowane, with whom he had lost contact for more than ten years. Bowane was in good form but his band, Ry-Co Jazz, had gone their own way to the French Antilles. Pleased to be able to assist this most respected elder, Franco gave Bowane a pile of money with which to re-establish himself. While making a road transfer from Togo to Ghana, to catch a Pan-Am flight home via Lagos, OK Jazz spent their spare evening playing an impromptu dance at an Accra nightclub run by the popular highlife bandleader Jerry Hanson.

Soon afterwards, OK Jazz made their second visit to Zambia where they played in Lusaka and the Copperbelt towns of Ndola and Kitwe. On their return home the musicians were surprised to hear that Franco had been detained at the airport. He reappeared after a few days and did not mention his detention to the band members, but the assumption amongst OK Jazz was that he had been caught smuggling something in or out of the country — either that or the President had some serious business to discuss with him. A short while later the band flew out once again for Sudan, where they spent one month.

In Khartoum they played in a stadium before a huge crowd of many thousands who stampeded the stage to get close to Franco, precipitating a crush in which at least six people died. Musicians recall ambulances carrying the dead and injured past the stage, where the band played on, frightened to stop in case the panic turned to anger. OK Jazz returned home via Bangui, the capital of the Central African Republic, where they played for the self-styled 'Emperor' Bokassa. Franco was reported to be personally offended when the eccentric ruler, who allegedly collected some 60 wives, took a fancy to one of the OK Jazz dancers, and the band cut short their tour.

There was more than one trip to Chad, whose President Tombalbaye was an ally and friend of Mobutu. In October, 1970 there was a summit conference in the capital city, N'Djamena (then Fort Lamy), attended by twelve heads of state from the OCAM alliance of Central African countries. During the evenings, following the banquets, OK Jazz and Rochereau's newly-created Orchèstre Afrisa were to give a showcase presentation of Zaïrean music. Rochereau was to present the première of the spectacular new stage show he was developing for his European debut, while OK Jazz were to offer their own well-polished rumba. In the words of one participating musician, it was a "most bizarre episode", not just because of what happened on the trip but also because of the sequence of events which occurred in Kinshasa before and after Franco's absence.

Franco had recently bought himself a new car, a Renault. On the first day he used it, he drove into a pedestrian, who suffered a broken leg, and from then on Franco seemed to lose interest in the vehicle. His brother, Bavon Marie-Marie, who was by now a successful performer, needed a car of his own for prestige as well as transport reasons, and pleaded with Franco to let him have the Renault. The night before the planned departure for Chad, Bavon and Franco were heard having a very violent discussion, which ended with Bavon seriously insulting his elder brother and breaking the rigid tradition of respect within the family. When Franco arrived at the airport the next day he was reportedly distant, vague and 'not himself'.

But the OK Jazz and Afrisa musicians, travelling together, soon had other things to worry about as their plane took off into a ferocious equatorial storm. They eventually arrived safely but the storm had followed them, and torrential rain flooded out the first night's show at which Rochereau was due to perform. The programme was rearranged and on the second night both bands shared the stage, with OK Jazz due on last. Rochereau had presented his showbiz routine, with its choreography and Western-style arrangements and Franco was eagerly expected to give a powerful response, not least by President Mobutu, who was anxious to show off his favourite music to the gathering of presidents. Franco failed to appear, however. Vicky led the band for what was to be one of his last shows with them, and Fan Fan took the guitar solo. They were nervous moments, but when all the heads of state began to get up and dance, the musicians knew they had saved the day. In the morning, Franco appeared at Fan Fan's hotel room beaming with pleasure and satisfaction, because the young guitarist had preserved the honour of OK Jazz. He gave him a massive present of 150 Congo francs, about fifteen times the normal bonus.

Franco, who normally travelled and lodged with his musicians, had spent the night in another hotel where, coincidentally or not, a certain girl was also staying. She had been on the plane from Kinshasa, apparently accompanying Youlou. For the return trip Franco loaded up the plane with ceramic tiles and as much building material as he could to help fit out some property he was developing. Heavily loaded, they flew into an even worse storm which buffeted the passengers and set their stomachs reeling as they seemingly tumbled from the sky more than half a dozen times. The aircraft had to make several circuits before it was able to land at Ndjili aiport. Relieved as they all were to be home, Franco had the unfinished argument with his little brother still waiting for him.

Brotherly love

Tshongo Bavon Marie-Marie, who was about six years younger than Franco, was often thought to have been a half brother, born of a different father. But Franco, Bavon and their sister Marie-Lousie were registered as the legitimate children of Emongo and Mama Makiesse. Like his big brother, Bavon became a guitarist and, not surprisingly, he often sounded just like Franco. As Sam Mangwana remembers: "Bavon Marie didn't play exactly like Franco. He was younger and he had his own style, but he had the same 'punch' to the guitar. He didn't copy Franco, but he had almost the same spirit. It is normal for two brothers to be alike. They had almost the same fire, the same charm when they played guitar." But Franco did not initially give his little brother much support. Unlike other sibling collaborators — Nico and Dechaud, or Dewayon and Johnny Bokelo — Franco and Bavon Marie-Marie did not play together in public. Indeed, when Franco first heard that Bavon was performing secretly at the Tshibangu bar in the Bandalungwa district of Kinshasa he tried to stop him. One of Bavon's companions recalled that Franco had turned up there to argue with the bar owner, Albert Tshibangu, who he knew well from having played there himself. Franco said: "Listen, Mr Albert, I have the greatest respect for you, but I prefer that my young brother doesn't play here anymore. I would prefer that he continues his studies at school. I know this business and I do not want to see my brother take the same route." Bavon was not so easily put off, however, and he continued to play in secret until eventually Franco gave up his resistance and offered him a guitar — in fact he supplied all the equipment for the Negro Succès band in which Bavon played lead guitar.

Bavon did not officially join OK Jazz, although there was a time in 1963-4 when some of Franco's collaborators, De la Lune and Edo, suggested that his brother should not be left to struggle in lesser bands and as he had the same 'punch' he would make a good second soloist. Some contemporaries believe that Franco was actually coaching Bavon to be the eventual leader of OK Jazz, although he did not want to diminish his junior brother's standing by making him the band's second-in-command, where he would always be in Franco's shadow. Later some records were released under the name of Bavon and OK Jazz, notably *Johnny Yuma*, on Editions Populaires, but it appears that Franco himself was playing solo and the credit was given as a form of tribute. Although he had, on occasions, played with OK Jazz, Bavon was not stylistically or temperamentally compatible with the regular members, or the clan of OK Jazz enthusiasts. One contemporary remembers that Franco and Bavon had made some recordings together on a portable tape recorder, which Franco re-recorded after Bavon's death. But OK Jazz never played his songs live.

Bavon was an original member of Orchèstre Jamel Jazz, founded in 1967 with saxophonist Empompo Loway 'Deyesse', but he achieved fame with Bolhen's Negro Succès, where he was known as a great showman, or 'animateur'. Bavon was undoubtedly pop star material, and he knew it. He was playing a faster, more youthful style of music and developing an image to go with it. With his skin bleached by mercury-based complexion creams, he proclaimed himself the most handsome man in Kinshasa and, like Franco a decade before, he found his greatest support among the economically liberated young women of the city. He was a controversial figure, embroiled in a highly competitive business, however, and his rise to success did not pass without comment and jealous gossip. Indeed, one rumour which gained credence, in a city full of malicious whispering, was that he had bought his success by mortgaging his soul to a sorcerer.

The relationship between popular musicians and *bandoki* (magicians or sorcerers) has not been as well documented as that of traditional musicians, for obvious reasons. But the subject of sorcery crops up so frequently in discussion with people involved in the contemporary music business that some credence must be given to its significance. It is often claimed that certain musicians (in fact, almost all the successful ones) have entered into

Bavon Marie-Marie: proclaimed himself the most handsome man in Kinshasa

some kind of pact with a sorcerer who has guaranteed a
limited period of success in exchange for control over the
souls of living beings. In some cases, it is said, this might
be a direct trade-off with, say, five years of stardom being
given in exchange for five years off the life of the artiste
himself. More commonly, musicians are believed to
nominate other people's souls and, if the exchange is to
have any value, the surrogate soul(s) are usually those of
close family members. Sometimes those chosen victims
find out about it and a round of bargaining ensues, with
the number of souls being increased as their value descends
from mother, wife or son down through the ranks of
family and friends. This exchange does not actually require

the sacrifice of the victim but is rather a symbolic form of possession by the *ndoki* — a debt which can be called in later or used as collateral. Should one of the victims die an apparently normal death, the *ndoki* would nevertheless be understood to have claimed his property. Such stories are still current in the 1990s among African musicians (not only Zaïreans) and, when questioned as to their reasoning, several have attributed the fabulous success of the Beatles during the 1960s to their 'sorcerers' in India. Although it is claimed that there are *bandoki* resident in every neighbourhood of Kinshasa, the most influential people are rumoured to seek their success through the medium of foreign (often Senegalese or Malian) sorcerers.

While Franco had been absent in Chad, Bavon's temper had obviously not cooled. On the evening after their return, on October 8, 1970 the OK Jazz musicians met up at the Vis-à-Vis club for their payment. Bavon turned up in a furious mood with Franco, alleging that he had been sleeping with his girlfriend, Lucy, the one who had accompanied Youlou to Chad, and who had also just arrived at the bar. He began shouting and further abusing Franco in a most violent row in front of the gathered musicians. Franco walked out as cool as possible. Bavon swung a punch at Youlou and then went for Lucy, who fled from the club and jumped into a taxi. Bavon, who now had a car of his own, gave chase along Avenue Kasavubu. He stopped the taxi a few kilometres away in Bandalungwa, by swerving in front of it, and dragged out the unfortunate girl. Angry, shouting and evidently distracted, Bavon packed the girl into his car, did a fast U-turn and, in the darkness, he drove head-on into a parked military truck which had broken down at the roadside.

It was a horrifying accident: Bavon was killed outright and Lucy lost both legs. News of the accident was brought to the house in the Rue Assossa where Mama Makiesse lived with her second husband, and she was one of the first to know her son was dead. She personally informed Franco who, with his inability to find death 'acceptable', was demoralised and virtually paralysed with grief. He would later record several songs expressing his sadness, including the moving folklore lament *Kinsiona* (Bereavement).

The rumours about Bavon's involvement with sorcery, however, were not laid to rest with him. It is still common in many parts of Africa for uneducated people to believe that any person's death should be directly attributed to their enemies. There is no such thing as a total accident. Every effect has to have an identifiable cause. Some people thought Bavon's credit with the sorcerer had simply run out, an idea supported by the prophetic quality of one of his last hit songs, *Libanga na Libumu* (A Stone in the Womb) in which he sang, 'I am crying because it is too late to have a child'. More suspicious observers searching for a culprit did not bother to look far. Franco's personal suffering at the loss of his young brother was only compounded by the ignorant gossips who claimed that, twisted with jealousy, he himself might have arranged for his brother to have an accident. Far from capitalising on this change of fortune, however, Franco retired from the music scene for a long period, seemingly detaching himself from the running of OK Jazz for the first time in his career.

Picking up the pieces

In creative terms Franco was now at one of his lowest periods. After Bavon's death, he withdrew from the limelight for several months, retreating with his private grief into a long period of mourning. One month after the burial, the musicians resumed work but the band was virtually ignored by Franco and, as one senior member recalls, OK Jazz was "really down, broken". Franco was able to live off the fruits of his past success, and from now on his relationship with the majority of OK Jazz musicians became less personal and more strictly professional; the close companionship and shared adventures of the early days were over. OK Jazz had matured into a commercial organisation, and Franco had achieved the status of PDG 'President Directeur-General', or managing director, of one of Zaïre's best-known businesses. But he was now spending more time supervising the construction of various properties, and was also becoming more heavily involved with Vita Club, a role which upset many of his musicians, particularly those who supported other football teams.

Worst of all, although the singles on the newly-launched Éditions Populaires label were selling well, OK Jazz concerts were often almost empty, causing some musicians to lose heart. At home they faced fresh competition from 'new wave' bands such as Thu-Zaïna, Zaïko Langa Langa, Stukas and Lipua Lipua. These young bands, while re-interpreting 'authentic' Zaïrean music, were actually structured more like Western pop groups than the classic orchestras. They played a more frenetic music for their student audiences, which did away with horns altogether and for the first time made a prominent feature of the snare drum. And they took much of the momentum away from the big dance orchestras. The core musicians of OK Jazz, however, ploughed their creative energy into keeping the band alive.

Even when Franco did turn up to play, his approach to the music was sometimes lacklustre and casual. Several songs from that period which came out on disc were recorded informally during rehearsals by Franco with a handful of musicians, and subsequently released without any re-recording, mixing or embellishment. The band was packed with creative musicians, however, and they were able to 'carry' their leader when he was off the peak of his form. For some time OK Jazz had been working on a quota system of composing two new songs each week. These would be performed for the dance public on Fridays and Saturdays and at the end of every month the most popular two would be recorded for release on the first

Saturday following. His long absences meant that Franco was growing distant from his band and losing touch with popular taste. As one of his colleagues commented: "All the musicians wanted him there. Everyone loved him and we were upset when he wasn't there. Franco's brain was indispensible to OK Jazz."

The revival came at the start of 1971, stimulated by Rochereau's fabled appearance at the Paris Olympia theatre in December, 1970. The show he presented to the European public was the one he had premièred in Chad in October. The first concert was televised back home and the brassy, flamboyant and tightly-performed spectacle was considered a great success. In the annals of Congo-Zaïrean music it is often considered one of the finest hours. Unfortunately for Rochereau, however, a second concert was later broadcast, which had none of the novelty value and was performed to a less appreciative Paris audience. In truth, the second show was considered a failure by the supporters of OK Jazz, who included President Mobutu, and Rochereau lapsed into a state of semi-retirement which was to last for about three years.

It fell to Franco to take the initiative, for which he was handsomely funded by the President. He devised and choreographed a stage show based on the national ballet of Guinea which featured 40 musicians and dancers. He recruited most of Rochereau's dancing troupe, the Rocherettes, and renamed them the Francolettes. And, as if in response to the 'look, no-horns' phenomenon of the new-wavers, no fewer than four new trumpeters were taken on. Barami-Miranda, Adamo Seye, Kapitena Kasongo and 'Vieux' Kalloux were expected to boost the excitement level with piercing fanfares. "From now on," Rondot observed, "when the saxophone played a solo part, the trumpets would play the reprise. Even if there was no sax player, the trumpets could play the sax part, although this system meant there was less opportunity for improvisation."

The band's resurgence came with a package of songs which had originally been recorded by the would-be renegades Bitchou, Simaro and Fan Fan. Two classics of that period, Bitchou's composition *Infidelité Mado* (Mado's Infidelity) and Simaro's *Ma Hele* (My Helen) were among the batch of tapes and record masters which Franco had retrieved from Verckys and destroyed. The songs were now dusted off and re-worked, with Franco taking the solo. *Ma Hele* provided one of the most difficult challenges to Franco, from a suprising quarter.

One of the newly-recruited trumpters, 'Vieux' Kalloux, was a slow-speaking, retiring character who had rarely contributed to musical debate. After listening to Franco rehearse his guitar part, Kalloux quietly dropped the observation; "Chief...I may not...be...a...guitarist ...myself...but...even I...could play...a better ...*sebene*...than that." Franco bristled with anger and embarrassment but was obliged to hear the trumpeter's suggestions as, under the band's constitution, every member had the right to speak out. After a painful wait while Kalloux explained his idea of a suitable *sebene*, singing the notes in slow motion: "tang, atanga, tang, ting", Franco set out again. "No, no, no", he was told over again by the trumpeter. After five hours Kalloux was still not satisfied, as Franco's pride and the honour of OK Jazz required he should be. A rehearsal was called for first thing the next morning, which the boss duly attended. It reportedly took him two days to get the part right, and when he did the effort bore fruit. Franco's *sebene* had a hard, metallic urgency about it which met the expectations of the young generation and *Ma Hele* became a massive success, as did the more romantic *Mado*.

The expanded horn section and the dancers had been taken on for the new stage show Franco was developing in response to Rochereau's European spectacular. The manager of the Olympia, Bruno Coquatrix, arrived in Kinshasa to negotitate with Franco, who had prepared a reception for the delegation of four or five Europeans, to which musicians of OK Jazz and past masters such as Vicky and Dewayon were invited. The food was to be prepared by Franco's companion, Paulina. On the day, however, when the guests assembled at Franco's house, neither food nor Paulina were to be seen. She had apparently gone out to buy supplies but had not returned. Franco grew increasingly annoyed waiting for her and eventually the guests decided to leave. Just then, Paulina returned in her car, which was loaded with provisions, but as one witness put it, she was "completely, first-class drunk". Franco flew into a rage, she retaliated, and the couple launched themselves into a violent brawl in front of the assembled guests. Only the physical intervention of Brazzos kept them from seriously injuring each other.

OK Jazz never did play at Olympia. Some observers believe Coquatrix could not come to an agreement with the Zaïrean co-sponsors but Franco claimed to have his own reasons for not wishing to appear there, as he later explained to *Bingo* magazine. "I play typically African rhythms. Consequently, I prefer to play in front of the African public who understand and can appreciate what I do. I don't think Europeans understand my music enough to realise its true value. So why do you think I should be tempted by Olympia? Anyway, that music-hall doesn't interest me. I don't have any desire to play for a public of one thousand people of whom there would be 700 Europeans and only 300 Africans."

Franco had been under stress from many quarters in recent months. The death of Bavon still weighed heavy; he had parted ways with Vicky and now counted several enemies among his ex-musicians. His personal life was also in a kind of turmoil, and his appetite for women was to provide him with further grief. Lately, Franco had been seeing a new girlfriend, a Mukongo woman of Angolan origin called Emma, whom Franco strongly fancied and who his mother believed would make him a more suitable wife than his long-term sweetheart Paulina. Franco had already started wooing Emma, and plying her with presents, when he discovered she was also seeing a rich and influential young politician.

Furious at being deceived, Franco sent his assistant, Jean-Jean, to recover the gifts he had bestowed on the woman, which included a television set and other domestic appliances. When Jean-Jean returned with the goods Franco was pleased to see that everything had been recouped, except for the TV antenna which was left on the roof as a gesture of his rejection. That night OK Jazz were playing at the Kimpwanza bar where Franco was in high spirits, satisfied at having punished the woman's duplicity. However, towards the end of the evening, one musician recalls, "The punisher was himself punished, when Emma arrived with her boyfriend, and the couple started dancing very close and initimately in front of the stage." Glowing with rage, Franco passed the guitar to his deputy and stormed out of the club. Later the woman's politician boyfriend came to the band's rehearsal to apologise to Franco in front of the musicians who had seen him humbled.

There was usually more than one woman in Franco's life, however. The musicians who had witnessed this unusual expression of passion were less aware that Franco had another girlfriend among the ranks of the Francolettes dancers who also inspired intense jealousy. Annie Mbule was the dancer alleged to have been been picked out by the 'Emperor' Bokassa during the show in Bangui, CAR. The musicians, who had been surprised to quit that tour prematurely, soon became aware of the reason for Franco's reaction — he had his own eye on Annie and intended to keep her to himself. When Bokassa made a private visit to Zaïre, allegedly to track down Annie, Franco hid her away, and when the band was recalled to CAR, she was ordered to stay behind. The highly polygamous Bokassa must also have had a serious crush on the woman, and when he learned that she was not travelling with OK Jazz, he reportedly sent a private airliner to Kinshasa just to pick her up. Franco cancelled the tour and returned to Kinshasa where he complained to Mobutu about this interference in his personal life by the president's friend.

Franco managed to hold on to this girlfriend and, perhaps looking for some calm in his stormy existence, he discreetly married Annie later in the year. When he told Paulina of his intentions, she said simply: "Well, you are my husband, but you prefer to forget everything we have suffered together since our childhood, and now you are happy to marry a younger woman. I can't spend my time as a rival to Annie. So I'll leave you to live with her and I will continue with my life and look after my children." As one confidant remembers: "That is all she did. She didn't make any trouble. On the contrary, Franco even insulted her in a song. But it was nothing serious." With the money Franco gave her as a settlement Paulina moved into a house in Matonge and started in business trading goods between Brussels and Kinshasa. Annie was to remain with Franco for the rest of his days, and to mother several of his children.

As a state-sponsored band, OK Jazz turn out in the uniform of the MPR:
(l-r) Dele Pedro, Rondot, Musekiwa, Bitchou, Checain and Youlou

CHAPTER FIVE

The Authentic Voice of Zaïre

"Happy are the people who sing and dance."
President Mobutu Sese Seko, 1973

THE FIRST DECADE of Congolese independence had
seen Franco grow from an ambitious but naive young pop
star into a national celebrity. He was a commercial success,
and the wealth he was beginning to accrue underlined his
growing status. Wealth on its own equated with power.
The fact that he had survived several low points, including
public rows and defections from his camp, and could
bounce back when all around were saying he was 'going
down' made him a winner. For all the competition, when
Franco put his mind to it he could outplay and outsell
anybody. When another competing band was on a run of
success Franco would sit back and observe, even sending
his musicians on vacation if necessary, and he would
either let the new stars burn themselves out or plunder
the competition, recruiting one or two of the most creative
members.

Although he had developed some snobby, ostentatious
traits Franco never deserted his people, for most of whom
loyalty was absolute. Even the harsh way he sometimes
treated his musicians only consolidated his authority. He
behaved, and was treated, like a paramount chief. The
allegations of sorcery, which he personally found tedious
and annoying, did nothing to diminish that authority. On
the contrary, Franco obviously had the strongest fetish. If
that was where the source of his power lay, there was no
point in trying to fight it. If not, then Franco himself must
have had the resources to defeat any witchcraft directed at
him. Although the source of his power rested with the
band, there was an inevitability about Franco's rise, which

ran parallel with the Congo's troubled growth as an independent country. A country which was also run by a self-appointed paramount chief, who recognised and valued Franco's contribution.

In October, 1971 President Mobutu made the first move in the introduction of a cultural revolution which followed his predictable success in the presidential election of 1970. The name of the country was changed from Congo-Kinshasa to Zaïre. The river and the currency were also renamed: the 'Three Zs' were 'One country, one river, one currency'. A massive festival, gathering all the great names in Zaïrean music, was held at the stadium, to launch the new national anthem, *La Zaïrois,* composed by a certain Lutumba (not Simaro). All the professional musicians were obliged to play three numbers from their repertoire. The unfortunate Dr Nico struggled to remember the songs of his youth. Franco, however, could have played all the numbers in his repertoire and was also able to accompany a host of past masters on their own material, staying on stage practically all night. Thus all the practising musicians of the new Zaïre, and the general public, acquired a deeper and lasting respect for the man which transcended matters of personal preference and musical taste.

Mobutu's programme of 'Authenticity', designed to unite the disparate peoples of the country in a single nation, was modelled on Sekou Toure's policy in Guinea and Mao Tse Tung's example in China. Although considered by many observers to have been a self-serving sham, designed only to consolidate the President's own position, Authenticity was in many ways a positive force, certainly in the development of Zaïrean arts. As Zaïre's prime communications medium, OK Jazz was chosen by Mobutu to educate the people on the new changes, and the need to adopt a national Zaïrean identity rather than cultivate ethnic differences. In the song *Oya* (Identity) Franco praised Authenticity as the greatest expression of an individual's freedom. After stating that a people has to define itself and find an identity, he goes on to exhort each of us throughout the world to present ourselves as we really are, with our own mentality, habits and customs. OK Jazz was called to accompany the President on a tour of the country. At each of the regional capitals the presidential address would be followed up by OK Jazz playing political propaganda songs and, by introducing more local folklore traditions into the music, Franco brought the message home to a diversity of peoples. For these official performances the band members, who usually dressed casually or wore slick stage jackets or matching shirts, were obliged to perform in the militaristic khaki uniform of MPR (Mouvement Populaire de la Révolution) militants, complete with army boots and caps. The MPR was now the country's sole political party, of which all citizens were automatically made members.

Authenticity coloured every aspect of Zaïrean culture, and Mobutu started by renaming all those places without African names, before imposing the same indigenisation on the people themselves. "We have decided to bury once and for all the vestiges of our colonial past by renaming those of our towns, villages, regions, and zones which bore foreign sounding names. In the name of our return to ancestral sources, we have rejected borrowed names," said the President in his address to the nation. In explaining his new plan, he continued: "The return to authenticity is not a spirit of narrow nationalism, a blind return to the past but, on the contrary, an instrument of peace among nations, a condition of existence among peoples and a platform for the cooperation of states. For Authenticity is not only a deepened awareness of one's own culture but also a respect for the cultural heritage of others. . . Authenticity as we envisage it, lies in the strengthening of each people for the purpose primarily of reconciling it with itself and enabling it thereby to appreciate the culture of others. In other words, as far as we are concerned, a nation which despises the culture of another demonstrates its ignorance of its own culture."

Mobutu was undoubtedly referring as much to those ancient kingdoms and prospective nation-states which cohabited uneasily in the huge territory of Zaïre as to international relations with other countries. The reconciliation about which he spoke was an internal matter, and the forging of one unified national identity was the President's first priority. He reinvoked the non-tribal philosophy of Lumumba and even rehabilitated the late Premier, renaming the main boulevard which runs from the Ndjili airport into Kinshasa the Boulevard Lumumba.

Fashion police

The full force of Authenticity as a national doctrine was imposed in 1972, following Mobutu's visit to Mao Tse Tung in China. In addition to the name changes a dress code was introduced, which outlawed Western suits and ties for men. The national male dress was modelled on Mao's austere high-necked jackets, although much more elegantly tailored. The outfit was called the *abacost*, from the French 'a bas les costumes' or 'down with suits'. Women were prohibited from wearing miniskirts or trousers, on pain of arrest, while the approved wear was the *pagne*, or cloth wrapper. Taking further inspiration from the French Revolution the people were obliged to call each other 'citoyen' and 'citoyenne'.

As Mobutu doubtless intended, the Zaïreans turned this dress code into a national identity symbol. It also tapped their innate sense of style and made them even more design conscious. The *abacost* was not always tailored in business worsted or conference mohair; colourful wax-dyed prints or European furnishing fabrics were also acceptable and, for a European at least, it was pleasant relief not to see a collar and tie at even the most formal occasions. Informal dress included high-fashion shirt styles, cunningly cut so that a tie could never be worn. The women went to town with the *pagne* and blouse. The huge range of printed textiles available in the markets was probably more varied in colour and design than anywhere in Africa. The 'official' costume included three wrappers (one of which doubled as a scarf or shawl) and a matching blouse, often tight and low cut. The sleeves or shoulders were turned into pieces of virtual architecture with wired-up constructions of frills, flounces and cut-out shapes. Scattered throughout Matonge were dressmakers' shops with little parades of these blouses standing outside.

It was actually illegal for women to wear miniskirts, jeans or wigs. The latter were often overlooked, as many of the 'authentic' traditional hairstyles involved plaiting with extensions, but it was not uncommon, even in the later years of Mobutu's Second Republic to see paramilitaries pulling respectable women off buses by their hair, just to see if it came away in their hands. A young girl walking towards a dancing bar in jeans might be tapped lightly with a policeman's baton and admonished: "Citoyenne, if you must wear trousers when you go out dancing, take a taxi to the door. You should not walk around provoking people." Far worse abuses of human rights were, of course, taking place throughout the new Zaïre but the way the people conformed to, and adapted, the fashion code is a kind of paradigm for the way Mobutism was allowed to work.

Although there were no written laws on the production of music, there were constant reminders that this too should meet the criteria of Authenticity. In his broadcast to the nation in December 1972, Mobutu declared: "We must at all costs re-evaluate our music. Until now I have been trying to retrieve from anonymity most of our artists and musicians. But that is a task for each of us and must not be reserved exclusively for the President of the Republic. What shocks me most in this regard is that many of us know the exact details — and it's not a bad point, quite the contrary — of the lives of great musicians like Mozart, Beethoven and Wagner, up to the point that they'll overlook nothing in the chronicle of their love lives, even the name of their last mistress. At the same time we know nothing about our own artists. It is a little as if our own musicians, the singers of our own Authenticity, had neither the talent, nor the love life worthy of being remembered by posterity. To remedy these deficiencies we have henceforth entrusted to the department of culture and arts, in collaboration with Our (Presidential) office, the preparation of an anthology of Zaïrean music. They will re-record the hits of the past by our old musicians, successes which stand out as the best of Zaïrean music before it became polluted by commercial influences." The first double album in a planned series of anthologies contained songs by several of the first generation recording artistes such as Wendo, Adou-Elenga, D'Oliveira, Bukasa, Eyenga Moseka and Feruzi.

The President was noticeably concerned about the growing commercialism in the music business which meant that, as more records were released more often, the content of the songs was becoming trivialised. In a speech the following year, announcing the formation of MPR 'animation' groups, later known as 'Groupes Choc', Mobutu declared: "Happy are the people who dance and sing." He was referring specifically to the propaganda and morale-boosting troupes attached to the various party offices and commercial companies to "educate the masses and develop revolutionary enthusiasm". Among other duties, this required employees to parade before the national flag each morning and sing and dance the praises of the President-Founder. A similar contribution was expected of the many 'ballet' troupes, which combined music with theatrical drama, dance and story telling. The formation of these mainstream cultural troupes provided a revolutionarily 'correct' counter-balance to the unashamedly playful music of the many 'shanty-town' bands. In the middle ground, able to straddle both extremes, were the country's now legendary dance orchestras.

Throughout the Sixties and Seventies dance was the name of the music game, but the rhythmic ambience generated by the great orchestras was not enough for those who expected a more didactic approach from the artistes at the forefront of the country's revolution. The political and social circumstances were hardly conducive to outright criticism, although Franco maintained his role as a mirror of the common people. Many of the songs were either simple, straightforward declarations of love or commentaries on affairs of the heart, such as the unforgettable love song *Infidelité Mado*, a classic of its kind, composed by Bitchou and sung by Franco and Youlou, and the mournful bolero lament *Lola*. But there

No mention of the name 'Franco' or his label on this official MPR release

was always room for the Sorcerer to insert a blistering guitar solo and, as dance fodder, the late Sixties' and early Seventies' singles decried by the President reached out to audiences across Africa. As Sam Mangwana later commented, anyone in Africa of that generation who had ever enjoyed dancing certainly would have stepped out to OK Jazz at some time in their life. And although formulaic, many of the songs of that period have endured well.

Functional songs were always part of the OK Jazz repertoire and in the run up to the 1970 presidential election Franco had contributed two pieces of party propaganda, *Cinq Ans Ekoki* (Five Years On) celebrating the President's first term, and *Salongo Alinga Mosala* (Community Service is Good Work) exhorting people to join the party-run schemes for keeping the 'quartiers' clean. Politically correct sentiments from Mobutu's point of view; vital OK Jazz music for those foreigners who didn't understand the lyrics but who later bought the records, regardless.

For all his criticism of contemporary 'commercial' music, Mobutu's arts policy was not unpopular with the bulk of Zaïrean musicians, who had no intention of diluting the cultural mix. Interestingly, even some of those musicians who later left Zaïre specifically to embrace different cultures still give President Mobutu credit for consolidating Zaïrean music. One of those is the 'International' Sam Mangwana. "I am not a politician or a fan of politics," he said later, "but you can honestly say that when Mobutu spoke of the need for Authenticity it gave the musicians many ideas. Authenticity never blocked musicians from playing other music, like soul or funk if they wanted. But Zaïrean musicians are very proud of their music. They play as they feel, and they don't feel the need to change for any other people. They play for the people of their time."

Ray Lema, a musical exile in Paris during the 1980s, agreed. "What Mobutu taught the people was that when the Belgians came one of the things they did was to destroy all our cultural background. They convinced people that everything we had before was just a kind of bullshit. And Mobutu said: 'No guys, from today you must know that what we had before was fantastic, Yes. But we are not trying to go back to those things. We want to try to learn them so that we can use them to survive in the modern system.' From 1972 until the early 1980s we didn't have any foreign music in Zaïre. Nothing on the radio or anything. It was strictly Zaïrean music, and that's how groups like Zaïko Langa Langa and Papa Wemba are so strong somehow. And they sound so different. There is no influence of Latin music or Western music. You really feel they were working in a closed system. I think somehow it was very positive."

Lema somewhat exaggerated the lack of outside music, which could be heard on foreign radio stations and in the downtown nightclubs of Kinshasa which specialised in imported sounds. The whole new-wave movement had actually been inspired by Western groups like the Beatles, even if the new Congo beat sounded nothing like that coming from the Mersey. But Papa Wemba, a pioneer of the new generation who was later to become highly critical of Zaïrean rumba's incestuous nature, shared Lema's conclusion. "When Mobutu talked of Authenticity many people confused 'return' with 'recourse'. Before, when the President-Founder proclaimed Authenticity it was a return. But then later he realised it was an error, that you could not return to authenticity — wearing raffia skirts and living in mud huts — but it was a recourse to authenticity. And for me and all the Zaïrean people it was very important because it gave us a personality."

The greatest personality on the scene, and the one to make the most of Authenticity was, of course, Franco who, not surprisingly, put his whole weight behind it. "Authenticity is normal for us," he later explained to British journalist Rob Prince. "In London, if you listen to the radio, you won't hear any songs in French. They just play American songs and English songs. That's Authenticity. Me, I take a dim view of French radio. They speak in French and then they'll play an American song or English song. That's not Authenticity. When President Mobutu began his Authenticity campaign, I wrote songs to help speed up the process so that people could understand what Authenticity means."

As a 'non-tribal' personality, whose parents had different ethnic origins, Franco was an obvious spokesperson for unification. Under the new doctrine, Christian and European personal names were banned and citizens were required to adopt African names: Franco became L'Okanga La Ndju Pene Luambo Makiadi, a combination of different names reflecting his father's and mother's origins — Tetela (Kasai) and Ngombe (Equator) on his father's side, and Mumboma and Mulemfu (sub-groups of the Bakongo from Bas-Zaïre) on his mother's side. Some observers have put a certain amount of Franco's popular acceptance down to this non-tribal identity. Although he was brought up in the culture of the Bakongo, he also exhibited some characteristics of his father's people — considered by the inhabitants of Bas-Zaïre to be more excitable and unpredictable.

Mobutu's cultural revolution was intended to guarantee internal stability after years of civil war and to generate international confidence, which he hoped would be shown in the form of financial investment. The USA was the main hope to bankroll the development necessary to regenerate Zaïre. In the public relations game any positive publicity was to be encouraged, and Franco made good journalistic copy. In March, 1973 a prominent article about the country appeared in the *National Geographic* magazine, with a full-page colour portrait of Franco, captioned: 'One must keep pace, believes Luambo Makiadi. The songwriter and singing idol had switched from romantic ballads to tunes with political lyrics long before a nationalistic 1972 law abolishing foreign sounding names caused him to drop his old name Franco. His willingness to change reflects the mood of young Zaïre, faced with the problems and growing pains of 20th-century nationhood.' Outside Zaïre, however, he retained the name Franco, so as not to disappear suddenly from an attentive and increasingly valuable international audience. However, the name of OK Jazz had probably penetrated further than his own, and even in Zaïre that very Western sounding name was allowed to survive.

The early 1970s was a period of great social change and, like everything else in Zaïre, OK Jazz was in an almost constant state of flux. For a while, when Franco was taking care of other business, the lead guitarist and 'sous chef d'orchèstre', Fan Fan, was virtually running the band. His compositions *Djemalasi* and *Mongando* were big local hits (although not offered for international licence). While initially playing parts laid down by Franco, Fan Fan brought a fresh charge to the *sebene*, injecting a faster, more frenetic style he called the *sebene* de Ba Yankees. "It was the start of the *soukous* style following the *boucher*, and it was for the younger generation. It put disorder into the order of OK Jazz." The new beat and the guitarist's compositions were popular enough that the band's vice-president, Simaro Lutumba, later admitted there was a period when Fan Fan could have taken over control of OK Jazz. The younger guitarist was too impatient, however, and feeling blocked inside OK Jazz he had already decided his own chance of success lay elsewhere.

During a period of suspension from OK Jazz, he had recorded several songs with saxophonist Dele Pedro and members of Johnny Bokelo's band. And since the end of 1969 he had also been recording with Simaro, Bitchou, Youlou and Empompo Loway for Editions Mi under a variety of names including Fan Fan and his Ensemble. This practice, known as *nzonzing*, is still a common way for musicians in the big bands to boost their income with some freelance recording work, and is a frequent bone of contention between bandleaders and their 'employees'. In 1970, under the name Orchèstre Mi, the freelancers scored a hit with *Mele*, named after the girlfriend of Franco's personal assistant, Jean-Jean. The delivery has been described as "like OK Jazz but with a bit more life".

When Franco found out who was responsible for the clandestine recordings he was furious. First he chased out Bitchou, a difficult and often argumentative character with whom he had clashed many times before. In 1972 the issue came to a head once more, with the same characters again at the centre of a big dispute. "Franco had become convinced that musicians from Congo-Brazzaville, like Youlou, were out to break up OK Jazz," said Fan Fan. "He was determined that they should leave. So Youlou went. Because I was Zaïrean I was allowed to stay. I thought that was unjust, so I left too." At the end of 1972 Fan Fan joined Vicky in Orchèstre Lovy before regrouping with Youlou, Bitchou and Kwamy under the name Somo Somo.

In the subsequent rebuilding of OK Jazz, the veteran rhythm guitarist Armando Brazzos rejoined after a three-year sojourn with Orchèstre Révolution. A new bassist, Mpudi Decca, had entered the line-up in 1970 from Orchèstre Vedette. Decca, then a small thin 28-year-old, provided the big, fat bass sound which was to power OK Jazz through the next two decades, providing the perfect fulcrum to balance the rhythmic identities of rumba and folklore. But the biggest coup for Franco, which pushed OK Jazz unchallenged back to a peak of popularity, was the recruitment in 1972 of Sam Mangwana from African Fiesta, via the Maquisards (many of whom, including Ntesa Dalienst, Jerry Dialungana, Dizzy Mandjeku, Michelino, Kiesse Diambu and Lokombe would at some time play with OK Jazz).

Sam Mangwana, who was born in 1945, has a smooth, slightly breathy voice which is almost liquid in its quality, flowing easily from the pits of emotion to the high ranges of desire and pain. His is a voice for love songs and heartfelt ballads, in which the pangs of yearning and denial are unmistakable, and which has charmed a wide cross-section of listeners. As a romantic crooner who played up to the role, Mangwana touched the hearts of many women but he was also hugely popular with his peers, many of whom express great admiration for his singing abilities, if not for his erratic progress as a solo voyager.

The popular press in Kinshasa was initially hostile to Mangwana, saying he was not serious; that someone who played the music of the African Jazz 'clan' was not compatible with the OK Jazz style. Sam rehearsed several numbers with the band but before the first show he received some hate mail from fans of Fiesta, who even threatened to burn his house, and he failed to show up for the first engagement. Franco left Sam alone for a week and then sent his bodyguard, Jean-Jean, to say that it was Franco himself who stood to lose most if things did not work out, and he was willing to take the risk. Sam should come and play one concert and if it turned into a disaster he would pay him a year's salary and give him a plane ticket to go somewhere else to get over things. The show went well, however, and Mangwana became a member of OK Jazz. The first songs he sang with the band were Simaro's masterpiece *Mabele* (The Earth) and *Ou est le Serieux?* (Where is the Seriousness?). Franco was so pleased he gave Sam a present of a car, the first the singer had owned.

Poetry and motion

The prolific output of OK Jazz continued, but there was a marked change of musical direction during the first years of Authenticity. Simaro's song *Mabele*, sung exquisitely by Mangwana, is a moving ballad; a long, slow talking blues about the impermanence of life, which confirmed the composer's status as 'Le Poet'. In the living room of his

The 'Poet' Simaro Lutumba (centre) at home with members of the band

mother's modest family house in Lingwala, surrounded by the trappings of a bandleader's life — two beer-stuffed fridges, two large TV sets, two hi-fi systems, a pair of reel-to-reel tape recorders and a photo of himself with President Mobutu — the 'Poet' explained how inspiration moved him to write his masterpiece.

"The idea came to me late one night as I sat gazing into a candle. As the flame burned down, the wax dripped on to the floor and eventually the light flickered and went out. I was reminded of the similarity with the life of a man. How he comes from the earth and returns to the earth in the short space of a lifetime. When the candle finished, I heard the cock sing and I wrote the first lines: 'The cock sings, day is coming/ Soon the sorcerers will be returning home/ when the day comes, somewhere there is always someone suffering'." Simaro is a reflective and philosophically-minded person, who has made peace with himself. 'I am an artist, my life is full of problems,' he writes half way through the song. 'I don't complain/My wife is the fly. My family is the earth.' After predicting how his friends will avoid him once he is a stinking corpse, he continues 'I know that when we die, we go with a white bedsheet, whether we are rich or poor'.

Franco's lament on the death of Bavon Marie-Marie, *Kinsiona* (Bereavement), was a similarly affecting 'slow', in which he mourned the loss of his brother in the Kintandu dialect of Kikongo, with a folkloric backing. Acoustic instruments, florid horn lines, augmented by the soulful saxophone of Rondot Kasongo, and rich percussion sounds, characterised these and other recordings of the period, like *Kinzonzi Ki Tata Mbemba* (The Wisdom of Old Mbemba) and *Mambu Ma Miondo* (Problems of Land). These classics were released internationally in 1974 on one of the band's most impressive albums *Editions Populaires* (360 056).

Other strong titles on that African label release were Mangwana's debut composition *Luka Mobali Moko* (Look for a Man), and *Monzo*, composed by the new vocalist Josky Kiambukuta, who had joined in 1973 from Orchèstre Continentale. In contrast to the avuncular hulk he later became, Josky was at the time a rather scrawny figure with the crown of his head beginning to poke through his thinning hair. His voice had a high nasal quality full of soulful expression, and his best compositions have always promised a manic kind of excitement. *Monzo* featured one of the simplest of hooks, which could foreseeably be capable of hypnotising a listener. A single guitar note rings out above the arrangement like a bell on some ghostly marker buoy — it is a haunting accent and Franco's *sebene* which eventually cuts through is brutally economical.

But as the companion album (number 360 053) demonstrates, there was always more than one side to the music of OK Jazz. As if to show just how good a commercial song could be, in 1973 Franco released what proved to be one of his biggest hits outside Zaïre, *AZDA*. This was the advent of the full-blown, big band sound which would become the trade mark of the latter-day OK Jazz. While many outsiders thought the song must have a heavily romantic lyric it was, in fact, an advertisement for the national Volkswagen dealership, whose acronym made up the title. The refrain 'Veway, Veway, Veway, Veway' is the local pronunciation of 'VW'.

Franco's working method was similar to that of other Congo-Zaïrean bandleaders to this day. He would basically let the musicians get on with things. Neither Franco nor most of his musicians could read music and, as several of them have explained, Franco did not formally arrange parts for people. He selected the musicians and chose who would play on which song. To work out a number, they would start with the singer and the melody which would have been dictated by the scanning of the lyric. This would already have been worked out on the guitar. For Franco's own songs he would accompany the singer with his guitar, while the band members sat and listened, working out how to fit in their contributions. The rhythm section, guitars and vocal accompanists would then begin to contribute and after a couple of attempts they would have smoothed out the errors. By the third run-through the structure would be complete enough for the musicians to inject individual ideas into the treatment. Then finally, horns would be added.

The rehearsal of one of Franco's own songs might take all day under his direction, after which the band would be ready to record or perform the finished number. With other people's compositions, the musicians would work things out themselves and Franco would come in just for his solo, without necessarily making any other contribution to the song. But however small Franco's involvement, OK Jazz always maintained a sound within which he could play, and although he might not have consciously moulded their style, it was inseparable from the sound of Franco. A vital attribute, without which Franco could never have progressed, was described by Fan Fan: "Franco really had good ears. He could hear everything, harmonies, mistakes, badly tuned instruments. If you didn't listen well, he could get very cross. Guitarists had to tune their own instruments and if you wanted to play his personal guitar, a Fender Jaguar, first you had to tune it exactly."

Heart of the ambience

Since 1971, OK Jazz had been recording on their own mobile studio, a system which was custom made by Televic to Franco's specifications to allow him to record on location. It utilised a 24-channel mixing desk directly feeding to a stereo ¼-inch tape recorder. There was no facility for overdubbing and the productions, which count for some of the best of all OK Jazz recordings, were cut 'live' in one take at the Vis-à-Vis club, near the Victoire roundabout, which Franco was now renting. When the band were recording a take, someone would have to go out to the street to divert traffic from passing too close to the open-air studio. The dance bar, which was to become Kinshasa's live music centre, had been moved after independence to its current premises: a small, roofless, walled enclosure, at the centre of Matonge.

Although Matonge is the pulsating heart of the cité indigène it does not appear on the maps of Kinshasa. It is a 'quartier' which, since colonial times, has been the playground for 'ambienceurs' who begin to gather on the sand-blown streets in the short equatorial twilight after work or school are finished to promenade in their freshly-ironed clothes. It is a crowded, bustling atmosphere, but good tempered. The poverty known by most inhabitants exists alongside the randomly disbursed wealth of the few, seemingly united only by social grace and demeanour — and a common sense of cool.

The cité is actually a vast urban collection of villages linked by meandering avenues. Most of the side streets are unmade, with rivulets of waste water running out from beneath the gates of the compounds. After school, children scream, skip, dance or play football amongst the chickens and ducks. Many streets are occupied by stripped-down hulks of motor vehicles which have sunk into the earth. It is a low-rise neighbourhood, which often appears to be in a suspended state of redevelopment. The few exceptions stand out like navigation beacons. Seen from the top of one such 'storey building' built in the late 1970s, Matonge is full of trees. It looks so calm. Only the dull red corrugated roofs rusting together in the various markets, the traffic-jammed junctions and the music which wafts continually over the neighbourhood give a clue to the activity below.

Down on the street the life really begins as the daylight fades, and reaches its peak in the small hours. Matonge is Zaïre's own 'music city' where 'banderoles' strung across street junctions and hand-painted 'tableaux' outside the clubs indicate which bands are playing where. Around the Victoire roundabout the bars fill with custom and lean young boys move between the pavement seats, balancing on their heads cardboard trays stacked with cigarettes, kola nuts, boiled eggs and other snacks and aphrodisiacs. 'Commercantes' set up tables to sell 'Thompson' (grilled mackerel) *kamundele* (kebabs), *soso* (chicken), *kwanga* (cassava dough) or fresh-made *mikate*, the small, round sweet doughnuts eaten with peanut butter and *pili-pili* (hot chili pepper). Along the Avenue Victoire, between the roundabouts occupied respectively by the Vis-à-Vis and Kimpwanza clubs, is a stretch given over to Sahelian sellers of *ntaba*, barbecued remains of the bleating goats which had been tethered outside during the afternoon. The flaming braziers add flickering movement to the scene and, for those choosing meat from the grill, they intensify the tropical heat. Whether waiting for a 'kombi' minibus after work, eating *ntaba*, or taking to the dance-floor, perspiration is inevitable, and for most people beer is the preferred liquid replenishment.

Matonge's reputation has spread around the world and, for many other African nationals and certain middle-

In 1973 OK Jazz embarked on an East African tour which took in Zambia and Tanzania, including the island of Zanzibar. Not surprisingly, the shows were packed out with enthusiastic crowds, who knew the music from hearing it played on radio and in bars as well as in copyright versions by local groups. One of the strongest regional bands, Orchèstre Volcano, so closely followed the OK Jazz formula that the leader, Mbaraka Mwinshehe, was not ashamed to be known as 'The Franco of East Africa'. From 1964 till his death in 1979, Mwinshehe developed his own version of African rumba using the Swahili language and a guitar style that would have slotted smoothly into the OK Jazz format. Following a show for the people at the Ammani football stadium in Zanzibar, OK Jazz played at the luxurious Mahrubi Palace, late home of the Sultan. The band also travelled west to Guinea and returned to play in Brazzaville for the first time in many years.

That year Franco's beloved Vita Club had reached the final of the African champions cup, and in December he accompanied the team to Ghana, where they beat Ashante Kotoko 4-2 in Kumasi. The final was played over two legs and Vita approached the return match as if the trophy was already theirs. But in one of the most dramatic sporting turnabouts Kotoko won 3-0 in Kinshasa and took the title. One of the Vita players, and also a Zaïrean international, was the guitar-playing composer Mayaula Mayoni, who hung up his boots at the end of the season and installed himself in OK Jazz as a songwriter and rhythm guitarist. At around the same time, the vocal front line was further boosted with the arrival of Blaise Mayanda (Wuta Mayi).

The strength of the guitar section was also consolidated with the recruitment of Thierry Mantuika and Gege Mangaya, original members of Thu Zaïna, the seminal new wave group which had inaugurated the 'authentic' new pop style later developed by Zaïko Langa Langa. Gege was then a 21-year-old virtuoso guitarist, who played solo and accompanying guitar as well as covering on bass. He also composed several of Thu Zaïna's biggest hits. Some twenty of their numbers were recorded for release on Franco's label, Editions Populaires, for which payment came in the form of instruments and amplifiers.

The big man's sponsorship of the original new wave group was not the blessing it first appeared. As Gege recalled, the deal had a kind of built-in self-destruction, which he suspects might have been planned deliberately by Franco as a way to neutralise any new competition. After two years all the band's equipment had mysteriously disappeared or broken and Thu Zaïna were almost destitute. Gege himself recalls 'losing' two guitars in circumstances which he could never unravel. He accepted Franco's invitation to sit in with OK Jazz, while still hoping to revive the fortunes of Thu Zaïna. One day, just before a show, Franco spoke to Gege alone. "Young man," he said enigmatically, "you see I have a big appetite and my stomach is not yet full. Remember, my appetite is still not yet satisfied." He then waved the youngster on to the stage. After the show, Gege conferred with one of the elders in the band who advised him that Franco was hungry to 'chop' any musician who challenged him. From then on, he had to accept that Thu Zaïna was finished, and that he had been absorbed into OK Jazz.

Rumba in the jungle

1974 was the year of the big international launch party for the recently renamed country, and the one event which brought the name of Zaïre to the world's notice was the legendary world heavyweight championship title fight between Muhammad Ali and George Foreman, publicised by the Western media as the 'Rumble in the Jungle'(even though the tropical rain forests are hundreds of miles from Kinshasa). The internationally acclaimed African horn players, Hugh Masekela and Manu Dibango, flew over from New York with the eccentric millionaire boxing promoter Don King, who had booked a suitably heavyweight musical contingent to play before and after the fight. On the bill were some of America's top artistes, including James Brown making a return visit, and 'King of the Blues' BB King, along with the salsa heroes Johnny Pacheco and Ray Barreto. The two-week long festival at the 20 May stadium also featured most of the national and local bands, including, of course, OK Jazz.

This was the beginning of another golden age for Zaïrean music, and a period of heightened competition among the groups of Kinshasa. It is impossible to deduce exactly how many bands were active in the capital at the time. The Zaïrean historian Dr Botombele, writing for UNESCO, says there were 64 orchestras, while Silvain Bemba, quoting *La Semaine Africaine* in April 1975, puts the figure five times higher at 360, although this might have included political 'groupes choc' and informal, neighbourhood outfits. The true total of professional dance or pop bands probably lies somewhere between the two, but personnel were moving from band to band with such regularity that many collaborations were short-lived, and more outfits failed than survived.

The history of one such group illustrates some of the difficulties faced in this competitive musical environment. In 1974 Orchèstre Somo Somo was founded by the guitarist Fan Fan, along with some OK Jazz colleagues. Fan Fan later gave a brief history of the group on the sleeve notes of one of his albums. "In 1974, I, Youlou and Celi Bitchou formed our own group under the name Somo Somo [roughly translatable as 'Double dread'], which originates from a song I composed while with OK Jazz called *Djemelasi*. However, as financial difficulties confronted us and we were unable to obtain good instruments, a misunderstanding arose, sadly breaking up the group. My friend Youlou returned to OK Jazz, Celi Bitchou joined Orchèstre Vévé and the late Kwamy joined Tabu Ley. Alone but

determined I swept aside any offer to join another group
or return to OK Jazz. I started travelling and encountered
many hardships on my safari, meeting many friends most
of whom laughed and scorned me, saying I was stupid to
leave OK Jazz. As I pause to pay tribute to my unforgettable
and dear late friends Mujos, Kwamy, Hippolyte, Simon,
Coster and Mbole for their sincere advice, morally and
spirtually while with the TP OK Jazz band, all my thanks
and credit, which words cannot express, go to my teacher
through whom I reached where I am today. Bravo Luambo
Landju Makiadi — Franco."

Among Fan Fan's hardships had been the initial
problem of obtaining a passport, a difficulty smoothed
over by the old maestro, Kabasele who, although semi-
retired, was able to give the young adventurer the benefit
of his advice. He travelled east: first to Zambia, then
Tanzania and Kenya, setting up bands wherever possible
by recruiting expatriate Zaïrean musicians. He released
two albums under the Somo Somo name and played with
several other East African-based Zaïrean bands before
eventually arriving in England ten years after leaving
Kinshasa. Back home, Youlou had not returned directly to
OK Jazz but had for a while retained the Somo Somo title
and released a short string of singles, before persuading
Franco to let him return.

The following year the 'Pigeon Voyager' Sam
Mangwana also flew the coop when he was tempted to
return briefly to Tabu Ley (the new authentic name of
'Seigneur' Rochereau), having felt his mission was
accomplished at OK Jazz. Sam too had ambitions of his
own, and he soon quit to further his career internationally.
He travelled to West Africa and in Côte d'Ivoire he joined
up with some dissaffected members of Rochereau's Afrisa
International, to form the first Zaïrean 'supergroup'.
Named the African All Stars, and including guitarists
Dizzy Mandjeku, Lokassa Ya Mbongo, Bopol Mansiamina,
Pablo Lubadika and Syran Mbenza, the band propelled

A section of Franco's guitar solo from Celi Bitchou's song 'Infidelité Mado'

Sam on his career as a solo artiste. The manager was Henri
Bowane. With the All Stars Sam synthesised a new
'international' style of Zaïrean music which borrowed
elements of highlife and beguine and which gave
prominence to a thumping, metronomic bass-drum line
which brought the music closer to the pop dance sounds
of the west.

To replace Mangwana, the singer Ndombe Opetum
was recruited from Tabu Ley's band, along with the *mi-
solo* guitarist Mavatiku Visi, 'Michelino', who came from
Franco's home region, where he had started out in the
Comet Mambo band of Matadi. Michelino was a master of
the *mi-solo* guitar, literally a semi-lead role which was so
crucial to the *sebene*. The saxophonist Empompo 'Deyesse'
Loway, who had a florid jazzy style, was also signed up to
OK Jazz. This 'poaching' of musicians reportedly deepened
the hostility between the two bandleaders which, although
patched up briefly in the early 1980s, was to develop into
another long-running feud. Until now, the two had
attempted to appear cordially competitive with little
animosity, despite the rivalry whipped up by their
respective fans.

By the mid-1970s OK Jazz had re-established itself
sufficiently to be seemingly able to ride smoothly over the
problems of personnel changes. Business was good, both
at home and abroad, with the catalogue of Editions
Populaires records now being marketed throughout Africa.
Thanks to a sponsorship tie-up with Volkswagen, whose
praises he had sung so splendidly in *AZDA*, Franco had
been able to give each musician a car (VW Passats on this
occasion). He was still supervising the construction of the
Un-Deux-Trois which was slowly transforming the open-
air Alex Bar into a three-storey entertainment complex.

Situated in a residential area at one end of the
Avenue Gambela, the building, with its Spanish/Moorish
arched windows, faced open ground planned for

commercial development and the eventual site of the Chinese-built Kamanyola stadium, only a short walk from Matonge. Designed by Franco himself, the Un-Deux-Trois had a dance bar on the ground floor, a nightclub on the middle floor and hotel rooms at the top. The construction had already been started by a European businessman who was unable to finish it off, and the building had been taken over by a military officer who was eventually disgraced. His property was seized by the state and 'Mama' Mobutu Marie-Antoinette, the first wife of the President, transferred the building to Franco to use as the headquarters of OK Jazz.

Franco spent much of his time at the club, supervising the positioning of every brick, including the construction of a secret doorway through the ladies lavatories, where chosen women could come and go to a private backstage room. While he was overseeing the builders he was fortified by a table full of food, and surrounded by an expectant entourage of beggars waiting to scoff the left-over *kwanga*. Franco's eating habits had become legendary and people still argue over whether he could consume 25, 50 or even 100 *kwangas* in a day. His habit of gobbling up feasts in public view had become a gross, if not obscene, indulgence, and there was undoubtedly an element of power display involved. He evidently found it amusing and he wasn't shy to discuss the subject in song — although characteristically he made a woman the object of his derision.

In the song *Mbanda ya Mama ya Mobali* (The Mother-in-law's Co-wife) Franco sang about a woman who could not stop eating. She became so huge that when she jumped in the swimming pool, all the water splashed out. She ate and ate until she got full, then she got fuller and fuller until eventually she exploded, leaving a foul-smelling cloud of guts and gore. A rumour went around that one woman had taken the song as a personal attack and was so humiliated that she committed suicide. Members of OK Jazz don't remember a specific target, however, and it is often pointed out that Franco did sing about reality, but he sang in a generalised way. For all his 'brutal' criticisms of women, his musicians say, he would not have been so cruel as to attack a defenceless individual.

A woman's place

Franco had always sang for and about women just as much as men and now that he was more interested in "telling the truth" than singing love songs, the behaviour of upwardly mobile women provided a wealth of material. The Zaïrean writer Mbamba Toko W. has documented the rise of the 'free women' of Kinshasa in a tone that is regretful and censorious. He points to a period in the mid-1970s when the moral climate began to change. First he blames the nationalisation of several hundred major businesses for creating a boss class of President-directeur-generals (PDGs) and their stooges, whose main interests were gathering and displaying wealth, and whose hobbies included the establishment of 'deuxième bureaux' households for their mistresses or concubines.

Until then respectable women had looked on prostitutes as 'untouchables' whose loose morals were probably contagious. During the 1970s, however, certain middle-class women claimed their own emancipation and formed a loose alliance with the 'free women' which blurred the edges of their own moral certainties. The women's openness offended not only the traditional male sensibilities but also the imported morality of the various Christian churches which flourished largely as an antidote to sorcery. Married women, particularly traders who in many senses ran the day-to-day life of the city, broadened their horizons by opening up their compounds as *ngandas*, or private drinking places. Meanwhile, Mbamba claims, the lowering of the female age of consent from eighteen to fourteen years was simply to make more young girls available to the new playboys.

Franco was by now living with his wife, Annie, in a big

*With members of the Francolettes dance troupe: Franco had an ambi-
vilent attitude towards women who provided the theme for many songs*

luxurious house, also provided by Mama Mobutu, close to
the Ivorian ambassador's residence in the select area of
Binza. In his driveway stood more than one Mercedes. He
was also undergoing a spiritual change which may have
placed him further apart from the world he appeared to
be growing out of. Despite President Mobutu's disapproval
of Christian names, Zaïre remained nominally a Christian
country, with the Catholic faith acknowledged as the
national religion. But in 1975 Franco, brought up as a
good Catholic, converted to Islam. The conversion was
not widely publicised, although people who asked his
religion would always receive a straight answer. The man
with so many names and titles had acquired another. He
adopted the Islamic name Aboubakar Sidiki, although he
did not use it for professional purposes.

In fact, those musicians who were close to Franco did

not notice any change in his behaviour. While maintaining respect for anyone's choice of religion, one of the senior band members later commented: "I don't like to speak for someone else, but what I saw of the way Franco lived — you will excuse me — but I thought it was a joke, really a joke. I couldn't understand why he became a Muslim, or what he did with it. It's true he told us he was a Muslim, but even though we lived together I never saw evidence of his religion. He still ate pork and drank alcohol. I never saw him praying."

The growing economic power of musicians was witnessed by Emmanuel Maradas, a Chadian journalist who studied at the University of Kinshasa in the mid-1970s. "The business sense, or money mentality, came very late to the music scene. Not until about 1975 did musicians and bandleaders realise there was some big money to be made with music. Before they would play, get paid and go home. Now they began to take more interest, especially following the success of younger groups like Bella Bella, Lipua Lipua and Zaïko Langa Langa. Even after independence Zaïreans did not really know the value of money." A serious economic slump occurred in 1975 when the price of copper, Zaïre's main foreign exchange earner, fell dramatically, leading to massive devaluation and an ongoing financial crisis.

Some people had spotted the music's commercial potential, however, and one prospective foreign investor was seen as a threat by Franco who, in one of his more ruthless business manoeuvres, had the man thrown out of Zaïre. The businessman had arrived from Europe during the early 1970s to invest in a new studio, called Sophinza, which was intended to nurture young talent. Initially, Franco collaborated with the newcomers and himself made some recordings at the studio in Kingabwa which were sold under licence to Kenya. Other musicians were invited, including several up-and-coming young artistes who were still unrecorded. Some observers believe that Franco and the other influential bandleaders had a vested interest in blocking this new source of popular music, but as Rondot put it: "Franco had them closed down because of exploitation. The musicians demanded to see the accounts. But Sophinza claimed they were not selling any records. Franco brought a case against Sophinza and the European producer was expelled from the country." Other musicians remember things differently. Taking objection to this outside competition, the alternative version goes, Franco had the man reported to the security police for allegedly defacing Zaïrean banknotes and he was summarily deported. Either way, Sophinza closed and the European returned home. The value of music was also recognised in high places and in 1976, twenty years after the formation of OK Jazz, Franco was honoured with the civil decoration, Officer of the National Order of the Leopard. Each member of the band also received a medal for their contribution to the arts of Zaïre.

In September that year, the singer Ntesa Daleinst was recruited after the collapse of Les Grands Maquisards, and he brought along his guitarist Jerry Dialungana, soon to become a regular feature of the band. Dalienst, however, was initially reluctant to join Franco. "Franco offered to give me a hand, to go to work with him. At first, I didn't want to. But after I had thought about it, I agreed. He had said, 'You know, Dalienst, you don't have the means to re-create Les Grand Maquisards. If you don't do something you will be forgotten. You can start again bit by bit, until you have the means to re-form your group. But in the meantime, I'd like you to come and work with me.' I accepted and I brought my friend, the guitarist Jerry Dialungana. Later Lokombe and Dizzy Mandjeku followed. Franco could see the value of what we had in Les Maquisards and didn't want to see young musicians stranded like that. But frankly, when I first entered OK Jazz, I was not very interested. The climate and the atmosphere did not suit me. So I left immediately. Two months later Franco called me back. He said 'No, no, no, you should not do this'. He pleaded with me, so I returned. That is when I contributed my first songs. There were three, *Tala Ye Na Miso* (Don't Mind Him), *Zaïna Mopaya* (Zaïna the Stranger) and *Lisolo ya Adamo na Nzambe* (A Dialogue between Adam and God)."

The third of Dalienst's compositions was a profound observation on the relationship between men and women, which brought a hostile response from the Church establishment, and made Franco think a bit about his own position. "The priests didn't like the song because they thought I was doubting their religion," explained Dalienst. "I was saying in the song that men always accuse women of sorcery. But if a woman is a sorcerer, who is it that bewitched the woman, who gave woman the ability to become a witch? God created man, and out of man he created woman. Therefore, it is man who has bewitched the women. We only know what our fathers told us when we were young: 'Be careful of women. Women are very sly, they are very weak, they will bore you with their nagging.' But me, if a woman is weak, I blame the man because he is strong. If a woman goes looking for gold, it is the fault of men. It is our fault. In my conception we are doing it all wrong. What is wrong with women is the fault of men. What is the most weakening thing for a woman? I believe it's a man." This went against the personal philosophy of Franco who believed, on the contrary, that women were the cause of men's problems. Nevertheless he did participate. "Franco sang the solo vocal," recalled Dalienst. "I said to him 'This is a song I'd like you to sing'. He sang it, but I am sure it gave him a problem."

In 1977, the band was chosen to represent the country at the Festac event in Lagos, with all the glory that was associated with that unique and extravagant cultural festival. Festac was a huge pan-African jamboree, hosted lavishly by the Nigerians like a cultural Olympics, to which artists, writers, musicians and theatre troupes were invited from each African country and for whom a new town was constructed. Culturally it was a qualified success; financially, a disaster. Zaïre was given four days of the main event, divided between OK Jazz and Afrisa, which as well as playing their own music served as national showcases for new talent. Rochereau was introducing some members of Zaïko Langa Langa, while OK Jazz also accompanied Ray Lema and introduced a 21-year-old handicapped female singer, called M'pongo Love. Originally coached by the saxophonist Empompo Loway, M'Pongo Love went on to become one of Africa's brightest stars before her untimely death shortly after Franco's in 1990. During 1977-78 two more distinctive singers were recruited into the vocal line-up: Dialu Lukoki 'Diatho' and Djo Mpoyi Kaninda joined Youlou, Josky, Ndombe, Wuta Mayi and Boyibanda. By now Dalienst had also decided to become a full-time member. The veteran guitarist 'Papa Noel' Nedule had also joined the squad.

Surprisingly, in view of the many business trips he had made to Europe, Franco was 40 years old before OK Jazz embarked on their first European tour in 1978, performing four concerts in Brussels and Paris for the Zaïrean expatriate community. In fact, the 'timing was not right' and the promotion was rather limp. Worse still, when OK Jazz returned home expecting the kind of glorious reception reserved for those who had 'conquered' Europe, the musicians received a shock. Franco's position as a national hero was enhanced by his growing international success, but on his home territory he had again been courting trouble.

Matters of taste

Playing for his own constituents, Franco was always outspoken and, towards the end of the 1970s, the shows at the Un-Deux-Trois had been getting decidedly controversial. But although he was by now virtually an unofficial ambassador for the country, especially since being honoured with the Order of the Leopard, Franco was not immune to censorship or the law. His self-confidence was legendary, however, and he once described his own role as to "see things with the critical eye of God", obviously believing in his own omniscience. But, for all his professed objectivity, Franco the citizen could not avoid the consequences of his work.

His satirical wit had already begun to annoy certain important figures who took personal offence at some of his more topical social critiques. Although Franco never named names, it was often assumed that his criticisms were directed at particular individuals. When challenged he said that was nonsense; he sang about generalities, but if people wanted to identify themselves with the villains in his little dramas that was their problem. This time, however, he had pushed the authorities, and his own luck, a bit too far and, in a bizarre example of popular justice, he ended up in prison. But the cause was not political and there was no question of anyone misinterpreting the offending lyrics. It was a simple matter of bad taste.

There were two songs which led to Franco's temporary disgrace, *Helene* and *Jacky*, each featuring women of easy virtue in songs described by one his peers as the "equivalent of a porno film". The obscenities can still shock the worldly Kinois, who found the songs outrageous. The topics ranged from oral and anal sex to Jacky's disgusting habit of feeding excrement to one of her boyfriends. As Franco later complained: "There is a censor, which is normal and justifiable. His main function is to suppress licentious gossip. But where the shoe pinches is that the official existence of the censor restrains creativity in general and forces the artist into self-censorship. In France, for example, when a musician has a mind to say 'shit', he says it, provided it is in a given context. Often a musician is condemned by default, without having the occasion to defend his point of view. And in any justice without defence, the accused remains vulnerable and risks being unjustly convicted." Here it was not so much the word 'shit' as the context which incurred the censor's wrath, however.

The lyric of *Jacky* was described by one of Franco's contemporaries as "infantile, the sort of thing no adult person would normally say. He was not just saying 'shit'; it was as if he was actually shitting in public." The songs were released in Kinshasa on cassette but when the Attorney General, Kengo wa Dondo, heard them there was official outrage. On his return from Europe, Franco was called to explain himself. He denied the songs were obscene but his inquisitors ruled that, as it was a moral issue, they should put it to his mother to decide whether the lyrics were acceptable. Franco apparently pleaded with them not to play the cassette to her but nonetheless she was summoned to be the arbiter of her 40-year-old son's fate.

Mama Makiesse was predictably shocked and Franco was duly tried, along with members of the band. Dalienst, who was one of the few musicians to escape being incarcerated, recalled the trial. "The musicians were imprisoned because they were badly defended. Franco had said to the judge, 'I am to blame. It's me who sang the song. Me who composed the offensive words. So don't blame the group. I have been doing this since 1956, and that is what has made me.'

"It is true he had asked me to sing on the song," Dalienst continued. "I sang, of course, but the important thing is that he composed the song. When I sang with him I didn't utter one obscene word. 'Mwana oh, Mwana oh, Jacky, Kitoko na yo ya nyama (This girl Jacky, she's a natural beauty)'. . . me, I stopped there. The prosecutor then posed the question that as I knew what Franco was singing, why did I not advise him against it. I told him that Franco had just stated he began all this in 1956. When I met him he was already like that. What can I do? I cannot condemn him. It's you who want to condemn him."

Condemned he was, along with ten of the musicians. They were sentenced to two months' imprisonment and Franco was ordered to hand back his medal for the Order of the Leopard. Dalienst was lucky enough to evade the punishment, as did some of the other musicians, who hid out at the band's rehearsal studio at Kingabwa.

Those taken to the infamous Makala prison in the heart of Kinshasa were Simaro, Mackos, Thierry, Flavien, Jerry, Gege, Papa Noel, Kapitana, Musekiwa and Checain — many of whom had played no part in the obscene songs. After a few days Franco's presence proved disruptive and he was moved to Luzumu prison in Bas-Zaïre. Twenty-two days later, the musicians were released by presidential pardon, although Franco was detained for a further eleven days, before being freed on medical grounds after he had been taken to hospital with a fever.

Ten years later the Voix du Zaïre radio played a song called *Jacky* sung by Franco, which brought embarrassment to some female listeners and giggles from the menfolk of Kinshasa. It was a version with sanitised lyrics, recorded at around the same time as the offensive material and, although the song had not been heard for such a long time, it immediately brought back memories of Franco's lapse into bad taste. Both *Jacky* and *Helene* were strongly structured compositions, with classic OK Jazz arrangements pushing home their overtly erotic message. Franco's solo guitar motif, used in the former song, was later revived for one of his most functional and morally correct compositions, *Attention Na Sida*.

Shortly after his release, Franco had a chance to snap back at the man who had sanctioned his prosecution when Kengo wa Dondo was appointed Prime Minister, and then swiftly demoted. Franco's song *Mokolo Tonga Abotoli Tonga Na Ye* (The Owner of the Needle has Taken Back his Needle), also known as *Tailleur*, was taken to be a satirical commentary on this event, and only exacerbated his conflict with the authorities.

In 1979 OK Jazz visited West Africa on a tour which took them to Gabon, Cameroon, Benin, Côte d'Ivoire, Togo and Senegal. In common with the African method of touring, the musicians did not know their eventual itinerary before leaving Kinshasa. Most African promoters would only be confident in promoting a band once they had them 'in their hand' so to speak, and few long distance tours were planned in advance. If promoters continued to offer dates the tour would continue to roll. In this case, as Dalienst remembers, "In Cameroon we played for a gentleman from Baffoussam. And when we had finished the tour for him, he sold on the contract to another promoter, a Senegalese, who took us first to Togo, then Côte d'Ivoire and back round to Benin."

The following year OK Jazz arrived back in Paris and Brussels, where they really made their mark. This time Franco wanted to take greater advantage of being in Europe. The recording technology was far superior to the facilities at home and, with a greater part of the band's records being marketed in West and East Africa, Europe provided a better business base. There were also family considerations, in the form of his children who were being born at the rate of about one a year. The eldest were ready for further education and Franco decided to set up a European home base as well. He bought a house in Brussels and an apartment in Paris.

Back in Kinshasa, Franco was installed as Honorary President of the musicians' union, Umuza, but more significantly he and Kabasele, the two pillars of Congo-Zaïrean music, were awarded the supreme title of Grand Maître (Grand Master). It is a deferential form of address reserved for the likes of judges, professors and sorcerers, which sat easily on Franco's increasingly bulky shoulders, and which he obviously felt was most appropriate.

CHAPTER SIX

Grand Master's Choc Tactics

"After we have dined well and drunken well, what shall we do? Ah, my dear Mangwana, it's simple. We dance. We'll dance all night with OK Jazz."

Coopération, 1982

FROM HIS NEW EUROPEAN BASE the Grand Master was poised to make his assault on a wider international market, in particular the USA which, in his own words, he was most anxious to 'conquer'. But although he was ready to redirect his energies outside the rather introverted Zaïrean music scene (the 'closed system' which Ray Lema identified), Franco had no intentions of ignoring his primary audience, the people of Kinshasa. In fact, from his outside perspective he seemed to draw new inspiration on his favourite theme of 'Mr and Mrs Everybody', and his distance from home only enforced his identification with his own culture. As a kind of roving ambassador he showed Zaïre's most positive image, but Franco was a straightforward, direct personality, whose diplomacy was limited by his integrity.

"I will not adapt the music, or the language, for new audiences in the West," he insisted before visiting America. "It is what we play, what we sing and dance to — what we understand. It is our music and people must accept it for what it is. We listen to Western music; even though we don't speak English we can dance to it. We make an effort to enjoy it. In Europe it is different, our music is considered just for Africans, not for them. But music has no frontiers."

Over the years Franco had built up a business relationship with Fonior, owners of the African label which produced and distributed OK Jazz records internationally from Belgium. The company was now in financial difficulties and, although he was invited to become a director, Franco decided instead to withdraw his capital. When Fonior was wound up in 1980, Franco was already primed to take personal control over all aspects of record production. In Europe he realised that albums had much greater commercial potential than singles, which were now a diminishing factor in most of the world's record markets. He had no intention of cutting down on his prolific output, however, and Franco embarked on a programme of recording which astonishingly produced some 30 new albums during the first six years in business, excluding re-issues and compilations released elsewhere. Initially he announced three new labels; Edipop for OK Jazz releases, and Visa 1980 and Passeport which were intended to showcase up-and-coming talent.

In fact, Franco inaugurated the Visa label himself with a powerful pair of 'comeback' albums entitled, appropriately, *Vraiment En Colère* (Really In Anger) Vols 1 & 2, followed by the equally strong double album *Le 24ème Anniversaire*. This was the third double album from OK Jazz: the first had been a 1965 Pathe Marconi collection of early singles repackaged in 1977, while the first 'concept' double was the *20ème Anniversaire*, with its fake applause. The *24ème Anniversaire* album, which for many Europeans is one of the prime examples of OK Jazz, included songs which were themed around the subject of wealth, including *Proprietaire* (The Landlord), *Locataire* (The Tenant) and *Heritier* (The Heir). There was also the curiosity of the song *Nalingaka Yo Yo Te* (I Don't Like You) which took up one whole side of the album *A Bruxelles*. On this song Franco indulgently picks at an acoustic guitar for 21 minutes, accompanied only by a rhythm machine and ethereal synthesiser. It was Franco's last release on the Visa label, before transferring his output to Edipop. The up-and-comers on Visa 1980, whose albums announced in large type 'Franco Presents', included Papa Wemba and

Lengi Lenga, both 'new wave' singers from the Zaïko Langa Langa family, or 'Clan Langa Langa'.

After surprisingly dropping the Visa label in 1981, Franco launched Edipop with a four-volume, 25th anniversary set titled *Le Quart de Siècle*. Although released as single albums, the records used the same sleeve design with the name of his youth, Franco de mi Amor. In the picture, however, he looked more like the Godfather — bulky, tough and sporting a trilby hat, large tortoiseshell shades, sideburns, moustache and goatee beard.

These are some of the most complete works in the OK Jazz archive. The band played with a mature, solid confidence and here can be heard the full majesty of OK Jazz. The first two Edipop records featured long compositions by senior band members, which stretched over the full side of an album. Dalienst's composition, *Bina Na Ngai na Respect* (Dance with Me with Respect) was the first in the series. Introduced by the spoken words of a young woman demanding such respect, the song is a tour de force for Dalienst, who coolly sings up and down the musical scale with a relaxed flowing delivery. POP 02 was Josky's *Bimansha*, then came Franco's *Tailleur* and Simaro's *Mandola*.

The albums in this set show the whole spectrum of full-bore TP OK Jazz: guitars entwined in exquisite embrace, harmonic force from the front-line vocalists embellished by florid horn parts, all powered by a deep, resonating rhythmic drive, and arranged with a dynamic tension which prolonged the release of the *sebene* almost until bursting point. Franco was now emphasising the *rumba-odemba* ingredient. These are each classic OK Jazz albums which also include compositions from Papa Noel, Checain, Gege, Mpudi Decca, Wuta Mayi and Djo Mpoyi, the singer who gave such a spirited interpretation of Simaro's *Mandola*.

Franco contributed one song to each album and played a memorably hard, syncopated *sebene* on *Bimansha*, but it was the third volume, with Franco's own composition *Mokolo Tonga Abotoli Tonga Na Ye*, renamed *Tailleur* (Tailor) which caught the Zaïreans' imagination. The popular music press reported that *Tailleur* was widely thought to be about the Prime Minister, Kengo wa Dondo who, as Attorney General, had imprisoned Franco on the obscenity issue. When asked in an interview with the Paris-based *Antilles-Afrique* magazine, Franco denied the song was targeting any particular individual, but the fact that he was spending more time outside Zaïre suggested to many observers that Franco was not on the best of terms with the country's leaders. He strenuously denied he was living in exile, quoting his domestic businesses and official obligations as evidence.

He was by now a partner in Mazadis, Zaïre's only record pressing plant, proprietor of the Un-Deux-Trois, and still honorary president of the musicians' union. He owned luxury apartment buildings in the Limete and Kingabwa districts of Kinshasa, mostly rented to Europeans who paid in foreign exchange, and the cattle ranch at Mont Ngafula. He also had a handsome, three-storey, chalet-style mansion built for himself at Limete, not far from the district of Yolo, where he had lived for so long.

As if to make the point that he had nobody to fear in Zaïre, Franco released a song for the local market titled *Na Mokili Tour A Tour* (As The World Turns), in which he asked sarcastically if he was really expected to leave the town where he belonged. 'I beat my head against a tree, the tree dried up', he warned in song. 'Stop provoking me. Must I leave Kinshasa, the town where I grew up?' He saves his most cutting put-down for the casual aside: 'Luambo used to know Mbelekete'. Mbelekete was a legendary name in Zaïrean social history, known by repute to people who were not yet born when he was active in the 1950s. He had been the top stunt cyclist in the 'quartier Far West' where Franco grew up, and was more famous than a certain person who was seeking to make his name in politics. Nevertheless, Franco did spend the best part of three years in Europe, having already prepared OK Jazz to continue in his absence. He was not shy about returning home and, a few years later, he even came back to haunt Kengo wa Dondo in his own house.

The Grand Master's 'authentic' identity had never been questioned but, while his business interests kept him out of the country for longer periods, there were those in Kinshasa who felt he was drifting away from them. He appeared much less frequently with the band, which he left in the competent hands of his vice-president, Simaro. With Franco spending so much time in Europe, there were now two OK Jazz orchestras functioning. The Brussels-based squad was the 'A team', while OK Jazz 'B' was the Kinshasa band under the direction of Simaro, who did not much enjoy travel and who kept the OK Jazz sound alive at the Un-Deux-Trois.

There was some interchange between the two camps, although certain musicians preferred to stay in Europe and others rarely left home. In Brussels the Grand Master was accompanied by Jerry, Gege, Decca, Dessouin, Pedro, Matalanza, etc., with singers Josky, Dalienst and, from 1980, Madilu System, who was destined to become the band's biggest star of the decade. In Kinshasa the line-up alongside Simaro contained Brazzos, Flavien, Isaac, Rondot, with singers Djo Mpoyi, Boyibanda, Diatho and the newcomer Lokombe, composer of the song *2ème Bureau Nganda*. 'Papa Noel', Nono Nedule, was also in the Kinshasa squad. Born in 1939, he is a solo guitar maestro who played the 'Franco style' without mimicking; he used a bit more vibrato and a softer finger technique. An imposing, somewhat studious figure, Noel was a descendant of parents from both banks of the Congo river, and as such he was able to play in both camps. On the Brazzaville side he had been a founding member of Les Bantous and later the Bamboula band, whose singer Aime Kiawakana had also joined up with OK Jazz. The organisation now had sufficient personnel to maintain a 16-piece touring band and an even larger orchestra at home.

Re-entry of the gladiator

In 1982 the full complement came together at the Voix du Zaïre television station for a grand comeback performance. During the two-and-a-half hour show the full splendour of OK Jazz was displayed. Among the singers who provided an hour of entertainment before the Grand Master made his entrance were Wuta Mayi, Djo Mpoyi, Josky, Dalienst, Boyibanda and Madilu. The instrumentalists, who were sitting in rows behind old-fashioned big-band music stands, included a front line of three guitars and bass, seated in pairs, with the horn sections on a tier behind them, saxes to one side and trumpets to the other. Perched above them all were the drummer and conga players. Throughout the show these musicians rotated, so that four different players took solo guitar, with as many on accompaniment, including Simaro, who also stood conducting the band on some numbers. It was a clear demonstration of the OK Jazz system.

When Franco took the stage he appeared triumphantly alone in the spotlight at the top of some steps wearing a white lace boubou and weighing, as he later told the TV presenter, about 120 kilos. He sang, unaccompanied, a slow, talking bolero-blues type song, *Kinshasa Mboka Ya Makambo* (Kinshasa, Town of Problems) in which he spoke directly to the receptive studio audience about his love for, and fidelity to, Kinshasa, the town of many problems, a town he would always love even though he was accused of deserting it for Europe, where people suspected he made his wealth by running drugs. It was the spectacular entry of a supremely confident star returning to his own people. He had the audience in his grasp as he descended the staircase, speaking out his feelings in a slow and soulful way before calling for the blue Gibson guitar and making that do the talking. Once ensconced in the wrap-around sound of the complete TP OK Jazz, Franco played a stunner, lest the people of Kinshasa had forgotten whose town it was.

But Franco was also an international businessman, and by now he had signed an agreement with an Ivorian producer in Abidjan to release albums which would tap a sudden boom in the market for Zaïrean music. This new craze had started in Côte d'Ivoire around 1976 and was spearheaded by Sam Mangwana who was selling records prolifically. Daniel Cuxac had set up the Disco Stock label and, in partnership with an American, Roger Francis, he signed a deal with Franco to release OK Jazz albums in West Africa. Their first release, in 1981, opened with the Dalienst song known as 'Musi', but titled *Liyanzi Ekoti Ngai Na Motema* (A Tick has Entered my Heart), which was a susbstantial hit in the region. As Dalienst said, "We toured a lot on the strength of that song." Disco Stock alone accounted for 75,000 sales in West Africa, while some 225,000 copies were sold out of Paris. Added to the other Zaïrean albums licensed to, or distributed by, Disco Stock, Franco's products laid a solid business base for Cuxac. But he wanted more. He had his own vision for some guaranteed smash-hit Zaïrean collaborations and made several propositions to Franco, which the big man accepted, reluctantly at first.

Cuxac's primary objective was to reunite Franco with Sam Mangwana, but he knew it would be difficult. "Franco was very disappointed when Sam Mangwana suddenly left Zaïre for Abidjan to make his name," Cuxac told the Danish musicologist Flemming Harev at the time. "In 1981, when Franco came here I said to him, 'My interest is to have you together. Everybody knows that Franco is a big name. Everybody knows that Mangwana is a big name. Why don't you put yourselves together and make something even bigger ?' I remember that day, when Franco told me, 'Daniel, I cannot accept Sam back in my group. I have five other singers now. Definitely, I cannot go with him.' So we discussed it for a long time. Then later he called me and said he thought he could do something with Sam Mangwana, and he was going to go back to Kinshasa and quickly do it. 'First to satisfy you Daniel, then maybe for Mangwana.' That is how it came about. They made the record in a few days."

The resulting album, *Coopération*, is one of the outstanding examples of mature Congo-Zaïrean music, with a rich, fruity sound and an irresistible energy. The title song opens with an exquisite, vibrant bass line and an introduction spoken in French by Franco and Sam, which contains the immortal definition of the music's purpose: 'After we have dined well and drunken well, what shall we do? Ah, my dear Mangwana, it's simple. We dance. We will dance all night with OK Jazz.' In East Africa that song was known as *Odongo* after a local trader whose name Sam had praised in one of the verses. Only two of the songs on the album had Franco's participation, while on the other two Mangwana compositions OK Jazz was under the musical direction of vice-president Simaro. Franco brought Mangwana back to Kinshasa for a grand reunion show, which stifled the various rumours surrounding the itinerant Sam's supposed 'disappearance'. Franco dashed Sam another car as a bonus and later the album was awarded the 'maracas d'or' by the French music business for its high sales in francophone countries.

In the meantime, however, Sam tried to release another album in Abidjan which contained a song from *Coopération*, entitled *Faute ya Commercante* (The Businesswoman's Fault). He brought the tapes to Cuxac who obviously recognised the song and contacted Franco to ask advice. Franco had already released the song in Zaïre and he told Cuxac not to accept it. But Sam, who had equal rights in the session, took the tapes to Badmos who released the song for sale in West Africa.

Cuxac's other project was to bring together for the

Ready to dance all night: Franco reunited with Sam Mangwana in 1982

first time Zaïre's big three bandleaders; Franco united
with Rochereau and Verckys, both of whom were also
popular in West Africa. To pull off the coup, Cuxac
devised a plan. Franco and Rochereau had, between them,
sold almost one-and-a-half million albums in the region
and the Ivorian decided to award gold discs to the two
maestros. In September 1982 he travelled to Kinshasa
with Roger Francis to make the presentation, which took
place live on television.

"As you know, everybody calls them the 'enemy-
brothers'," recalled Cuxac the following year. "It was a big
occasion for them to come together. Really they are

brothers, they are friends, but they are competing. Everybody knows they are always competing but for me it is so easy to think of them together. It was the first time they had been photographed together. Franco on my right hand, Rochereau on my left and Verckys behind. That was the first time I suggested that all three of them make a record together. Verckys was the first to say he couldn't do it, because he was not ready. Rochereau said nothing. Franco said nothing. Which was meaning maybe they were ready to do it. I could not believe it. I was very happy because I was discussing with them for days and days and days to let them know the importance of playing together, not just for themselves but for all Africans, for all African musicians. I think that Franco, Rochereau and Vévé [Verckys] are tacitly friends, but people need to believe they are enemies — to buy their records maybe. As people want them to be enemies, I believe they are playing a game. I believe so. I hope so. But this was the first time Franco and Rochereau had been in the studio together."

Franco did finally make peace of sorts with his long-time rival Tabu Ley. While they had usually been diplomatically polite about each other in public, and despite Cuxac's beliefs, it had been known for some time that a feud was running between them. In a publicised gesture they signed a 'peace pact' and collaborated for the first time in their long careers on a couple of important recordings. The first was *Choc Choc Choc 1983*, a heavyweight double album which introduced a new hi-tech gloss to the music and inaugurated yet another OK Jazz record label, CHOC.

Recorded without most of the OK Jazz regulars, the Paris CHOC sessions, which lasted for three months and produced some still unreleased material, featured a few members of OK Jazz, some from Afrisa and some new Zaïrean talent from the Paris studio scene, including the bass player Thoms Toroma Sika and drummer Boffi Banengola. Many of these musicians, as well as the guitarist

Jerry Malekani, who had played with Manu Dibango for some fifteen years since the break up of Ry-Co Jazz, had accompanied Franco at recent shows in Paris and Brussels. Franco's only son, Luambo Emongo, is also pictured on the sleeve holding a guitar in the studio. The CHOC sound used a hard disco beat with contemporary production values which, while leaving the musical integrity intact, was obviously aimed at the international dance floors.

The featured guitarist on the CHOC sessions, Michelino, also shared an album of his own with Franco, entitled *Bénédiction*, which was released on his own label. From the same sessions came yet another double album with Franco and Josky, also titled *Choc Choc Choc* (CHOC 002/3), on which Franco and Michelino combined to record no less than nine guitar tracks. With the exuberant *Chacun Pour Soi* (Everyone for Himself) and the side-long track *Partagez* (Share It) on the same album, Franco came close to achieving a 'crossover' club hit in the European discos which, at that time, were beginning to look for exciting dance music from previously unknown cultures. This was before the lame and lamentable effort to promote 'world music' diverted attention from Africa's finest, and from 1983 to 1985 Franco's CHOC records blazed a pioneering trail through the Western world. He had also made an uncredited contribution to what was undeniably the biggest African hit record of the period. *African Typic Collection*, recorded in 1983 by the Cameroonian Sam Fan Thomas, reprised the chorus and melody from Franco's 1970 song *Boma l'Heure*.

Now in charge of his own production and distribution, Franco kept a close watch on how his products were moving. At the time he claimed that, disregarding licensing deals, his albums were selling a minimum of 30-40,000 copies in Africa, with a bestseller topping 100,000. As he was often releasing five new albums a year on his own labels, the totals built up. But, ever mindful of piracy, he

Franco and Tabu Ley: signed a 'peace pact' and then recorded together

would rather keep one step ahead of the bootleggers by continually releasing new titles. These would be distributed first to Africa in cassette format and then, only when they had been delivered, would the record be released in Europe. That way customers could buy seal-wrapped, pre-recorded cassettes at the same time, and virtually the same price, as the first of the inferior, pirate copies. When the disc arrived later, Franco believed, it would still be bought by those who preferred their music on vinyl rather than cassette. For would-be producers or licensees, Franco had ready-mixed master tapes of albums available for outright sale at an asking price of some £20,000 sterling. His need for control meant he had a 'hands-on' approach to everything including the artwork for his album sleeves. These were 'designed' by Franco, who would sketch a rough layout, write in the title and provide a photograph for the printer. "It takes about twenty minutes to design a sleeve," he once said. "It's simple. I am used to it."

Franco had brought Zaïrean music a long way, with techniques that were radical if sometimes counter-productive. The other top solo artistes and bandleaders, like Tabu Ley, Verckys and Mangwana, were making varying successes of their own labels, with Verckys' Editions Vévé being the only general catalogue of other people's releases. Coming up behind the established big bands, the third generation groups of the Zaïko family were establishing themselves internationally: Zaïre appeared to have a music business with a future. At least the present was healthy, and the music's integrity had been retained, due to a direct linear connection with the roots of Congo-Zaïrean music.

The connection with the first generation was, however, broken on February 11, 1983. While Franco was busy consolidating the position of Zaïrean music, its founding father, the only other Grand Maître, Kabasele, died after a long illness in a Paris hospital, aged 53. Since the big break-up of African Jazz in 1967, the Grand Kalle had dropped out of the musical limelight, although his reputation and his works remained close to the people's hearts. In 1970 he had made a temporary comeback with the African Team, playing with Manu Dibango, the Cuban violinist Don Gonzalez and Roger Izeidi. It was mellow, vintage style Latin music with a subtle Congolese flavour. His influence remained strong, with most of the musicians in Zaïre who were not from the school of OK Jazz claiming allegiance to the 'African Jazz clan'. Rochereau, Mangwana, Vox Africa, the Maquisards and many of the new wave singers all claimed to follow in a direct line from Kabasele.

The 'Grand Kalle' had been seriously ill for some time and had only recently returned to Zaïre after a long hospitalisation in Paris. While there, he broadcast a show on Voix du Zaïre TV, accompanied by several old African Jazz members, which showed him to be in fine form. It was a temporary recovery, however, and he had since returned to the Paris hospital. Franco was staying at his Paris apartment at the time, and in the early hours of February 12 he was awakened by a telephone call from his business manager, Malambu, informing him of the Grand Kalle's death. Franco recalled that he immediately dressed and hurried down to the Bataclan club to inform Tabu Ley who was playing a show there. The following morning they contacted Kalle's uncle, Cardinal Malula the liberal Catholic prelate, who had decided to proceed with the burial immediately the body was returned to Zaïre. Franco and Ley were unable to get a flight home that day, and did not attend the funeral at Kinshasa's Gombe cemetery. They held a memorial mass in Brussels near the Zaïrean embassy, and a few days later Franco arrived in Kinshasa to pay his respects at the graveside. The people of Zaïre and the musical community in particular were in deep mourning for Kalle, the man they considered to be the father of their culture.

In a publication which came out in Kinshasa the following year, entitled *Hommage à Grand Kalle*, Franco spoke of his respect for his early mentor: "Kabasele, like myself, had his way of behaving which pleased some people and displeased others. There are two things which I appreciate about him. First his time in African Jazz which was his great idea. [Even when he was recording with other musicians he continued to think of African Jazz which he always wanted to revive.] But most important was his sincerity. When a musician colleague had done a good job, Kalle congratulated him straight away. He didn't fail to encourage those who were interested and if necessary would have long discussions about their work. He would often come to ask for a copy of the record to keep for his own pleasure." Franco summed up his tribute to the great bandleader: "Kalle has entered the pantheon of immortals.

I prefer to replace the past tense with the present: Kalle is well and truly a pillar of our music."

United in their shared respect for Kalle, the two remaining pillars of Zaïrean music, Franco and Tabu Ley, came together again to record a tribute song *Kabasele in Memoriam*, featured on the album *L'Evénement* (The Final Event) which was released on Rochereau's own label, Genidia. In the lament, the two sing in duet, calling for a magician they can pay to reverse the death of 'our Kalle'. Franco comes in with two verses towards the end, closing with the sentiment: 'Brothers, what bad dreams before the tragedy. But waking is worse than the dream, because it is true. Where can we find enough tears to shed for the father of modern Zaïrean music.'

The tears were shed, however, and after a period of mourning the musical life of OK Jazz resumed. With the solo guitarist Dizzy Mandjeku now on board as bandleader and Papa Noel also back in the fold, OK Jazz set out on a tour of Kenya later in 1983, which made up for their failure to arrive for an advertised tour in 1982. On his return to Kinshasa, Franco was now living at the mansion on 12th St, in Limete, but he travelled frequently to Europe, particularly to set up the arrangements for the first OK Jazz tour of the USA, scheduled for the end of 1983. Franco took the US tour very seriously. He had a letterhead printed in English, reading 'Franco and the TP OK Jazz on European, American and African Tour', and a small booklet in English and French giving brief biographical details and lyrics of some of the songs the band was to perform.

Although well aware that he should not change the music, and proud of the fact that he was not going to, the matter of presentation was to pose a problem. He had seen many European and American artistes on television in France and Belgium and he had noticed that the big stars offered a mixed repertoire to show the range of their talents, while often showcasing various members of the band. Franco had acquired a personal preference for his near-namesake, 'Franky' Sinatra, whose lush orchestral ballads often provided the sound track on Sunday mornings while Franco lounged at home. Like most African bands, OK Jazz were used to playing a selection of international 'variety' numbers to warm up in front of home audiences. These would include some Latin rumba, maybe a jazz standard or two and possibly a recent Western pop song. Franco assumed that foreign audiences would also like to be led into this new, and possibly strange, musical experience by way of material already familiar to them. As he was to discover, this internationalism was not necessarily what foreign audiences wanted. Those keen to hear Franco's music were enthusiasts who had little in common with the mass audience for European cabaret or light entertainment television.

In 1983 the band eventually landed in the new world for shows in New York and Washington, but the logistics of touring with such a large orchestra meant their arrival was not straightforward. OK Jazz was always a flexible organisation, and on this occasion the inducement of an American holiday had seen the band's ranks swell. As promoter Ibrahim Bah told Gary Stewart: "I spoke with Franco several times and we had agreed we were going to have 25 people in the group. . . and I applied for the visas and got the visas. A week or so later he got pressure from his quarters that some people must be in the band and he called me and said, 'Look Ibrahim I cannot come with just 25. I've got to come with 45 people.' I said 'You mean 45, four five?' He said 'Yes 45'. He gave me the additional names and I applied for visas for the rest. And immigration said, 'Hey, one moment this group is 25, the next minute they're 45, what kind of group is this?'"

The pre-show publicity announced a seventeen-piece band accompanied by a twelve-piece traditional troupe. "Tradition is a great influence in my music," Franco told the *New York Times*. "In my music I put all my soul and all my spirit. And my soul is a traditional one, because I was born in a family that respected tradition. My mother was always singing traditional songs. The traditional music lacks some sounds, while the modern music has the guitars, the saxophones and many other things. But the spirit of the music is the same." The hastily arranged debut at New York's Manhattan Centre in November, 1983 attracted some 1,000 expectant ticket holders but, it seems OK Jazz tried a bit too much variety for the audience's tastes. The Zaïrean liking for prefacing live shows with a leisurely workout of cabaret numbers did not go down well. Only when Franco was cranking his guitar were the Americans satisfied, and they did not see enough of the big man. For one reviewer, Franco brought only 'brief flashes of Congo heaven'. Franco had not adapted his music, but it seems he had chosen the wrong form of presentation. Instead of a showcase of fleeting glimpses, he might have done better with a few long, classic songs and extended *sebenes*.

Shortly after his return from the States, Franco was closing the contractual arrangements for his first visit to Britain. The debut performance was to be at the prestigious Royal Albert Hall in the Kensington district of central London as part of a one-night African music festival, featuring far too many acts on the bill. It was a big moment for the growing number of African music fans, and especially the many African students throughout Britain who made travel arrangements to come to London that Sunday. Unfortunately, due to the increasingly familiar excuse of 'visa problems', the show was postponed at the last minute. Coachloads of dejected Africans returned to the British provinces still holding the tickets they had bought in advance. It was only the first of many bungled attempts to promote OK Jazz in Britain. The band did return one month later, in April, to play at the Hammersmith Palais, a more appropriate dance hall venue, but the momentum had been lost and due to the lack of public confidence the attendance was not what it might have been.

When OK Jazz eventually hit the London stage, however, they delivered all that anyone could have asked, except that two and a half hours of OK Jazz is never enough. Franco provided a show which was tighter and less casual than the home-based dance performances, and he appeared to have learned from the American experience: there was no 'variety', it was strictly *rumba-odemba*. The music of this superbly disciplined band was dynamically orchestrated and the presentation spot on. Fronting the excellent outfit were the full-throated, emotion-packed voices of Dalienst, Josky and Madilu, whose operatic delivery was enhanced by individual bulk almost equalling that of Franco. As ever with OK Jazz, power radiated from the stage, particularly the power of the Grand Master.

Following Franco's first, and what transpired to be his only, British appearance, OK Jazz returned briefly to Africa for a tour of Uganda. The Grand Master made a triumphal entrance into Kampala in a red Mercedes convertible, and reports told of a virtual slump in the commercial sector as business people stayed up all night to dance to the music of OK Jazz. But on his return to Europe a rather chagrined Franco complained of being escorted out of the country by soldiers, without receiving payment for his shows. He bounced back to play more European dates including a grand all-night midsummer dance at the Cirque d'Hiver in Paris and a big music festival in a football stadium at Delft, Holland.

Mamou meets Mario

The record releases on Edipop continued to flow regularly with several new classics, including *Tu Vois?* (You See?), better known as 'Mamou', a duet between Franco and the newcomer Madilu Bialu 'System', which was to remain a great favourite of his Kinois followers. Madilu, like Franco, has his family roots in Bas-Zaïre. He had joined OK Jazz in April 1980, after a ten-year singing career which had taken him through two of his own bands and Tabu Ley's Afrisa, where he spent two years, before being abandoned at Ndjili airport when Ley left for Europe. Like several Afrisa musicians before him, the smoky-voiced Madilu found greater glory with OK Jazz.

There was a portent of Madilu's coming stature in the band when he became the first member of the group to be invited by Franco to introduce himself on disc, during the song *Non* on the 1983 album *Chez Fabrice*. But the number which linked his name indelibly with OK Jazz was *Tu Vois?* (You See?), on the second side of the album, *Très Impoli* (Very Impolite). The title song was a tirade, in the inimitable telling-off style of Franco, against someone who behaved with no social graces and no consideration for his fellows. This stern admonishing, while musically a class-one OK Jazz epic, was probably a bit too severe for the Zaïrean audience, who much preferred the lighter, more humorous, and occasionally hilarious, domestic argument taking place around Mamou.

The theme of *Tu Vois* is a conversation between two women, the speaker, who is a divorcee with children, and her friend Mamou, a married woman who has accused her of trying to break up her marriage. Vocalist Madilu takes the lead role in this plaintive criticism of Mamou's morality. Mamou has accused her friend of being a prostitute. In fact, Mamou has been using her friend as an alibi to cover her own adventures. Mamou is now living in Europe with her children, and the husband has arranged to telephone twice a day. In between calls she sprays the bedroom with insecticide to help keep the children asleep while she slips out of the house for her secret assignations. The telephone call, delivered in a cracked falsetto by bassist Decca, invariably provoked howls of laughter among Zaïrean audiences as the wife tells diversionary lies to her husband.

Franco often seemed to be happier and more creative

when criticising women. He was often accused of taking a 'brutal' approach but women were themselves the most critical and loyal members of his audience, and he had to be able to please them first with tenderness or ironic humour before getting to his point. To do this he had literally to enter their world, from where his attacks were intended to be perceived as a form of self-criticism by the women. The parts he sang most earnestly were often in the words of women. Franco certainly knew enough about their appetites and aspirations to charm himself into their confidence and into their consciousness. But he was also able to upset whole sections of womanhood. For a long time it was the 'liberated women', *bandumba*, who felt the strongest tongue lashing, even though this loose class of females, ranging from innocent teenagers, widows and divorcees to adulteresses and outright prostitutes, often made up Franco's most loyal audience. Later he turned his attentions to the shortcomings of married women. Even so, however much he annoyed some people, he never totally alienated his listeners, who would have already grown up in a world so coloured, described and enlightened by OK Jazz, that they could be excused for accepting Franco's world as the 'real' one. Compared with the close identification shown by Western audiences for fictional TV soap operas and 'manufactured' pop idols, the Zaïreans' involvement, and even participation, in the world of OK Jazz, is normal and healthy. The world of OK Jazz is real.

The reality of this world was brought home directly, without metaphor, satire or irony, on the 1984 album *Chez Rythmes et Musiques*, a concept album on a different aspect of the extended family theme — trouble with the in-laws. That is the subject of the song *12,600 Lettres*, which Franco had been composing on the notepad he carried with him in London in April. He had received that many letters from his constituents, about specific problems between wives and their husbands' sisters. In what is

With Jerry Dialungana at Hammersmith Palais: Franco's only UK date

apparently a common situation in the matrilineal Bakongo
society especially, the sisters-in-law begin to mistrust the
wives and try to take over their domestic duties, while
frequently insulting them. Franco spills out some of the
wives' complaints in argumentative style, while the chorus
lets you know he is telling it in America, in Brussels, in
Paris. The subject is then taken up in *Le Débat* (The
Debate) when, following a genuine discussion around the
microphone, Franco covers the problem from all sides,
even coming on in full haranguing power as the Sorcerer
himself.

After his flirtation with the international disco crowd,
Franco had returned wholeheartedly to his Kinois
audience. In *Kimpa Kisangameni* (Meeting of Witches),
sung in a minority Kikongo dialect over a funked-up
folklore backing, the Grand Master reverted to the theme

of sorcery, with a back reference to his dead brother, Bavon Marie-Marie. Aside from the heavy lyrics, OK Jazz inevitably and indefatigibly kept the people dancing with songs like *Pesa Position* (State your Position). And kept them pointed in a politically 'authentic' direction with the official campaign song for the sole candidate in the 1984 presidential election, *Candidat Na Biso Mobutu* (Our Candidate Mobutu). This album, which carried no mention of the name Franco, but which was credited to Luambo Makiadi and OK Jazz, was supposed to be distributed free to the 'citoyens' of Zaïre, but was being sold alongside Franco's other records in European music stores. He followed up with an average quality praise number for a Gabonese football team *FC 105 de Libreville*. After the glorious records of the early 1980s, and the penetrating CHOC sound, some listeners felt Franco was retreating into parochialism, singing for a diminishing, older generation. The form of the compositions was also changing from the song-and-*sebene* structure to a single-speed format in which the lyrics often lasted one complete album side, and on record the *sebene* was often truncated or left off altogether. But with OK Jazz things were always in flux.

Nineteen eighty five was to be another watershed year for OK Jazz. Franco was unable to participate in the Tam Tam Pour L'Afrique famine benefit organised in Paris by Manu Dibango, Mory Kante and other francophone Africans in response to Live Aid. But he contributed to the cause of African famine relief by helping to organise an all-star benefit show in Abidjan, capital of Côte d'Ivoire, featuring Pamelo Mounka from Congo and Abeti Masekini among others. Through no fault of Franco's, the event was marred by poor organisation and recriminations between the promoters and the aid agencies. But OK Jazz gave their services to 'Africa For Africa'. Back in Europe, however, following the appearance of an independent 12-inch maxi single by Momy and the OK Jazz band, without even the name of Franco, the realisation dawned that Josky and Dalienst, the two stalwart frontmen, had left the band, the former working as artistic advisor for Production Tshika, who released the maxi single. Dalienst claims he quit in 1984, although he was to return as a collaborator on record and on stage. The vocalists Bonyeme and Lokombe stepped to the fore and OK Jazz regrouped once again.

Then, late in 1985, while the gossips discussed yet another crisis in OK Jazz, Franco bounced back with Madilu System sharing the vocals on *Mario*, a two-volume, epic narrative which proved to be Franco's hottest selling record for several years, inside and outside Zaïre. Stretching the listeners' attention span even further than before, Franco split the song over two album sides, released on two separate discs. Presumably originally intended as a double album, *Mario* was released in Europe in two parts within weeks of each other, with identical, un-numbered sleeves and A-sides that were virtually indistinguishable from each other — except to those Lingala speakers who rushed to buy both episodes of the soap opera with its adventures of 'Mario', a fading gigolo or 'toy boy', whose days of loving and living off older, rich women are coming to an end.

Thirty years on

Despite the bizarre marketing of the *Mario* story, which ensured that fewer people bought both records than if they had been better labelled, the band's 30th anniversary year, 1986, began with both episodes at the top of the African charts. The ever-prolific Franco was already recording new material at the 48-track IAD studios in Brazzaville, a modern and far better facility than any of the Zaïrean studios. By April he was in Paris mixing the tracks. OK Jazz played some more shows in Europe before moving on to Cameroon, and then in June the band travelled to Kenya, which by now had become the most profitable market place for Franco's music. Instead of

The big man indulges his prodigious appetite while on tour in Kenya

returning to Kinshasa as expected, Franco spent June 6, the 30th anniversary of OK Jazz, in Nairobi.

The first of several 'anniversary' albums was *La Vie Des Hommes* (The Life of Men), subtitled 'Birthday Present', which reintroduced Djo Mpoyi to the vocal line together with the 25-year-old newcomer Malage de Lugendo, another charismatic singer who had recently been recruited. Following the success of *Mario*, with which it shared a musical structure, *La Vie des Hommes* confirmed another shift in Franco's position: he had turned his attention from women's shortcomings to those of the men. Asked on television what had brought about this new attitude towards women, Franco said with a sideways smile, "I have grown up. I am 48 years old now, and you have to accept I am allowed to change my mind." As if to underline a new-found respect for women, Franco simultaneously released the first recording he ever made with a female artiste. *Le Grand Maître et Jolie Detta* gave welcome exposure to the young singer who performed two numbers on the album, notably *Massu* which made her name. Detta, the tall, elegant daughter of Greek and Zaïrean parents, first performed in Kinshasa with Choc Stars (a Zaïko family spin-off and no relation to the CHOC label), before joining the Francolettes dancers. She made her singing debut with OK Jazz during their month-long tour of Kenya in May/June 1986, and then moved on to link up with Bozi Boziana's Orchèstre Anti-Choc.

After the usual gossipy concern about whether Franco himself would turn up, the big man had arrived in Nairobi one week later than expected, with a supremely powerful complement of talent and several familiar names amongst the band. These included that reluctant traveller, rhythm guitarist and vice-president of OK Jazz, Simaro Lutumba, who had recently made up his differences with Franco over the release of his album *Maya*, recorded outside the OK Jazz system while Franco was in Europe. With tremulous vocals by Carlito Lassa, the title song had become a big hit in East Africa and, although it had not originally been sanctioned by Franco, it was performed by OK Jazz during their Kenyan visit — presumably in deference to public opinion. Malage de Lugendo sang Carlito's part and he was joined by Kiesse Diambu, Ndombe Opetum, Djo Mpoyi and Madilu System. Malage and Madilu were the men the Kenyan fans were shouting loudest for, after Franco that is. Dizzy Mandjeku and Papa Noel took on the solo guitar parts. Reports in the Kenyan press told of wild scenes with up to 10,000 people at some of the shows. But the four-hour long performances were not enough for many of the fans, and when one show was started with a version of the Live Aid song *We Are The World*, it was greeted with catcalls from the crowd. They wanted authentic OK Jazz. Switching the repertoire, the band moved into *Pesa Position* and the crowd's mood turned from anger to wild delight.

The headlines said it was Franco at his best. OK Jazz on form. In fact, Franco had appeared on stage for short periods only, and at some of the shows there were serious disturbances as fans showed their frustration. It transpired that he and several band members had been suffering from malaria. Detta, Isaac Musekiwa and Madilu suffered badly — as did Franco. Isaac was hospitalised for several days. The promoter had been thinking of cancelling the last performances but, true to showbusiness tradition, Franco took the stage. The tour ended in tears, however. Following a show at the Rift Valley stadium the band were locked in their dressing room by an angry promoter, who insisted that Franco had broken the terms of his contract. Among the many names he used to describe the bandleader was 'shark'.

While Zaïrean fans had been waiting in vain to celebrate the group's birthday at the Un-Deux-Trois in Kinshasa, Franco was winding up the Kenya tour. From there he moved to Zambia, playing at three venues including the Independence Stadium, where he performed in front of a tearful President Kaunda, singing a specially composed praise song and leading the whole orchestra in waving handkerchiefs, the trademark of 'KK', who sat weeping and watching appreciatively. OK Jazz records had for a long time been available in Zambia on the Teal label and the expectant crowds included some of his keenest followers.

Franco had flown in the band's equipment in a chartered Boeing 737 which greatly impressed the

Zambian fans, many of whom apparently regarded Franco as a kind of god, and massive crowds appeared at the airport as well as at the shows. According to a Lingala-speaking member of the Zambian paramilitary assigned to protect him, Franco himself was nervous about the high level of security. Mindful of past experiences, the Grand Master had taken the precaution of demanding his money up front. From Zambia, Franco travelled, via Europe, back to the USA for his second tour. In the meantime he released the best of the 30th anniversary discs, *Testament Ya Bowule* (The Testament of Bowule), composed by 'Le Poet' Simaro Lutumba and jointly credited to both of them. On the face of it, Franco and TP OK Jazz were starting their fourth decade in better shape than ever.

*OK Jazz reached a new peak with 'Mario', but few of Franco's fans
realised that a long and productive era was coming to an end*

CHAPTER SEVEN

Setting of an African Sun

"Yes, Franco was a prophet. A missionary who well understood his mission. If he was considered a trouble-maker it was only because his message was frank and direct and challenged the consciences of his listeners."
Funeral address, Nôtre Dame Cathedral, Kinshasa

IN MARCH, 1987 Franco announced from the Brussels office of his company, African Sun Music, the release of an album which was at once frightening and morbidly fascinating, as well as being a very sensual music. Later, in view of the rumours surrounding Franco's demise, the title song took on a painful significance. *Attention Na Sida* (Beware of Aids) was one of the Grand Maître's masterworks. Against a heavy folklore rhythm, mixed to give the drums as much prominence as the delicate interwoven guitars, Franco spoke out in thunderous, preacher-like tones about the disease itself, the moral background and ways of avoiding HIV, which in Africa is mostly spread by heterosexual contact and non-sterile injections. He warned against the use of unclean needles and the dangers of injecting drugs, exhorting all sections of the community to protect themselves and subsequent generations from infection. He sang in clear French as well as in Lingala in order to reach the widest audience, and even in anglophone countries the song's success was matched with some understanding of the subject's gravity. Although English speakers didn't know exactly what he said, people listened, and trembled when they heard Franco's vocal outburst, particularly when he growled out the portentious reference to 'Sodom and Gomorrah'.

The song was recorded without OK Jazz, most of whom were not in Brussels at the time. In their place

Franco called on members of the visiting Kinshasa band, Victoria Eleison, under the direction of the rhythm guitarist, Safro Manzangi Elima, who brought in guitarists Akwesa and Lutula, bassist Pinos and drummer Djou Djou Che. Vocal accompaniment was by Dalienst. Ironically, Franco's introductory guitar phrase was a repeat of the gloriously erotic *sebene* used on the 'pornographic' song *Jacky* which had so outraged the population of Kinshasa. This may have been just another example of Franco's mischievousness or, more likely, it was used as a conscious link to emphasise the connection between Aids and the unsafe sexual practices catalogued in that earlier song. While in Brussels without OK Jazz, Franco had also called on Zaïko Langa Langa to back him at a private dance hosted by a director of Air Zaïre. The fact that two such groups from a much younger generation, and a different 'school' of Zaïrean music, should be able to accompany Franco shows just how familiar his music was to all, and how close it remained to the core of Congo-Zaïrean culture.

A few weeks later, OK Jazz joined up with Franco in Belgium, bringing Josky back with them into the fold. Simaro was also making a rare sortie outside Africa, and the impressive line-up for their first show in Brussels included Jolie Detta among the vocal section. Although no one suspected at the time, this Good Friday all-nighter was to be virtually the European swansong of Franco in full force; he was at the peak of his powers, playing for his own people, and there was no need to cater his show to European tastes. With plenty of imported Zaïrean 'ambience', the Belgian shows were usually at least as good as Kinshasa performances — and taking into account the superior sound equipment and plush dancehall environment, they were sometimes even better. Here, as at home, Franco was surrounded by his cronies. He was relaxed and looking fit, with his well-rounded shape further exaggerated by a bold check suit.

There were 27 musicians at the Salle Arlequin, with

up to sixteen on stage at any one time. The singers wore green shirts, the instrumentalists red. OK Jazz played a 'typique' show, aimed squarely at the mainstream Zaïrean audience. They warmed up with a variety spot, including a taste of country and western and the song which so upset the Kenyans, *We Are the World*, before embarking on some classic rumba drawn from 30 years of music history, including one of the original successes, *La Rumba OK*. During *Pesa Position* there was a dose of the Sorcerer's magic, when the whole band seemed to freeze with hands in the air while Franco's talons did their work on the guitar fretboard. There was a folklore number that sounded like one of the roots of zouk music.

Then came *Testament Ya Bowule*, delivered in piercing style by Malage, with a *sebene* which saw the four trumpeters dancing in line, waving their horns from side to side, leaping and going through the motions of patting a basketball, like a group unto themselves. Across the wide stage stood two saxophone players, who came into their own with *El Manicero*, (The Peanut Vendor). Another lovely old number was *Josephine*, a sultry Fifties-style rumba, delivered with romantic passion by Franco and just a handful of musicians, which recalled the small size of the original OK Jazz squad. Jolie Detta sang *Massu*, and a few other recent successes were aired; the crowd were delirious for Franco and Madilu's 'Mamou' duet. But the song which ran away with the night was Josky's *Mata, Kita, Bloqué* (Get Up, Get Down, Jam); played three times, with Franco cranking up the *sebenes* to fever pitch.

In Britain, for the second year running, an OK Jazz appearance was announced and then cancelled at the last minute. The band was due to perform on the last weekend in June but the London promoter was informed at very short notice that OK Jazz had been ordered to return to Zaïre expressly to play for President Mobutu at the June 30 independence day celebrations. As it turned out it was probably just as well for Franco's peace of mind and the reputation of OK Jazz that they did not appear in London at that time. The main show might well have been a sell-out, but there was also a second gig scheduled, at which OK Jazz had been booked to play as a kind of side-show on a secondary stage at an indoor festival in the cavernous Earls Court arena. Even in such unknown territory, OK Jazz deserved to be a top-of-the-bill act, and neither Franco nor his fans would have been pleased about him being side-lined so disrespectfully.

Despite Franco's absence from Europe, his records continued to sell rapidly in the West as well as in Africa, and he kept them coming at a prodigious rate. During 1987, some nine OK Jazz albums were released, including a live recording from Holland of a dynamic if somewhat frantic show, and a compilation of old material on the RetroAfric label, entitled *Originalité*, which made available some of the first OK Jazz tracks recorded 30 years previously at Loningisa. There was a hard-driving electro-folklore album, *Ekaba Kaba*, released by the French Celluloid label, and towards the end of the year a retrospective pot-pourri, called *Animation Non-Stop*, in which Franco acknowledged the 'retro factor' that was bringing his earlier work to a new generation of foreign enthusiasts. The medley of old and new songs included follow-ups to his two most popular soap opera stories, *Mario 3* and *Mamou 2*. There was also a song of rare international topicality called *Iran-Irak* and a brief guest appearance from 'Le Prince' Youlou Mabiala. OK Jazz were riding a flood tide generated by Franco's outpouring of creative energy.

Hostilities resumed

Back in Zaïre, Franco was in 'turbulent' mood. The reason for the band's recall to Kinshasa from Europe had, in fact, been to play at a private birthday party for the daughter of the old adversary, Prime Minister Kengo wa Dondo, who had now apparently made up his differences with the Grand Master. But Franco embarrassed the host and guests by playing the controversial song, *Mokolo Tonga Abotoli Tonga Na Ye*, about the tailor taking back his needle. The song was popular the first time around, and once the people had indulged in their reverie, they demanded that Franco play it a second time. Joining in the joke against himself, and no doubt looking to minimalise the loss of face, Kengo wa Dondo then requested he play it a third time. Franco handed his guitar to Simaro and left the band, and the party, to get on with it.

The Grand Master had a more serious, professional conflict to deal with. He was now at the centre of a verbal slanging match with his old adversaries, Tabu Ley and Verckys. The root of Ley's complaint was the defection of his great female singing star and companion Mbilia Bel, who had boosted Afrisa's appeal so much during the mid-1980s that Afrisa's music had become at least as marketable as Franco's. Ley had nurtured Bel's career since discovering her as a dancer with Abeti Masekini, Zaïre's first lady of showbusiness. After half a dozen successful duet albums, Bel had become the first truly pan-African female superstar, with an image as the continent's most glamorous woman. The fact that she had borne a child by Ley did not diminish her appeal, although when, during the pregnancy, she was replaced at centre stage by Faya Tess it signalled the beginning of the end of their productive partnership. She eventually left Tabu Ley in 1987, apparently enticed by a wealthy Gabonese politician and record producer. The ensuing row was well documented in the Zaïrean tabloid press with accusations, threats and legal injuctions flying.

Ley was allegedly furious at losing his star attraction. But his anger was multiplied when Franco coincidentally decided he needed a female focus for OK Jazz and selected Baniel Bambo, a member of Afrisa who had been a virtual understudy for Mbilia Bel. In 1987 Franco released an album starring Baniel and Nana Akumu, recruited from Johnny Bokelo's band. The title song, *Les On Dit* (Hearsay), was widely believed to have been directed at Ley, with the two women singing pointedly about the wife of the chairman, and the difficult life of an unmarried woman.

The hostilities continued over the 'Zaïko affair' in which the top youth group split up, reportedly due to the same Gabonese interests which had separated Bel from Ley. Franco called the feuding Zaïko members to a discussion at his house in Limete but, according to an aide, the two leaders of the band could not be reconciled. Ilo Pablo listened to his advice, while Nyoka Longo did not. In the Kinshasa pop weekly, *Stars*, published by Verckys, Franco was accused of using his power as musicians' union president to give certain Zaïko members permission to work in Gabon where, it was alleged, they encouraged the enticement of Bel. When Zaïko Langa Langa split in two, Franco was already identified with the breakaway faction led by Ilo Pablo, so Ley naturally sided with the rest of the group who stayed under the leadership of Nyoka Longo. The Zaïko feud became the most bitter of all such disputes and Franco and Ley remained on opposite sides of the divide. The musicians' union eventually put a six-month ban on either band broadcasting or advertising under the disputed name of Zaïko Langa Langa.

There was another power struggle going on with Verckys, who had his own problems with both Ley and Franco, each of whom were competing for their slice of a diminishing music market. By 1987-88, Zaïrean domestic record sales had slumped to a dismal low point, at which time the Soneca receipts for the highest-selling album in Zaïre showed only 5,000 sold in one year, compared with over 50,000 some years earlier. This was as much a result of cassette piracy and smuggling of imports as the inability of Zaïrean manufacturers to obtain vinyl. The largest total of royalties paid out by Soneca in 1987 and 1988 was the equivalent of US$10,000; a cheque which undoubtedly

less and less, had reportedly increased his own slice of OK Jazz's earnings to 60 per cent. Franco did manage to hold the band together for a while longer, but already musicians were drifting away.

The guitarist Gege Mangaya was so discouraged after a lifetime of music, that he quit the business altogether, only to be rehabilitated into the ranks of Nyoka Longo's Zaïko Langa Langa. One of the newest recruits, Malage was already making mutinous noises in the pop press. Mandjeku, Djo Mpoyi, Madilu System and Lokombe, amongst others, were reported to be looking for a way out. Other OK Jazz members were virtually destitute in Brussels. Some musicians, including the new women members, Baniel and Nana, were in the USA. Josky, surprisingly, turned up again in Kinshasa, while he and another returned prodigal, Dalienst, were featured on the first two OK Jazz releases of 1988. Although his compositions *Mamie Zou* and *Dodo* became hits, Dalienst retreated back into his European exile. But Josky stayed aboard OK Jazz, making the most of his dynamic song *Mata, Kita, Bloqué* , which proved to be a durable hit throughout the year.

The Grand Master was already sickening, however, and in Kinshasa his name was spoken with increasing tones of sadness. Rumours abounded, and one particularly strong one reached Europe in the summer of 1988 saying Franco was dead. The story was refuted in early June, when he appeared on-stage with the band at the Faubourg night club. While the Un-Deux-Trois club was seemingly frozen in the middle of a major reconstruction, OK Jazz's current 'siege' was a white-walled, open-air enclosure in a residential area close to Matonge, with mature trees growing in the compound and hanging light bulbs illuminating the dancers. Outside, the parade of Mercedes and BMWs dropped off the clientele of 'big men' who had grown plump and prosperous along with Franco, accompanied by their stately womenfolk, self-consciously rolling their buttocks and flapping their colourful, multi-layered, wax-dyed wrappers like giant butterflies.

Franco played, sang, danced and made most of the public announcements himself. Although he had lost a lot of his previous bulk, which a year before weighed in at 140 kilos, he gave the impression that he was recovering from whatever mystery illness was afflicting him. With a thinner profile, some friends wistfully imagined he looked more like his younger self. He insisted that doctors were unable to diagnose his condition, but his symptoms included high blood pressure and diabetes. He also believed he had a heart condition and suggested he was deliberately losing weight to reduce the strain. In the week of his 50th birthday, on July 6, 1988, Franco made a brief appearance on stage, played some guitar, and left the Faubourg early. It was not the last time he played in public, although many people secretly feared they would never again see Franco on form. He could sense this sadness from the way people looked at him, and he tried to console his fans and wellwishers by telling them not to worry, OK Jazz would always be there.

From Europe Franco kept up the programme of frequent record releases with *Réponse du Mario* (Mario's Reply) and a companion album, featuring the two women, Baniel and Nana, entitled *Cherche une Maison à Louer Pour Moi, Cheri* (Find a House to Rent for Me, Darling). For these albums Franco called on the services of a keyboard player for the first time since the band was constituted. The musician Franco invited was also the first white person ever to play with OK Jazz.

Vincent Kenis is a Belgian multi-instrumentalist and record producer who, by strange coincidence, discovered later that he was the nephew of Gilbert Warnant, the keyboard player at Opika some 35 years earlier. Kenis recalls that Franco expected him to play his parts on these new songs straight off after the first listen. "Franco then went off and finished two other tracks while I worked out my part," recalled Kenis. "When we were ready I recorded my part at the same time as he was laying down the guitar solo. We played straight through together, recording the basic tracks 'live', and he was looking hard at me the whole time from across the studio." The albums were fairly makeweight, even though a slight 'techno' edge was introduced into the production. More successful with the Zaïrean audience was a two-song, 33rpm maxi-single with Franco, Pepe Ndombe (Opetum) and OK Jazz, called *Angela*.

In December, 1988 the Grand Master called Sam Mangwana to join him on two albums to be recorded in Brussels. No money was to change hands, but each would have the services of the other for free, and an album of their own to market. The first to be released early in 1989 was the Mangwana disc *For Ever*. The opening track *Toujours OK* (Always OK) recalled the creative mix the two had achieved with *Coopération* six years previously. Sam and Franco made a similar introduction, Sam delivered his soulful lyrics and Franco sang and played with his usual verve. There were only a few members of OK Jazz on hand, with an international team of session musicians on horns and vocal accompaniment.

The second product of what proved to be Franco's last sessions was released some months later. This was Franco's own album which he had sold to the French label, Rythmes et Musique. It opened with a hard, Bakongo folkloric number *Lukoki* and had more of the OK Jazz sound than Mangwana's album. Sam, however, believed that Franco would normally have made a better job of the mixing. It could, he thought, have been another masterpiece.

In the open-air bars and *ngandas* of Kinshasa people continued to dance as normal while the speakers pumped out the latest Francos. The first record, *For Ever*, should have been a bigger hit. The music was popular enough, but many Franco fans could not bear to see the photo on the cover, which showed a terrifying picture of an emaciated Franco.

At the time of the recording Sam knew well that Franco was seriously ill. He had lost about half of his bulk and the 'big man' now looked small, wrinkled and much older. His jovial expression had been replaced with a mask of worry. Even so, during the recording, Mangwana remembers, "He said he was better at the time, and he was even dancing in the studio. But he would not admit he was close to death. I think he just could not accept it." For someone who had never found death acceptable, his own proved to be cruelly drawn out and degrading.

In March, 1989 Franco was booked to play again in London, in a rare event, supported by Mangwana. This time the publicity was adequate and all 2,000 tickets were sold in advance. People flew into London from as far afield as Africa, the USA and Scandinavia, to be met by a scribbled notice on the dancehall door. The show was postponed until the next day, a Monday. On the Monday it was obvious Franco was not coming. Although it was not

The upsetting photo on the album sleeve from Franco's final recording session

the first no-show by Franco in London, this was undoubtedly a worse fiasco. It was not his health that had prevented Franco playing. Once again the perennial visa problem was at the root of the trouble. The people had once more been deprived of seeing the Grand Master, who was waiting with the band in a bus at a Belgian ferry port unable to embark for Britain. Mangwana did cross the English Channel but was refused permission to enter.

Back in Kinshasa the problems with band members continued, and the popular press reported dissatisfaction from several musicians, including the singers Malage and Lokombe, although OK Jazz had regrouped under vice-president Simaro and had begun playing again at Le Faubourg. The position of Madilu, the star singer, was in doubt. His family, at least, was ensconced in Europe, and there was much talk in the press and on 'radio trottoir' about his alleged personal problems.

On the other hand there were still musicians ready to claim an unconvincing allegience to OK Jazz. In July, Voix du Zaïre radio carried an interview with the vocalist Wuta Mayi, who had left OK Jazz some eight years previously to pursue a solo career and became a founder of the soukous 'supergroup', Les Quatres Etoiles. Wuta Mayi talked of working once again with the band and stated that, even after eight years away, he would always be a member of OK Jazz. There were also some newcomers recruited to the band, in particular the soft-voiced singer Carlito, who had made a name for himself as a regular member of Choc Stars, and a frequent collaborator on record with Simaro, notably on the hit song *Maya*. Carlito's voice was in many ways similar to that of Malage, the ambitious young man who had, in July, decided to quit OK Jazz and transfer to Zaïko Langa Langa Nkolo Mboka.

In Brussels, Franco was growing further distant from the running of the Kinshasa operation, and from his primary audience. He was seen on television frequently but, instead of entertaining he was there in an educational role, appearing in a public information broadcast to warn against the dangers of Aids. His stern, serious demeanour was heightened by the spectacles he now wore to correct his fading eyesight, while the shrinking, wrinkled skin amplified the gravity of his facial expression. One friend claimed he really noted Franco's decline from the moment he started wearing European cut shirts. He had previously been so bulky that his custom-made shirts were constructed more like African robes. In August, Voix du Zaïre television carried an interview with an even more haggard-looking Grand Maître, recorded in Paris, in which he denied the stories that he was, himself, suffering from Aids. His own problem, he now said, was kidney failure. When asked outright if he was scared of dying, Franco replied, "I'm not scared of death, because it comes to everyone. I'm not scared. When it comes, I will go."

Although the received wisdom has it that Franco died of Aids, he always denied it when asked. In fact kidney failure is a common cause of HIV-related death. If Franco did have the virus and did not wish to announce it that was considered to be his own affair. Some Europeans, in particular, find this hard to accept. However, in Zaïre, where heterosexual Aids is undoubtedly rife, the stigma attached is different. In a country where cerebral malaria, typhoid, tuberculosis, various fevers, deliberate poisoning and witchcraft are regular killers, there is often no accurate diagnosis, and society's way of dealing with fatal illness is often to accept its inevitability. With Franco's professed inability to accept death, it would have been impossible for him to admit even to himself that he had a terminal condition. Presumably his doctor knew what the verdict was, although no autopsy result was announced.

Franco was also asked during the interview about sorcery and whether he thought he had any enemies who (by implication) might have been using it against him. That was when he replied with the remark about the

Cameroon football team taking sorcerers with them to the World Cup; from which it could be implied that, like everybody else, he probably was threatened by and/or practising sorcery himself. If so, he managed to conceal it from the closest of his musical associates. There is no reliable evidence, but on the busy streets of Kinshasa there were as many theories about Franco's decline as radio trottoir had mouthpieces. At an informal roadside bar in an unpaved side-street close to the Un-Deux-Trois, a woman called Chantal who sold smoked fish in the Gambela market gave her opinion, based on a wide knowledge of the rumours which flourished in the market — that barometer of public opinion.

A gaunt young woman with a work-worn appearance, Chantal's expression was bright and confident as she sipped an ice-cold Primus beer. The problem, she proclaimed with certainty, was sorcery: Franco's own sorcery, which had by a cruel stroke of fate been turned against him. It was well known, Chantal insisted, that Franco had 'chopped' many of his musical competitors during his career. Had there not been seventeen musicians who died mysteriously? Were there not the same number of plants growing in front of the Un-Deux-Trois? Did this not mean that the souls of those seventeen were imprisoned there? This was the only proof she needed to establish that Franco was involved in sorcery.

Now, according to this most sensationalist of rumour-mongers, all Franco's health and personal problems had only come about because his powerful spell had been broken by an event which had happened quite recently. Across the road from the Un-Deux-Trois is the plot of land on which the new Kamanyola stadium was being slowly constructed by Chinese labourers (believed to be prisoners on forced labour). A small river bed ran through this land and at one point there was a road bridge which the workers had to rebuild. Beneath that bridge, however, the market woman claimed that Franco had hidden the powerful gris-gris which were his insurance policy. Unfortunately for him, the builders' heavy equipment dug it all up and destroyed everything. From then on, the smoked fish seller opined, Franco was finished. That was but one of the more fanciful stories circulating about the Grand Maître's condition.

The final KO

Franco was still taking on business obligations and he had a contract to fulfil with the London promoter whose March show, reuniting him on stage with Sam Mangwana, had been cancelled. In order to restore confidence among the British press and public, Franco was brought to London some weeks before the prospective appearance to give press and television interviews. An unfortunate air of suspicion and mistrust surrounded the meetings and Franco made a very negative impression.

The British press met an ailing man, too weak to rise from his bed to be photographed, who seemed, against all character, to be bitter and introspective. He realised that, in certain circles, he was a famous and respected figure but he implied he was offended that no Western pop stars had ever come to him with an offer of collaboration. Taking a defensive stance and a weak line of argument, Franco claimed African music was stronger than European music. "I'll explain why. In European music you start to sing. You reach the chorus and then, that's it. Finish. You might hear it twice, but in our music you hear it three, four, five times." Several people who met him then agreed that Franco should never have been brought to London in his condition; that it seemed like a last-ditch attempt to exploit cynically a fading star.

Back in Brussels, Franco checked into the Saint-Pierre hospital, where his personal secretary, chauffeur and sax player, Rondot, took a cot alongside the Grand Master, to be on constant stand-by. Franco, however terminal his condition appeared to be, was not prepared to give up without resisting to the end. But his remaining strength was draining away and he was bitterly resentful of his inability to function. He had earlier visited Lourdes, looking for a miracle cure which never arrived, and now he began to lapse into longer, and more troubled, fevers. On September 22, Rondot remembers, Franco was lying in bed when he suddenly sat up and demanded news of his band. When told they were playing in Holland that night, he struggled to get out of bed. "My Tout Puissant OK Jazz are playing," he said anxiously, "I must be there. Quick, bring the car and take me there."

Rondot believed Franco had decided he was ready to die on stage, and his colleagues were concerned this might well happen if he attempted to perform. Dressed in a stage outfit that was tightly belted against his shrunken body, Franco was driven across the border to the Melkweg club in Amsterdam, and was slowly walked to the stage by his tour manager Manzenza and the guitarist Mayaula. A chair was pulled up and Franco called for his guitar, but he could only play a few bars. This was the last time the Sorcerer touched a guitar and the notes he played had a ghostly, foreboding quality. Unable to continue, Franco left the stage for the final time and returned to his bed.

A few weeks later, when OK Jazz made it to London for their long-awaited second appearance, the farcical nature of their relationship with the British public reached its peak. The band came on-stage at the Brixton Academy and warmed up the audience for half an hour, with serious OK Jazz music. Then one of the musicians announced that Franco would not, after all, be appearing. The promoter appeared to panic, the plug was pulled and OK Jazz were humiliated.

Even more serious than the band's humiliation was the condition of Franco who was now hospitalised in Belgium, first at Saint-Pierre, where he consulted a prominent Belgian Aids specialist, Dr Nathan Clumeck, and later at the University Hospital, Namur. Members of his family, including his sister Marie-Louise and wife Annie, were at the bedside, along with the faithful Rondot. On the night of Wednesday, October 11, his old colleague Mose Se Fan Fan paid a visit to the Namur hospital which left him chilled with apprehension: Franco, whom he had last seen in full force, was barely alive, but he was still living. Rondot recalls that during the night Franco was ridden by crises. His heart stopped beating three times, and twice Franco managed to resist. Eventually the man who always found death unacceptable could struggle no more and had to come to terms with it. The next day, Thursday, October 12, 1989, the Grand Master was dead.

Like his mentor, Kabasele, Franco had died in Europe. A mass was held at Saint Boniface church in Brussels. The body was flown to Kinshasa on the Saturday, accompanied by Dessouin and Isaac Musekiwa, the two longest-serving members of OK Jazz, and constant companions of Franco. At 6am there were thousands of mourners at Ndjili international airport waiting for the arrival of the Air Zaïre DC-10. As the casket was carried off the plane, mourners distraught with grief jostled and pushed to touch the remains of their hero. There were traditional drummers with large, fan-shaped *lokole* slit drums, and a group of Kimbanguist horn players blasting a mournful fanfare alongside the pall bearers.

The route into Kinshasa was lined with thousands of people, many holding branches of green leaves, to watch the battered American hearse, draped with the flambeau national flag and accompanied by a police motorcycle escort, drive up in a wail of sirens to the Palais du Peuple, where Franco was to lie in state. Nowhere were the crowds thicker than along the Boulevard Lumumba, which passes through the zones of Limete and Yolo, where Franco had spent most of his life. Many of the grief-stricken Kinois ran desperately to keep up with the cortège.

President Mobutu had declared four days of national

Pallbearers carry the casket with Franco's body from the Brussels church

mourning, during which the Voix du Zaïre radio played a constant programme of OK Jazz music. For four days the Zaïrean people were reminded of the songs they knew so well, which had accompanied most of them through the whole of their lives, and which had provided the comfort of continuity in a most precarious society. Mobutu himself was out of town, at his residence in the south of France, and he did not attend the funeral, although a wreath was laid on his behalf by the Secretary of the MPR. The President did later pay his respects at the graveside — a gesture that he had not made for any other musician — and visited Mama Makiesse, Annie and the family at Limete. He also picked up the expenses for the funeral.

After the lying-in-state at the Palais du Peuple, during which OK Jazz played for the long file of ordinary citizens who came to pay their respects, the funeral service was held at Kinshasa's Nôtre Dame cathedral, with a special mass composed for Luambo. In his address, the priest gave high praise to Franco by acknowledging his unconventional contribution, without qualification.

"Franco lived a very full life," he said from the pulpit. "Yes, Franco was a prophet. If he was considered a trouble-maker it was only because his message was frank and direct, and it challenged the consciences of his listeners. He was a missionary who well understood his mission. As he himself said, his mission was to provoke, denounce and tell the truth."

The body was buried in Gombe cemetery on October 17. Through the densely-packed crowd mourners carried to the grave Franco's blue Gibson guitar and a large framed photograph of a cocky young man with sideburns and a yankee baseball cap worn at a jaunty angle. He had been posthumously awarded the country's highest order, Commander of the National Order of the Leopard, which took precedence over the rank of Officer, which he had previously held. The medal and ribbon of the Order were placed on the coffin, where Franco's embalmed, emaciated face could be seen through the open section of the casket lid, lying on a pillow of white satin.

First the Prime Minister, then Simaro Lutumba, the vice-president of OK Jazz, and lastly Franco's wife, Annie, paid brief tribute. Franco's mother, Mama Makiesse, spoke directly to her deceased son about the band's future. Referring to Simaro, who stood alongside her, she said: "My son, here is the person I have chosen, with unanimous approval, to take over your dream and direct the orchestra. Give him the strength so your work can be continued and come to the fore, as when you were alive." She raised her head and repeated the declaration: "Here is the person I have chosen to maintain OK Jazz so the music continues to attract and please the public." Simaro responded directly to the still form of his old companion, "In all truth, I pray you give me the courage to continue your work, so that I can look after your mother and the children who are now my responsibility." The lid was closed, the casket lowered and the body of Franco Luambo Makiadi, the man born to suffer, was laid to rest.

BOOK TWO: The Legacy

An outspoken social commentator, Franco had the good of his people at heart

CHAPTER EIGHT

The Human Comedy of Africa's Balzac

"The managing editor of the African 'Comedie Humaine'. This holy giant plays guitar and sings. Indestructible, immovable, he victoriously confronts time and fashion. One cannot see who could stem the flow of moral criticism from this singer-joker before the year 2000."

Sylvain Bemba, *50 Ans de Musique du Congo-Zaïre*

THE ZAÏREAN PEOPLE's sense of loss at the death of Franco was profound. He was so much a part of the collective psyche that his departure was mourned more deeply than even that of a blood relative. To many it seemed the heart had been cut out of their very identity. More than any person or institution Franco had endured, as Sylvain Bemba said, indestructible, immovable. That the 'flow of moral criticism' was now stemmed well before the year 2000 was itself a shock to the sense of security, a sharp reminder of everybody's mortality. There was also the grief at losing the man: the country's greatest artist and most charismatic figure, who could make you laugh, cry and, most importantly, dance. But the greatest shock came at being cut off from the only line of continuity to have lasted during 40 years of immense change, which saw his people progress from a village existence which had remained unchanged since life began, through to nationhood and world citizenship in the space age.

Whatever rung of the development ladder a person was on, whether a village youth fresh in the city, a hardworking, independent market mama or a millionaire businessman back from a New York trip, Franco was able to communicate with them in the most direct, economical manner. Where there were no newspapers, Franco would inform. Where there was no understanding Franco would educate. Where there were no role models, Franco would give examples of how, or how not, to behave. Where the disorientating maze of urban life made people dizzy, Franco would give directions.

Although Franco was never considered a poet like his vice-president Simaro Lutumba, or a vocal charmer like Rochereau in his heyday, he was very much a spokesman of the people, whose method invariably conveyed a message. Having acquired the role and status of what in some African cultures would be a senior and respected *griot*, Franco set standards for himself that were as high as those he expected from others. Zaïre, even before the regime of President Mobutu, had never been noted for freedom of speech and, although Franco steered clear of the more overt political issues, he tried to maintain a strict moral line. Sometimes the morality was highly personal, but he believed he had a duty to express himself. He was well aware of the effect that shock can have on catching listeners' attention, and outrage, provocation and even obscenity were some of his most potent weapons.

Franco was a troublemaker, but he had the good of his people at heart. Had he committed only half the number of outrages he might well have been crushed by the state, but he was so outspoken and prominent that he became virtually unassailable. The sheer volume of his outpourings wore down any moral opposition. But he was keenly aware of the restrictions imposed on him and usually knew just how far he could go before his tongue would run him into trouble. "I love the truth, I whip falsehood in all its forms," he once said. "When, in my songs, I take a theme of truth, it is because I think that truth can liberate ignorance. But, here too, I have learned to my own cost that all truth is not always good to say."

Just to listen to Franco's records, or to have seen him perform to a strictly Zaïrean audience, is to realise that there is a great deal to his music which fails to impress upon a large number of his fans, Africans and others, who do not understand Lingala. Franco was fond of saying that his music had no frontiers, and while he might have used the odd line or two of French, he never intended to start singing in English. Occasionally, to express a particularly personal emotion, he sang in minority dialects of his mother's Kikongo tongue, but Franco's medium was Lingala, the language of his people, and in particular the vernacular 'street' language of the argot-loving Kinois.

Lingala is a tonal, primal-sounding language, which is melodious and easy to sing along with without knowing the sense; it has even been remarked that the language sings itself. It is one of the few inter-ethnic languages on the African continent, having originated as a *lingua franca* or trade language. Lingala is a comparatively young tongue, which is one of Zaïre's four national languages, and the everyday vehicle in western Zaïre and Congo-Brazzaville. It has become the main language for Congo-Zaïrean musical expression, which has actually helped the language expand and grow.

As with most African languages there is a great deal of word play, in the form of metaphor, simile, punning, double entendre and any other device. The Kinois are particularly keen on twisting the meanings of words and inventing or adapting others from different languages. They also appreciate *mbwakela*, the stone-faced irony at which Franco excelled. In Zaïrean songs as in life, both traditional and contemporary, things are often not what they seem at first sight.

Ultimately, almost everything boils down to a metaphor for money. The cheapest cooked fish on the street is known as 'Thompson', after a 'cheap' foreign architect whose university building collapsed soon after construction. The currency became known as the *shaba* (copper) when the price of that mineral collapsed and the state named after it tried to secede. A 'flambeau', or flaming torch, as in the MPR flag, describes a tightfisted person. In popular music there is sexual innuendo aplenty, and in Franco's songs it is often combined with the money theme. Four examples of neologisms culled from Franco's works: 'Boma l'heure', meaning 'killing time', signified a prostitute, as did 'passe-partout'; 'Locataire'(Lodger) describes a prostitute's client; *nyama* (bushmeat) meant a woman's sexual organs, by association with blood.

Franco's social commentaries were never short on irony, particularly in the more dead-pan observations, but his preferred style was satire, at which he was an acknowledged master. The objects of his real anger and rage were the new bourgeoisie who burgeoned after independence, and in documenting their excesses he did, indeed, take on the role of a Balzac. Throughout his career he maintained a constant criticism of the middle classes, openly expressed in early songs like *Nani Apedalaki Te?* (Who Has Never Cycled?) in which he railed against the arrogance of motorists, taking the side of the more vulnerable cyclists, and pointing out that before independence everyone was content to ride a bike. The specific target of Franco's anger was not named but inhabitants of the cité knew it was an attack on Kasavubu who had graduated to the presidential limousine from a bicycle of his own. In fact, the rattling chainguard on Kasavubu's Raleigh bike was a familiar sound to the neighbours as the future president used to cycle home late at night. The word 'pedaleur' came to signify the poor working class. The attacks on pomposity continued through the middle years of Franco's career to the latter-day epics such as *Très Impoli*.

Franco was a prolific songwriter, and often sang the lead part on other musicians' compositions, but he could not really be considered to have a great singing voice. His voice had character and emotional expression and he enunciated the words clearly, but his range was limited and his gruff tone was hardly sweet like some of the great

Franco was always ready to note down song lyrics. Here in London with Manzenza looking on, he drafts the song '12,600 Lettres'

altos who sang alongside him. When Franco reached for the high notes his voice sounded strained, adding an element of pain which served to heighten the soulful delivery. He was most comfortable in the middle range, where his style turned more towards oratory than singing. He began recording at a young age when he still had a squeaky schoolboy voice, and as his work matured so his voice acquired a gravity to match his increasing stature. Eventually he even began to echo the charismatic, authoritarian tones of the Zaïrean president, Mobutu. After 30 years at the top of his trade he was singing with a vocal power equal to the band's strongest contribution.

On OK Jazz's recordings from the 1980s the guitar pyrotechnics and fluid saxophone solos of the previous decade had given way to massive waves of big, male-voice harmonies accompanying the solo singer, taking Kazadi's 'harmonic force' to the maximum. It was often sufficiently satisfying to revel under this tropical downpour of sound, appreciating the voices for their instrumental quality alone. But when Franco's gravelly voice takes over the lead something serious is obviously going down, and when it comes to epic conversational pieces like *Mario*, *Très Impoli*, *Suite Lettre 2* or *Attention Na Sida* it is nice to have some idea of what the Grand Master is saying.

Basic instincts

The subject matter of Franco's songs ranged widely but never strayed far from his listeners' experience. Among the topics were those traditionally dealt with by *griots* throughout West Africa, such as praise songs for chiefs (politicians usually), laments for the recently deceased and historical proverbs or parables as a guide to contemporary life. He also dealt with perennial African themes like tribalism and sorcery, and the wider implications of nationalism and black pride. As his commercial status grew, Franco was called to sing about consumer products and football teams.

Alongside the catalogue of documentary themes there were as many compositions about love affairs, or at least male-female relationships. In his first songs, *Bolingo Na Ngai Na Beatrice* (My Love For Beatrice) and *Marie Catho*, recorded at the age of fifteen, he sounded very much the besotted teenager. The latter, with its raw, zestful arrangement heralded the arrival of a dynamic new star, and became Franco's first smash hit.

Beatrice:
Even if someone insults me
Even if they kill me, it is no problem
Between you and me there is the band
of a wedding ring

Marie Catho:
When you go out, think of me

When you return, think of me
When you think, think only of me

Love has always been the prime subject matter for popular music the world over, but in pre-independence Congo it was a somewhat radical topic. Sexual relations were one thing, marriage was another, and there were rules of social behaviour to guide both. But love was something different. The Lingala verb *kolinga* means to want and to like as much as to love. Franco explained the concept of 'romantic love' with the phrase '*Bolingo ya Sentiment*' (literally 'Love with feeling', or passion). The respected Dutch anthropologist Johannes Fabian, who spent fifteen years in Zaïre, has suggested that, in pre-independence times, the format of the love song might also have been used as an ironic metaphor for the relationship between the Congolese and their colonists.

By all the evidence, Franco certainly knew about passionate love. Often he transposed the singer's role to voice it from the woman's viewpoint, as in the impassioned 1984 song *Temps Mort* (Dead Times) in which 'this painful thing called love' is equated with suffering in the heart, the head and the stomach, and with patience. Many years previously Franco had sung about his own passion in the song called *Majos*, dedicated to a married woman who was also believed to be the subject of several of his more personal compositions. In the early 1970s Franco was joined by Youlou to duet on some classic love songs from the man's viewpoint, notably the Bitchou composition *Infidelité Mado* (Mado's Infidelity), and the moving appeal to a love-object called *Celine*:

Save me, save me love
Death will soon swallow me
My heart is looking for a place
I am scared to admit how beautiful you are
Celine, o
I am scared to show my love

Love made frequent appearances in Franco's compositions, although he later said he preferred to provoke rather than croon. But the underlying theme of his work, particularly in the long songs of his later years, was the human condition. Here money and material considerations took precedence. Franco was not a priest, but he was a great entertainer and master satirist, who was never better than when ridiculing the vices and follies of his peers. As such, his completed works comprise the longest-running soap opera never made for television. As Franco told *Antilles-Afrique* magazine in 1983: "Each satire I compose is interpreted differently by everyone according to one's sensitivity and understanding. While the characters in my songs represent Mr and Mrs Everybody, people often try to stick a precise identification to them. Because of such speculations I can come into conflict with such and such a personality who, because of his being too sensitive, can lose his cool and order me to be jailed. The everyday worries of my people are the source of my inspiration and people are pleased because they can identify themselves in my songs. It's true my satires hurt some people. But this has nothing to do with me because I don't criticise anyone in particular, whether in private or political life. I am only an attentive observer of the morals of our society."

When Franco describes the subject matter of his songs as the 'lives of Mr and Mrs Everybody' it sounds a bit pat. As if he picked things at random and had no real theme. But he was so inextricably woven into the fabric of Kinshasa life that he was in contact with, and interested in, the social affairs of his musical constituency, the people of Kinshasa. Often letters from his listening public made up the subject matter, at other times fans would bring him poems or ideas for songs, but it was usually his own personal observations which caught the mood of the times. Franco sang in response to the village people deep in the forested interior of Zaïre, as well as to the smart Frenchified

Kinois, and as he acted out their situations, their lives and his often merged. Songs were frequently in the form of a conversation between two participants, often talking about a third party, sometimes with a commentator/narrator as the fourth member of the cast. Franco himself might be taking all the parts, as would a classic storyteller. Franco was no mean actor. He sometimes lived those parts so convincingly that separating the man from the work was impossible. And in Kinshasa, the big man's presence was everywhere.

The bewildering milieu of Kinshasa over which Franco presided, and which provided the bulk of his subject matter, was succinctly described by Tshonga-Onyumbe in an article published in *Zaïre-Afrique*, titled *Les problemes socio-economiques dans la chanson zaïroise moderne*. "Modern Zaïrean music is a phenomenon of city or semi-urban life. For the musicians and the world they create, which is reflected in their compositions, the environment is evidently the city and its multiple social problems. We know the attraction which this milieu holds for rural people. People of different origins come together to live and work. They leave their villages in a rural exodus to move into the city. At first they naturally carry over the mentality of the village in to the city. They succumb easily to temptation, believing that the extended family, tribal solidarity, hospitality and respect for tradition will be there to suppport them. But the city is not the village. It seems like a permanent party, disorientating and huge, where one can easily get lost in a forest of buildings and people."

As he points out, without the cultural, psychological and moral support found in the village, people have to struggle to find a regular home and a job, and then run a constant gauntlet of bandits, prostitutes and parasites. The big cities are distinguished from the villages essentially by the use of money, which rules and restricts all social relations. Even today money is of little use in the villages, whereas in the city it is essential. And as Tshonga-Onyumbe concludes, "Everyone must struggle for money, mostly by work, but with money comes new anxieties."

Tshonga-Onyumbe, who also wrote analyses of the roles of women, men, children, marriage, magicians, money and death in Congo-Zaïrean popular music of the 1960s and 1970s, identifies the 'most virulent' problems dealt with in popular song and puts them in order of immediate importance as real issues rather than songwriting subjects. He lists them as clothing, food, pleasure, parasitism, housing, unemployment and prostitution, and emphasises that these are problems which only money can solve. Franco sang about each of these subjects. Clothing, which is barely necessary in the village, takes on undue significance in the city, where modesty and the law require more garments. Its importance is compounded by the availability of new fashions, the need to create a self-image and the pressure to compete. As it must be paid for, clothing can also become a metaphor for money, as in two obvious examples from Franco's mid-1960s compositions:

Quatre boutons (Four Buttons)
Louise, I have plenty
When wigs were in (fashion) I had one
How many buttons did it open?

Cesar Aboya Yo (Cesar Scorns You)
You insult us when we meet on the road
Cesar scorns you no matter what
Since he rejected you, you are destitute
You no longer wear 'wax' wrappers

In the 1964 release Zuani Nabala Na Mbongo (Jeanne Who I Married With A Dowry) the desired object is food, and the plaintiff is a man:

Jeanne (Zuani) who I married with a dowry
Mistreats me

She goes to market like it's her job
While I and the children are starving at home

The pleasures of the city have proved to be almost irresistible to certain characters, like *Polo le Chipeur* (Paul, The Layabout), another Franco composition from 1963, which reportedly upset many of the Kinshasa citizens who bore that name, especially the more self-righteous ones:
Paul, believe it your day will come
You only want the pleasures of Kinshasa
Paul, stop, stop, stop your thieving hands
Paul, you only like the company of women
Your friends never see you
Paul, when the women leave him he's going to cry

When the money runs out, the women will certainly leave him and the fun will finish immediately. The moral of this simple story is that the pleasures of life often lead men to tragic endings. Those who carry on the fun without having money will be forced towards crime to maintain their lifestyle with the inevitable decline. This basic lesson has to be learned afresh by generations of urban youth throughout the world, and while it was not a particularly radical, or visionary, observation, Franco made his point felt by enlisting the audience in condemning the foolish young man.

Parasitism by members of the extended family is another aspect of the money problem Franco addressed in song. The demands posed by brothers, cousins, parents and in-laws, Tshonge-Onyumbe points out, represent a kind of tax on family members. The inevitable retreat from the extended family results in an increase in individualism, separation from others and cultivation of the two-adult, nuclear family. Franco illustrated some of the problems in the 1962 song *Lopango Ya Bana Na Ngai* (My Children's Compound):
My family, today I will die

I leave my children with you
I don't want you to mistreat them
I have left the house for my children
I don't want you to confiscate it
If there is a problem
Wait till I explain it to you in a dream
My poor children
My cousins, it's over between us
I am leaving the house for my children
I don't want you to seize it.
To be an orphan is very sad, mama
Very sad, for sure
To have your mother and father within the family
Makes the heart happy
We orphans grow up suffering
It is very sad for us

As well as the subject of inheritance in a matriarchal society, this song also addresses the problem of housing, a serious dilemma for people moving from the country to the crowded city. In Kinshasa, as in other metropolitan cities, people are at the mercy of landlords demanding high rents for mediocre premises, and a system of letting which involves a third party agent, known as a 'commissionaire', who takes his or her percentage for finding accommodation. The alternative has been to build an 'anarchic construction' or unauthorised 'squat' of their own, on land which is either vacant or fraudulently occupied. On a deeper level of meaning the song is a plea to the officials who repossess such property and a rebuke to the government for expropriating communal land.

Without work there is no money, except from cheating or theft or the 'parallel economy', which has been so effective in Zaïre that it could almost be considered work. But money must be found, even by selling cigarettes in the street or shining shoes, and Franco made the point in 1966 with the song *Tango Nazalaki Somele* (When I Was

Unemployed). *Somele* is the Lingala version of the French word 'chomeur' for unemployment.

When I was unemployed, o
I was selling cigarettes in the market
Always brushing shoes in the market
I made enough to feed the children
In this life, boss
You must look after the wife and children
When I was selling cigarettes
I made enough to feed the childen
You owe me ten thousand, o
And you pay me late
In this life, boss
You must look after the wife and children

The sentiments of this song were no doubt sincere when Franco wrote it in 1966, and on record he plays it with sensitivity. Soon after, however, Franco deleted it from the repertoire. As one ex-member of OK Jazz remarked with wry amusement, it was one song that Franco would never play, once he himself had become the patron who was late with the wages.

Women with formal employment in Africa are a fairly recent, urban phenomenon. And Franco has frequently explained that unmarried women, or those without a man to support them, must also feed and clothe themselves and have somewhere to live like anyone else. If they cannot do some small business, like trading or dressmaking, one way to survive is by becoming a second or third wife, or prostitution. In this nominally monogomous society, polygamy is generally disguised, with a man's mistress euphemistically described as the 'deuxième bureau' or second office, a concept explored by the OK Jazz singer Lokombe who composed a song of that name. The mistress of a businessman, politician or senior official does have a kind of security. The less fortunate *ndumba* (literally 'free woman'), who is obliged to work as a prostitute, knows her life will be precarious. *Bandumba* have to set themselves up while they are still young, beautiful and able to attract men. These same men are also the cause of many married women's problems, as Franco suggested in the 1964 satire *Ngai Marie Nzoto Ebeba* (I, Marie, Whose Body Is Crumbling):

> Those husbands of yours
> They came and followed me
> I look at how I'm unmarried
> The man is good looking, generous
> How can I deny him?

The key word is 'generous', because in any social transaction the bottom line is payment, as spelt out definitively in Simaro's song *Mbongo* (Money):

> To bury someone you must have money
> Even at the hospital you must have money
> Households break up because of money
> Families break up because of money
> Friendships break up because of money
> One gets money from his sister
> The other inherited his goods from the family
> This one spent his wealth with sorcerers
> The other cheated money from the state

The topics of Kinshasa life gave Franco and the other composers of OK Jazz an unending source of subject matter, but there was also a background of more traditional themes which the Grand Master addressed quite frequently. Fetishism, or African animist religion, has always had a place in the OK Jazz repertoire. Franco was the spokesman for the ordinary people, the very ones to whom fetishism, traditional medicine and sorcery were most important. Such beliefs were what had shaped their lives and, in trying to understand the modern, urban world, they would turn desperately to *bandoki*, sorcerers or *banganga*, traditional doctors. Franco's references to sorcery were most often critical. In *Kintul* (The Sorcerer), he tells the story of an uncle who has cast a spell on his nephew: the elders know he is guilty but he does not accept their judgement. Franco himself then goes on to denounce sorcery as the killer of many boys and girls, and he appeals to heads of families not to get involved with sorcerers who, he says, have the power to deny the future by destroying it. He often parodies sorcerers, but also at times appears to identify closely with them. This is noticeable in a classic song from the CHOC sessions, *Suite Lettre No 2*, which tells a lot about Franco's history and how he works. The drift of this very long song is a reply to a letter Franco has been sent by one of his listeners about fetishism and gossip-related troubles. He says he knows that if you take a photo of someone and stick a pin in the eyes, they will go blind. He knows such things because he has been cut (initiated) by a fetish priest in his youth. He sings about a ritual of putting up a cross with a lamb hanging on the left side to indicate innocence, and a lion on the right side to indicate strength.

But, in a personal aside to his listeners, Franco emphasises that his profession is music, not sorcery. He sings because it is his job. When he sings about someone, people think it is someone specific. He knows that people gossip about him too. Even when he is singing in Europe, he explains in a plea for the listeners' understanding and sympathy, he can never leave Kinshasa, which will always be his home. Then Franco talks about his youth; how he learned to play guitar at the Wenze ya Bayaka market in the 'Quartier Far West'; how he knew all the local characters, from the trick cyclist, Mbelekete, and the boys who tried to imitate him on their mopeds, to notorious gangsters. And how he hung out with the tough-guy 'Yankees', whose style of street-wise posing is parodied in a syncopated chanting section of the song.

The confusion of identity which Franco referred to,

in which any words that come out of his mouth are naturally assumed to be expressing his own opinions, was something he normally did little to explain away. His primary audience was well aware of the hidden meanings to Franco's songs, the sub-text, which was what the story was really about. Even when Franco insisted there was no hidden meaning, the Kinois fans would invent something plausible to fit the occasion. They were also fully capable of understanding the difference between a social satire and a commissioned praise song.

Praise and patronage

In *Kaful* (Renaissance), Franco sang about the social effects of the rebellions and schisms which had marked the first five years of independence. It is an overtly anti-war song with the moral line that peace is beautiful and necessary because without it no people can progress. The song was composed during the early years of the Second Republic inaugurated by Mobutu's coup in 1965. In commenting on that 'difficult period of our national history', Franco compares the days when brother fought brother with the new-found 'tranquility which reigns over our country'.

From the last decade of colonial rule to almost the end of the Second Republic, Franco sang the praises of many politicians, both inside and outside Zaïre. This kind of eulogising is a common function of African music and did not necessarily indicate political allegiance or support. In the early days of independence OK Jazz provided party political space to Kasavubu (*Kodi Yaya*, *Oya*), Lumumba (*Lumumba Heros National, Liwa Ya Lumumba*), Tshombe (*Dr Moise Tshombe*) and later, of course, he gave propaganda support to Mobutu. One of the early, optimistic praise songs was *Au Commandement*, in which he celebrated Mobutu's takeover of the presidency:

> After Lumumba, God has been merciful.
> We have found another prophet.
> The face of Mobutu is like the face of Lumumba

Once the regime was established and the sole political party, the MPR, ensconced, several functional songs were released on record, notably *Cinq Ans Ekoki* (Five Years On), *Salongo* (Community Work) and *Candidat Na Biso Mobutu* (Our Candidate Mobutu). In 1975, under the name Luambo and OK Jazz, Franco released an album titled *10ème Anniversaire 1965-1975*. The anniversary being celebrated was Mobutu's first decade in power and the songs were all MPR party pieces, including *République du Zaïre* and *Belela Authenticité Na Congress* (The Call for Authenticity at Congress).

Franco was always clear about his obligations to the state. "It is my job to explain Mobutu's actions to the public," he once said. "The songs are not political, but we use music to spread information, for the government and on other topics." When asked, on another occasion, whether his role was patriotic or political, his immediate reply was, "patriotic". But then he conceded that being patriotic inevitably meant being involved in the political process. Even such a piece of overt propaganda as *Candidat Na Biso Mobutu*, the campaign song for the 1984 presidential election, contains a kind of back-handed praise. The inevitability of the result in a single-candidate election is made clear; and to repeat the song on two sides of an album could also be interpreted as a sly joke or casual devaluation of the message. Being a musician, Franco had to accept patronage and, while he was politically neutral in the affairs of other countries, he did honour the heads of some other African states, in songs like *Mobutu na Bokassa* (of the CAR), *President Eyadema* (of Togo), *Papa Leon Mba* (of Gabon) and *President Kaunda* (of Zambia), which were straightforward public relations exercises.

Patronage has always been essential to the running of a big band, and after the state the most reliable income comes from business sponsorship and advertising work. As Franco's commercial status grew he was called to sing publicity-praise songs for a variety of clients. Having proved their effectiveness in Zaïre, these commercials were then exported to non-Lingala markets where the people took them on their musical value. Among the products Franco endorsed were soap, in *Savon Reward chez Marsavco*, cigarettes in *Cigarette Leopard*, Volkswagen cars in *AZDA*, and beer. The late-1960s song *Lisaso ya Kronenbourg* extolled the imported beer of that name distributed from Brazzaville. In a spirited piece of endorsement Franco sang of how 'Women drink it everywhere; Franco drinks it at home; Vicky drinks it in bed; Verckys drinks it in Europe.' Twenty years later, in *La Bralima et Brasserie 2000*, he sang the praises of the Primus brewery who sponsored OK Jazz in the last years of Franco's tenure. Surprisingly perhaps, OK Jazz rarely propagandised for the Vita football club; that would have caused too many problems with members of OK Jazz who supported rival teams. However, there was one salutation in 1973 when Franco wished them Happy New Year in *Bonne Année Bana Vea*. He later provided a free publicity plug, *Chez Fabrice*, to his friend, a Brussels tailor of that name who used to outfit the band. It was offered as a personal gift for Fabrice's birthday.

There was also a long-established convention of recording self-promotional songs, featuring the name of the band and extolling the virtues of 'Bana OK', the OK Boys, the efficacy of their rhythms and the allegiance of their fans. Among those releases, which were mostly recorded in the early years, were the following song titles:

La Rumba OK	(Franco)
On Entre OK, On Sort KO	(Franco)
Wapi OK Jazz?	(Edo)
Rhythmo de l'OK Jazz	(Franco)
OK Jazz Makila Mabe	(Franco)
Groupo OK Jazz	(Franco)
Amida Muziki Ya OK	(Franco)
Bana OK Babomi Mboka	(Mujos)

OK Jazz Kisangani	(Mujos)
Nous Deux Moziki Ya OK	(Piccolo)
OK Akeyi Sango	(Franco)
Ona Renseignment na Bana OK	(Franco)
Athenee Muziki ya OK	(Musekiwa)
Meet the OK Jazz	(Pedro)
OK Yasolo Okatisi Ebale?	(Vicky)
Ngai Se Mwana ya OK	(Vicky)
Sango Epanzana Mpo Na OK	(Franco)
Jardin de l'OK Jazz	(Edo)
Botika OK Amata	(Edo)
OK Asuakana Te Mpo na Mwasi	(Boyibanda)
OK Jazz Elombe Nganga Te	(Boyibanda)
Toujours OK	(Mangwana)

Speaking out

Parallel with the light-hearted dance numbers, however, there ran a constant stream of more serious contributions. Some of the grander themes always appealed to Franco. He has sung about Black Consciousness in *Pouvoir Noir* (Black Power), a contribution to "the great, global battle for the freedom and dignity of Black people". Their plight is not the fault of man, he claims, it is God who is unjust. In *Mambu Ma Miondo* (Problems with Land), he sings about territorial disputes, where 'even the brotherhood is broken up':

Go to Lebanon, brothers
They are fighting for land
Go to Chad, brothers
They are fighting for land
Go to Grenada, brothers
It's the same problem of land

He brought a more personal, and local, perspective to the problems of inter-ethnic harmony when he sang about tribalism, in *Mawe* (Oh Mother):

If they insist on a tribal marriage I shall not marry

Tribalism provokes a lot of problems
I shall not marry
Stop trying to force me
I refuse an arranged marriage
There are lots of pretty girls
Today marriages are made without thought of tribes
I do not want a tribal marriage

Another typically African theme — and a subject which he dreaded — was death. From his youngest days Franco recorded several laments to dead friends or those he held close, such as *Liwa ya Wechi* (The Death of Wechi), *Liwa ya Champagne* and *Liwa ya Lumumba*. *Liwa ya Wechi* is a song from the early 1960s, which Franco revived for his overseas tour twenty years later. A song of overriding sadness, set against a bolero rhythm, it is a memorial to François Wechi, a friend from his childhood days at the Vita club. The original version, available on the first volume of the *Authenticité* series, is hauntingly poignant, with delicate clarinet playing by Essous, a founding member of OK Jazz, and a plaintive vocal from the young Franco:

What sad news, what sad news
Our friend Wechi is dead
Leaving us alone with painful hearts
You have not served your time
So why are you dead little Wechi?
Your friends from the football club Vita
They are all crying, Oh François
Everyone is still surprised
By little François' death
Oh, oh, oh, poor little Wechi

The song was later recorded by the South African 'Empress of African Music' Miriam Makeba. When it was released on her first international album, however, the song was said to be a 'lamentation of a South African woman whose husband has left to work in the mines'. After Franco's death, Sam Mangwana adapted the song very slightly, substituting the Grand Master's name for Wechi's and bringing a slow reggae feel to the old-fashioned bolero. The song became *Liwa ya Luambo*.

One of the most personally emotional songs in Franco's repertoire was *Kinsiona* (Bereavement), a lament for his young brother, Bavon Marie-Marie, expressed in the Kintandu dialect of the Kikongo language:

I am crying for my brother, Marie-Marie
They are all sitting there calling me
Mother and father
Oh, bereavement, who has done this?
This is the wisdom of the ancestors:
Be strong, be wise, stand firm.

He mourned Bavon again in the 1984 recording *Kimpa Kisangameni* (Meeting of Witches) which also condemned sorcery, rumoured to have been a factor in his young brother's death.

An established favourite from the OK Jazz repertoire, which Franco dusted off to play on his American tour in 1983, is the early 1970s song *Kinzonzi Ki Tata Mbemba* (Old Mbemba's Sense of Justice). This is a folkloric number, which on disc sounds as if it could be played on a deep, resonating drum and marimba — until the saxes burst through, hauling the song into the urban world. Here Franco pays tribute to a wise elder, Mbemba, while criticising those who lack his sense of justice:

Let me go...
Wisdom and sense of judgement
Are in one's blood
See Old Mbemba's example

Let me go
Those who are unable to judge

Are thrashing people in Kinshasa
See Old Mbemba's example
Grandpa Mbemba
Your sense of justice is in the blood
But those others
Are joking and thrashing schoolboys.

This clear indictment of people in authority who, being 'unable to judge', resort to thrashing schoolboys, is typical of Franco's method of satire. The object of the song's attention is not Mbemba himself but 'those others' who do not have 'justice in their blood'. The song was a part of Franco's continuing crusade on behalf of the common people. From the same period came *Mwana Oyo* (That Child) about a naughty child who needs to be told off, 'Oh what a child' and all the gossip that goes on about him, '*Balobi, baloba*', people say what they say.

Serious gossip did get Franco into trouble at least once with a government minister and he crossed several other important citizens in his years as the people's mouthpiece. To be a mirror for society is not an easy role, and for someone to shout aloud what others only dare to think in private can lead to complications. Franco had found that out for himself in 1978, when the people's champion was imprisoned, along with most of the group, over the obscenity content of the songs *Jacky* and *Helene*, in which he catalogued a series of deviant sexual practices. This was during one of Franco's 'turbulent' and provocative periods, when the PA speakers at the Un-Deux-Trois club were blasting hard-core pornography over the peaceful neighbourhood of the zone Kasavubu, to the displeasure of many respectable residents. Some contemporary observers believed, however, that there were deeper, underlying reasons for the action of the authorities.

As Olema Dephonvapi noted in 1984: "Since 1974 his [Franco's] theme has been to discuss social and political problems. *Cherie Bondowe* included the monologue of a prostitute. *Toyeba Yo* (We Know You) denounced the exploitation of the masses by administrators and police. *Ba Beaux Frères* (Brothers-in-law) accuses the intellectual elite of corrupting morals. It is probably following the success of his new songs, inaugurated with *Cherie Bondowe* in 1974, that Franco was imprisoned." If Olema's observation is correct, it puts a different perspective on Franco's supposed role as a stooge of the state, as these songs were recorded at around the same time as some of his most militant and 'authentic' material. And, if the popular press was right, Franco did not let the imprisoning issue drop. Following his presidential pardon, he carried on the battle with the authorities who sentenced him, in the song *Mokolo Tonga Abotoli Tonga Na Ye* (The Owner of the Needle has Taken Back his Needle), released on album as *Tailleur* (Tailor). This was widely believed to have been an attack on the capabilities of the minister who had caused him to be prosecuted. Franco stuck to his familiar defence that he never criticised particular individuals. But for good measure he threw down another challenge in *Na Mokili Tour à Tour* (The World Turns), interpreted by his audience as another thrust against the old adversary:

I beat my head against a tree
The tree dried up
Stop provoking me
Must I leave Kinshasa,
The town where I grew up?
Luambo knew Mbelekete

In 1984 Franco released a long tirade, *Très Impoli*, in which he hammered on at someone in such a relentless and personal attack that he must have had a particular individual in mind. For this album only, Franco provided the helpful addition of lyric translations of the songs, and for the first time non-Zaïrean listeners could make direct, line-by-line sense of the Grand Master's oratory. The song does not give an edifying picture of its subject, whose gross and anti-social characteristics are itemised, right down to his smelly armpits and dirty socks. Franco was the last one to sweep unpleasantries under the carpet. "I am a painter," he once said. "I reproduce what I see. If I see someone with torn trousers, I say that he is wearing torn trousers."

Sexual politics

For all his attraction to, and identification with, the womenfolk in his audience, Franco was also often highly criticial of women, particularly in their domestic behaviour. When asked about this by *Zaïre Digest* magazine in 1987, his reply did not sound too convincing. "I attack women because they have a lot of problems. There are women who deceive men. A wife will say she will cook at midday. When the man returns she hasn't done it. She's out driving around. That makes men wild. Women have problems and I sing about them." Franco stuck to this line of thought for most of his life, convinced that women were more deceitful than men. What he did not like to accept was that in the new, urban society women could gain economic power by selling a commodity that many men were willing to pay for.

During the 1980s his attitude was modified somewhat after being persuaded to sing Dalienst's song *Lisolo Ya Adamo Na Nzambe* (A Dialogue between Adam and God), which criticised men's attitudes to women as being negative and counter-productive. Dalienst had written the song as a criticism of men who, in their foolishness, turn women into their worst enemies. Franco agreed to sing the solo vocal and Dalienst believes it must have set him thinking. He did start to give women some benefit of the doubt, although one of his most popular later songs was *Tu Vois*, best known as 'Mamou', a scurrilous dialogue between two women accusing each other of infidelity and prostitution.

Years later, talking to Rob Prince of *Folk Roots* in one of his last interviews, Franco tried to set the record straight. "I've never been against women. Women say that because sometimes I write songs that don't interest them. For me a woman is a mother. Your mother brought you into the world. You get an education, you become who you are and you marry a woman. And that woman becomes your 'mother'. When she is at your place, in your home, that is what she is. Me, ever since I started out I've sung about women. Why? Because woman have many, many problems. For example a woman might have three boyfriends, three guys. And those three guys will fight over that one woman. That's not good. So a woman has got plenty of problems. That is why I sing about women. I don't insult them but I make 'critiques', so that they might listen to me. I am not against women. It is just that women have so many problems. Women everywhere."

In fact, some of his heaviest criticisms during the 1980s were directed against men. The epic songs like *Très Impoli*, *Mario* and *La Vie des Hommes* which castigated men, were some of Franco's longest and most serious compositions. They were great sermons, although lacking some of the humour, and possibly the affection, with which he attacked women. Franco's most severe diatribe, painted on the biggest canvas of his career, was reserved for *Mario*, the young gigolo whose decline and fall were documented over two sides of separate albums, then a

A cartoon representation of Mario from the magazine l'As des As

short Part Three, before he was finally given his chance to reply in *Réponse du Mario*.

Mario was a genuine epic, given an operatic gravitas by its sheer scale. It uses a simple arrangement with light, understated guitars, inserts by soprano saxophones and an absence of heavy choral accompaniment behind the duet between Franco and Madilu System. The record had the requisite dance ingredient expected from any Franco release, but its musical excitement was limited. There was a simple, catchy melody, however, and the record became a massive hit, not only in Zaïre, where the listeners could at least keep track with the 'vulgar' monologue, but also in many other countries where no one understood Lingala. In some African countries the name Mario became applicable to any young man considered to be a gigolo or 'toy boy'.

Mario is the tale of a young man loving and living with an older, rich woman in Europe. Franco was apparently inspired (and shocked) by the memory of the singer Edith Piaf's marriage to a younger man, or 'petit poussin' (little chicken); a relationship he considered bizarre, and un-African. This *'mama mobokoli'* (foster mother), who has provided Mario's clothes, food, shelter and the other necessities of life is now tired of his sponging ways and is telling him it is time to go. Although he holds five diplomas, Mario remains a waster with no intention of getting a job. Now comes the end of their relationship. The mama is fed up with disputes, arguing and fighting with her young lover and as she throws him out of the house she denounces him for all his faults. Mario returns to his family home, to the same old bed he used to sleep in, with his long legs too big to fit it, and the old mattress full of insects.

For the first of the OK Jazz 30th anniversary releases, *La Vie des Hommes*, Franco stayed with the *Mario* format, using a slightly reworked version of the music as the backing for another long song chastising men for their bad habits. He sings from the point of view of a woman

'If I see someone wearing torn trousers, I say they are wearing torn trousers'

who has been sent to Europe on 'enforced' holiday, so the husband can direct his energies elsewhere. She (Franco) catalogues some of the husband's typical faults, including infidelity, selfishness and inconsideration, like making the children ride to school in a bus while his company car is on hand. As one Zaïrean listener observed, Franco was now singing to please the women. In the past he had often told them things about themselves they would rather not have heard. But now he was exposing the failings of men, Franco was once again the women's champion.

The topics dealt with in Franco's continuing soap opera might sometimes appear trivial, but they are fundamental issues which will have taken up much of his listeners' time. For most people, after all, the immediate daily priorities are rarely world-scale events. In 1987, however, the Grand Master released his last major work, a song which spanned the gap between international affairs and personal behaviour. *Attention Na Sida* (Beware of Aids) is a supreme example of the functional imperatives of African music and, as such, must stand as Franco's masterpiece, even though the music is subordinate to the message, which in this case had terrifying topicality. In view of the circumstances of Franco's death, the thunderous lecture he gives on the dangers of Aids takes on an added poignancy, which possibly increases its validity. For the song Franco seemed to have unearthed one of the most powerful and insistent rhythms in his repertoire. Following a short, introductory motif on guitar, which reprised the sensuous *sebene* of the pornographic *Jacky*, the minimal backing is intense and urgent as he unleashes a fifteen-minute monologue in French and Lingala against the perils of Aids. French was chosen deliberately to bring the message across to as big an audience as possible, with alternating verses in Lingala for his own constituents. Had Franco the facility of a few words of English the message could undoubtedly have penetrated much further.

In the song, Franco explains how Aids can claim

victims from all walks of life; the ways in which it can be transmitted from mother to baby, by unclean syringes, or indiscriminate sexual behaviour. Directly addressing sections of the community including mothers, youths, workers and bureaucrats, he calls on people to protect their own bodies, to choose carefully before taking a lover, to avoid prostitution and to guard against the dangers of drug taking. He warns doctors and medical workers to be aware of contaminated syringes, while urging them to attack the virus without fear. He encourages the Press, television and radio to inform the public, and he calls for a united international research effort to find a solution to Aids. Although musically sparse, the song is highly danceable. Its overall impression, however, is awesome, terrifying. Franco's monologue is gravely serious, but it is also a very human response to the problem. He sings with great compassion, and for once everyone believed that Franco was speaking for himself. Whether or not he knew he was writing his own epitaph is unclear. We must await the posthumous release of the song *Rumeurs*, which he was recording at the time of his death, for the definitive last episode of Franco's epic chronicle.

A Man of His Word

Some of the following translations of song lyrics have been abridged and do not correspond with the original lines.

POUVOIR NOIR (Black Power)

I am always wondering
Why I have been created Black
I never know
If my skin is punishment

I ask God
To answer me, but He cannot
And I suffer a lot

In many countries
Black men have their hands chained
In some countries
Black men have their lips closed with locks

I ask God
To tell me why, but He cannot
And I suffer a lot.

If I think that I shall die even tomorrow
I wonder what I am doing here down
In this pain of my people
Oh God, no
What an injustice

If you gave the same colour to all of us
If you created us with the same nose
If you gave to all of us the same cleverness
Black men would not be slaves

CHAPTER NINE

To White men you have given everything
Even the right of killing us
Do you feel proud of that, oh God?
What an injustice

But anyway
I am Black and I feel good in my Black skin

MWAMBU MA MIONDO (Problems Of Land)

Brother,
There is now a problem of land
And things are going to hot up
Things are going to hot up,
My brother

Go to Lebanon, brothers.
They are fighting for land.
Go to Chad, brothers,
They are fighting for land
Go to Grenada, brothers,
It is the same problem of land

Go to South Africa,
They are fighting for land.
Go to Namibia, brothers,
They are fighting for land.
Things are really going to hot up,
Always and everywhere for the same problem of land

COURSE AU POUVOIR (Race to Power)

You are running me down everywhere
My brother
But I take it as a joke
You insult me even in my private life
What jealousy !
Today it's my private life
Tomorrow you will reach my family
Yesterday you called me 'my brother'
And now you say I'm in opposition

You have become a wanderer
Like a poor orphan
And everything you say about me
Is just the product of your race for power
You say I have stepped on a tick
But you, my brother
You have put your foot on a thorn bush

You seem to forget
All I have done for you
You don't like me to succeed.
Because we are childhood friends
You suffer when you hear
That Franco has done this or that
You wish Franco's name would disappear for ever

God kindly created Judas
But Judas gave a mortal kiss to God...

MABELE(The Earth)
(Composer: Lutumba Simaro)

The cock sings, day is coming
Soon the sorcerers will be returning home
When the day comes it brings trouble
When the day comes some are happy
But somewhere there is always someone suffering

Where are you my love, Mbole?
Caddy, you gave a place for anger in your heart
The candle cries because it suffers
When man sets fire to its head

I am crying because you my love are missing
You don't realise that behind you
There is someone suffering for a love
which is priceless
Oh Earth ! I cry for you.

A young man wants to save money for retirement
He is afraid that when he grows old he will suffer
His savings will help him survive
When he grows old he changes his mind
I'll use all my savings because they are mine
When I die people will misuse my money
But they haven't done anything to deserve it

When I get old, Masivi, I know that I will be walking
with a stick
To beg for small money
People will ask themselves - Wasn't I married?
Didn't I have children?
Even those I helped have started criticising
And laughing at me

I will tell them that during my life
I have not had any sorrows
If such a life happens, it is destiny I will accept

Oh Earth ! I cry for you
I have no sorrows, Dilumengo
Hey Deko, Tchitatchima

The day I die there will be thunder
It will be a sign in the family
That we have lost somebody who sang about happiness
and sorrow
It will be a sign we have lost
Somebody who sang for the living and the dead

Tchitatchima, you have the duty of explaining
The last words of my last breath
They will have to cut off my head to make a monument
All the strangers coming to Zaïre,
Give them this message
My rivals will be happy
At all the beautiful women I have left them
The family will be happy at everything I leave them
While my enemies will rejoice and say I was too proud
There is no mourning for a cock's death

I am a great artist, my life is full of problems
My life is like one who has no sorrow
I have no sorrow, I don't complain
My wife is the fly
My family is the Earth
That is where I came from
That is where I will return
The Earth

LISOLO YA ADAMO NA NZAMBE
(Dialogue Between Adam and God)
(Composer: Ntesa Dalienst)

Eve was made from Adam's ribs
Adam saw the sun before her
Adam spoke to God before her
Did he speak about the devil too?
But the Bible ...
I can't find the chapter

How come woman became a devil to harm men?
Who taught us this devilry?
You'll say Eve was the first to eat the forbidden fruit
Who gave Eve the fruit?
Did you learn that a female angel
Quarrelled with God
In order to harm you?
Men, you're solely responsible for your troubles
With your fellow men.

(Chorus) You look at your friend's wife
You want to court her
You look at your neighbour's daughter
You wink at her
When it's about your woman
You look for judges
You want to find something wrong with them.

You see your neighbour's wife
Let her go by. Let her go by
You see your neighbour's child
Let her go by. Let her go by
Remember that you too have a wife and children
Remember that this is your friend's case too.

He whose plot of land is next to yours
You don't feel pity for him
You enter his house
To find his house
Why, dear friend
Be careful of your behaviour

Your neighbour's child
Who was created before your eyes
Your neighbour's child
Who grew up before your eyes
Because her breasts have grown
You desire her and want to marry her
Aren't you ashamed ?

When you were poor
You married an ugly woman
Now that you are wealthy
You begin to desire beautiful women
First you get rid of the ugly woman
To marry the beautiful one

Today you have acquired a Mercedes
You say you love a French-speaking woman
When you married your wife
You didn't know then that you were going
To become rich
See how anything can happen
We don't want that

Leave your old hypocrisy behind
We know you
Respect your neighbour's wife
Stop being a hypocrite
Your friends know you
Stop denying it

Leave alone the wives of those who work with you in
the company
They all know that you are only interested in their
wives
But leave them, leave them
Leave your friend's wives alone

For you, beautiful women can be bought for money
Your friends have married beautiful women
When they were in dire straits
Today you think you can hurt people
Because you have money

You see your neighbour's child
You start acting like Louis-the-old-man
You buy sweets for her
And give them to everyone in the street
Stop being a hypocrite
We know you, we know you

Now that you're wealthy
You badly treat your fellow men
All you do at work is to send the concierge
To get your colleagues' wives
But think about the past, present and future

Your eyes, that wink at the women of other men
Will be gouged out some day
Those eyes, that wink at the children of other men
Will be gouged out someday
Beware of the women of other men
Beware of the children of other men
You're looking for trouble

When you have a rendezvous with the wife of
another man it always takes place in a hotel.

If they ask for money
You'll only take them to a hotel
We know you. We know you
Leave these forbidden things alone.

TRES IMPOLI (Very Impolite)

You are very impolite. You are very impolite
You are very impolite, But why?

Why do you do so?
Why do you do that?
You say things without taking care of the listeners
You say anything you like without any sense of shame
Why are you so lewd
You enter someone's house with shame
Why do you do so?

Why do you do so?
You enter someone's house without knocking
And you go straight to the bedroom
Why are you so impolite?
Why do you do that?
Without cleaning your mouth
You want to talk near people
Why are you so ill-bred?

Why do you do so?
You enter someone's office with your
Hat on your head
You enter his office with a cigarette in your lips
Although he never smokes.
You have to use your cigarette pack as an ashtray
Why do you do so?
You enter his office and want to read everything

Why do you do so?
You go to see people with your hair unkempt
And you ask them for a comb
Why are you so ill-bred?
Why do you do so?
Your childhood friend has become responsible
And you are asking him for money
During a procession.

Why do you do so?
You enter someone's house and take off your shoes
Showing the holes of your smelly socks
Why are you so ill-bred?
Why do you go to visit people and
Put your feet on the table
When they use this table for their meals
Why are you so ill-bred?
Why do you do so?
Why do you do so?
You spend your night wherever you like
And as your friend lives in the neighbourhood
You go to his house and run to his refrigerator
Don't you know he has to feed himself
And you keep eating his food till 2pm
Do you know the price of food products nowadays?

TEMPS MORT (Times Passed)

The delicate thing called love
The strange thing called love
You cannot know, you never know
Who will be accepted in your heart
Nor whom your heart will throw down
Love is a punishment
I love him because he is not a liar
As other men are,

Loving me today, and another tomorrow
That's why I love him

This thing called patience
I am patient to see if it can change,
I keep quiet, hoping that he will change
Because I cannot follow fetishism
Love is a chore

The man I love is, unfortunately, engaged
He doesn't take me out but once a month,
He has too many doubts to come and visit me
Oh, love is so painful

Tis' a strange thing called heart
When it falls in love, it refuses any advice,
When it falls in love, it refuses any noise,
But when it rejects love,there is no witness
The heart is the motor of love

This painful thing called love
How painful is your heart
Your eyes are fixed on the street,
Your ears are glued to the lock
How painful is patience
This thing called suffering
You lose weight because of the pain in your heart
As the heart never expresses all it contains
You shall die with your secret in your heart
Love is suffering

This thing called love
As a result you get stomach ache
As a result you get high blood pressure
And, at last, you go to the doctor
Love is a punishment

This thing called love
This thing called suffering
This thing called patience
This thing called heart
This thing called love
This thing called suffering
This thing called love
This thing called patience
This thing called heart

CANDIDAT NA BISO MOBUTU
(Our Candidate is Mobutu)

Zaïrean people
Get out in the street
Run through all the zones
Shout as loud as a roll of thunder
To support the candidature
Of Marshall Mobutu Sese Seko

Let us say it sincerely and frankly
Let us drop hypocrisy and ingratitude
Who, better than Mobutu
Can take care of our nation's destiny?

For all of us
Mobutu Sese is our candidate
Our only candidate
Is Mobutu Sese Seko
Mobutu, you have been sent to us by God

You, members of the Central Committee
Pay attention to the sorcerers

Because they haven't given up the fight yet
When you'll have to retain Mobutu's candidature,
Look each other straight in the eyes.

Mobutu, there are still wizards in the family

In the buses and the cars
Our candidate is Mobutu
In the trains, planes or boats
Our candidate is Mobutu
For the patients in the hospitals
Mobutu is our candidate
Even if you are in prison for your mistakes
When you are out
Remember that our candidate is Mobutu
(Refrain)

Workers of all the companies in Zaïre
Gecamines, Kilo-Moto, Miba, Onatra, O.N.P.T.Z.
Air Zaïre, Sozacom, Sonas, S.N.E.L., Regideso
Bralima, Unibra, S.B.K.,Midema, Agetraf,
Ozacaf, Voice of Zaïre, Azap, Elima, Salongo,
Mobutu is our candidate.
Afrisa, OK Jazz and Zaïko
Our candidate is Mobutu
(Refrain)

Let us pray, Let us pray to God
For our candidate is Mobutu
Catholics, Kimbanguists and Muslims
Mobutu is our candidate
Protestants, adherents of Mahi-Kari
Salvation Army, Bima and Mpeve ya Longo
Let us pray God to give him long life
So he can stay at the head of our country Zaïre

TU VOIS? (Do You See?)

What have you said?
What have you said, Mamou?
You said that I am accusing you to your husband.
You said that I am a sneak,
That I am trying to disturb your house

Madilu, let her talk as she likes
Doesn't she know what she is doing?
In the streets where she walks
Many people meet her
In the houses she visits
The walls talk and accuse her
At the corners where she kicks her heels
The taximen see her
Why does she shout everywhere
That you are the one that gives the game away.

I am the one who defends you, Mamou
I am the one who knows all your secrets, Mamou
Today I have become a bad fellow, Mamou
Remember my interventions
When things start to hot up, Mamou
I am leaving you, but you will regret me, Mamou
Even if you are calling me a prostitute, Mamou.

Oh, Mamou
I am so surprised
I was always thinking that you were my best friend
Because you know that I know
Even your strongest secrets
What surprises me a lot today, Mamou,
Is that you have insulted me
You told Moussa that I am nothing but a prostitute
You know, however, that I got married, that I divorced

I have my children
And today, Mamou
You, the one I trust
You call me prostitute
It is not a sickness to be a woman alone
Nor a punishment
But you, the married woman,
Know that you always surprise me.
You go out for a walk with a big handbag
In which you have put
A loincloth, your toothbrush, as if you were travelling
Turkish slippers, a lot of kola nuts
You do know, Mamou
That I am an alibi for you
When your husband surprises you talking to any
other man
You claim quickly that he is a boyfriend of mine

I've never wanted to break your house
Because I hope that your kids grow serenely
I've never liked to get involved in your domestic
business
Because I fear what people say about me
Look at this woman alone who broke
A brave man's wife

What are you looking for, Mamou?
What do you like, Mamou?
You have already won the signature (at the bank),
Mamou
Please respect your wedding ties, Mamou
It's because of your marriage that you're living in
Europe
Stop being unfaithful to your husband, Mamou
When he rings you up, admit that you go out, Mamou.

Mamou, now again
You'll call me a prostitute if I say even a word
You told me yourself
Your husband sent you to Europe
In order to take care of your kids
That's the reason he gave you the signature
Since you are here, as you told me
Your husband calls you twice per day
At 6am and at midnight
But, just after his midnight call,
You spray insecticide in the house
So that the kids sleep deeply
Until the moment you come back home
Just in good time to wait for your 6am call
And when your husband rings
Listen to what you tell him

"Hello, my children's father,
Everything is okay with all of us
But how wild your kids are
The younger boy who resembles you so much
He is surprising me
He has broken the plate
On which your photograph was printed
Because I wanted to keep your face near me
This young boy is really turbulent
Exactly as you were in your childhood
As your mother told me
My children's father, I've no more to tell you
Just send us money for food"

You are the one who is misbehaving, Mamou
You are making mistakes yourself
You don't respect your husband, Mamou

ATTENTION NA SIDA (Beware of Aids)

Oh, Aids. This terrible sickness
Oh, Aids. A disease which does not pardon
A disease which spares nobody
Aids is a plague
Which leaves doctors impotent

Look after your body, and I'll look after mine
Protect your own body, I'll protect mine
Aids is taking the country
Aids does not discriminate against race
Aids does not discriminate against age
You mothers, beware
You fathers, beware

What can I say, mama?
Aids is dividing peoples
Aids has broken marriages
Aids has divided families
Those who used to eat and drink with me
Have started to ignore me
They say I have got the Aids sickness
All my friends are cutting me off
Who can I complain to?

Aids is ravaging all peoples; they are frightened
Europe and the USA accuse Africa of being
The source of Aids
Recently Asia and USA were invaded by the sickness
Today every country is under attack
Aids is not stopping its sinister course
All sections of society are victims of Aids
Babies, children, youths, adults, the old,
Workers, bureaucrats, managers,
Men, women and even doctors.
Aids can attack anybody. It can kill

It will kill all who do not protect themselves
You, brothers and sisters who already carry the virus
Do not behave in a way that contaminates others

Aids has made us forget all other illness
If a person is sick, they say it is Aids
If a person has a fever, they say it is Aids
If a person becomes thin, they say it is Aids
If a person dies, they say it is Aids
But why do we forget the other illnesses
Oh God, Oh God, Oh God. Only you ...
Sickness, Oh where are you coming from?
We forget other illness and only talk of Aids

You pregnant women, you can carry the virus
You can transmit it to your babies
They may be infected, although you do not know
Ladies, avoid getting pregnant
If you know you have the virus.
It is bad to ignore this, as your child could die young
Youths, beware, Aids can attack you
You are the life force of society
If you let it kill you, who will lead the people?
Avoid dangerous sex. Students beware unknown
partners. Be careful who you take money from
It could get you in deeper trouble.
Avoid occasional partners
Youths, beware of drugs. If you inject drugs with
needles you can become infected
Don't take drugs. It is very bad for your health

This sickness o, this sickness
Can make you go bald
It will bring you out in spots
It will give you diarrhoea.
Avoid picking up just anybody
Think before you make love

Even if you desire someone, be careful. Think first

You gentlemen, citizens
Beware of prostitutes
Avoid multiple partners
And you, ladies, citizens
Take measures for your own protection
Workers, in workshops, factories and offices
When you are talking together
Do not neglect the subject
Time passes quickly, and every day
Death takes the victims of Aids
The best way to avoid death is to protect yourself
Oh God, we pray to you

Priests at mass, pastors in church, rabbis in synagogues,
Imams in the mosque, you each have an obligation
A great obligation to society. Use your office to help
Preach what society must know about Aids
Do not hold back. It is your duty to tell the people that
Aids is a punishment from God; it resembles
Soddom and Gomorrah in ancient times
Ask God to deliver us from this sickness
Use your prayers to ask God the way to salvation
All my family have run away from me
Because I have Aids. I am left with only my mother,
Who has to suffer again all the sickness of my childhood

Teachers, instructors, professors
At school, in class, at home
If you have a free moment discuss it,
It is part of your scholarly obligation
Teachers at school, college and in universities
The parents count on you to educate their children.
Parents, don't be shy, tell your children and the youth
All you can about Aids
Tell the whole world, tell everybody to beware

It is for you to fight against Aids
We are waiting for a vaccine. We wait for medicine
It will take a long time to come,
Maybe five, seven or ten years. Change your behaviour
Time is pressing, the sickness spreads fast

Doctors, be like Pasteur, Flemming, Curie and other
Geniuses of the last century
Now is your turn to conquer this plague which
Terrifies humanity and defies medicine
Don't waste time finding the medicine, wherever it is
Get this plague out of the human body
Doctors you know well how Aids is caught
Do not show the disease that you are afraid
Do not discourage the sick by your behaviour
The medical profession looks to you to find courage
To conquer this sickness
Doctors beware, the patient's file is secret
It concerns only the patient and close family
Don't talk so much that you creat panic
Your duty is always sacred. Your profession is sacred
Your duty is to find a medicine
If there is a miracle it will come from you
Doctors be careful with needles,
Always wear gloves when you touch blood

Governments of rich countries, help the poor countries
Lead the way in the struggle against Aids
Don't sell them arms to kill,
But provide arms for the War against Aids
Brothers and sisters of the United Nations,
Between yourselves combine experience and
Spread understanding
Political authorities, use the radio, television and the
Press to inform the people of the dangers of Aids
Tell us how to protect against and combat Aids
We must all be mobilised against Aids.

Discography

To compile a complete and defintive discography of Franco and OK Jazz is an impossible task. Details of the 78 rpm releases from the early years have proved particularly difficult to trace. Fortunately some examples of these fragile discs have remained but catalogues of the Loningisa label, for which Franco recorded as a session musician for six years, have been even harder to find than the records. Those releases listed in the first category below comprise a small amount of the sessions on which Franco was known to have played a significant part. Several of these existing recordings have since been re-released on albums by RetroAfric, Sonodisc and Crammed discs, details of which appear in the album section.

A regular flow of releases streamed out of Loningisa, and the competitors' studios during the 1950s. Initially the discs were pressed in Europe in a single edition. The most popular records would be played hard over the first week of their release and would often be unplayable by the following weekend, by which time there would be new releases on the market. When the Congolese studios invested in their own pressing plants the situation became even more precarious, as worn records were bought up to be recycled for pressing new releases.

Finding documentary evidence of anything in Zaïre is fraught with difficulty. Most of the research that went into this discography was necessarily conducted via the catalogues and release lists of European labels which had licensing deals for OK Jazz material. There are, therefore, substantial gaps in many periods of Franco's career and the catalogue numbers of certain key songs, notably his first solo hit *Bolingo Na Ngai Na Beatrice,* have proved impossible to confirm.

More evidence was available about the release of 7-inch, 45 rpm singles, to which Congolese musicians converted around the time of independence in 1960. By then, however, Franco and the other members of OK Jazz were recording for a host of labels and the story becomes confused by the sheer number of recording deals, and sub-licences to labels in other parts of Africa and Europe.

An additional complication is that from time to time other band members have recorded under their own names as leaders, singers or composers. Vicky Longomba, for instance, used to release records on his own label, Viclong, and CEFA. Mujos, Kwamy, Boyibanda and many singers 'fronted' OK Jazz recordings. On other occasions composers such as Bitchou, Simaro or Verckys took the credit. This discography, therefore, includes releases by OK Jazz even without Franco, and occasionally Franco without OK Jazz.

Among the labels which released recordings by Franco and OK Jazz at various times were: Loningisa, Ngoma, HMV, Pathe Marconi, EMI, Decca, Surboum African Jazz, Boma Bango, Epanza Makita, CEFA, Viclong, Zebi, OK Jazz, Editions Populaires, Fiesta, African, Polydor, ASL, Makossa, Discostock, Celluloid, Africa Mama, Crammed, Sonodisc, RetroAfric, as well as Franco's own 1980s labels, Visa 80, Edipop, CHOC, and African Sun Music. Records were pressed up in Kenya, Nigeria, Ghana, Congo, Côte d'Ivoire, France, Belgium, USA, Holland and Britain, and probably a few other places besides Zaïre.

Compiling a list of albums has been less arduous, as catalogues exist for most labels. It falls short of the total of 150 albums which Franco claimed back in the mid-1980s, but no doubt some of those were collections of singles for the African market which were released in Europe in different compilations (or not at all). A posthumous series of CDs from Sonodisc, now owners of the African catalogue, includes several songs not previously released in Europe amongst more familiar material.

For reasons of space and difficulties in tracing full credits from catalogue lists, the names of composers other than Franco have not been included. OK Jazz did occasionally record without Franco, but even when the band is 'fronted' by another singer or composer he was usually present. Only when Franco recorded without OK Jazz has this been noted.

In some catalogues, printer's errors have attributed other people's recordings to OK Jazz; where possible these have been checked and deleted from the list. The order of 'foreign' releases follows the particular labels' own numbering policies and may not tally with the sequence of original Kinshasa releases. There is some duplication within the various lists, but as several songs appear in different permutations the lists have not been merged. If known, the dates of original release are shown.

This discography was started by Ronnie Graham, doyen of that craft, in 1986 and has been updated frequently, by him, by myself and by a small group of enthusiastic correspondents, notably Vincent Kenis, Richard Noblett and Flemming Harrev. Profuse thanks go to all of them: even so there must be dozens, if not hundreds of missing items for which we can only apologise and keep searching. Titles marked * are compositions attributed to Franco.

78 rpms

Loningisa label (1953-56)

Dewayon, (Ebengo Paul) and Watam group with Franco

100	Nyekesse / A yebi kobota
111	Tuba Mbote / Esengo ya mokili

Luambo Francois:

112	Bikunda / Group Watam

Bowane:

115	Angelika / Bonne Année

Dewayon:

120	Nainu ngai na kufi te / Bana Bosenge

Luambo Francois with Watam and Bana Loningisa :

122	* Kombo ya Loningisa / Lilima dis cherie wa ngai

Dewayon:

130	Nicodeme Lulu / Nalekaki na nzela

De la Lune:

131	Komeka te /Mia bella Boza

Nganga:

132	Bolole ya mwasi oyo / Liwa ya nkoko

Dewayon:

133	Locia wa ngai / Vis-a-vis
136	Sidonie / Oh Cheri na ngai
137	Na yebi elingi yo / La rumba La Pampara
139	Mwana akimi tata / Nakobala se yo

Vicky:

140	Nalingi ozonga / Mokili mobongwani

Pholidor:

141	Oyo elengi motema / Rumbamba

Rossignol:

143	Therese d'amour / Wa bolingo

Roitelet:

144	Cherie Margot / Houlala Mopanzo

Dewayon:

146	Dit Antoinette / Mabele yo okanisaka

Vicky:

147	Viclong Julie / Bolingo elei kisi

Vicky & Pholidor:

148	Mwana pause / Maria Antonia

Bemi & Vicky:

150	Palabras amorosas / Nabosani ndako

Franco, Vicky na Rossignol:

151   Wapi yo? / Osili obebi
152   * Tango ekoki nabatela mwana/ Tika bizeti
       Roitelet:
153   Anduku Lutshuma / Banzanza
       Franco:
154   * Makambo Mayisa Mazono / La rumba OK
157   * Tika kondima na Zolo / Meya te, kaka elamba

HMV (Loningisa LON series)
       Vicky, Franco, Rossignol, De la Lune:
1001   * On entre OK, On sort KO /La Fiesta tcha tcha tcha
       (plus Essous):
1002   Nini Cherie / Passi ya boloko
1003   Mado ya sango / Na bosani yo te
1004   Lina / Se pamba
       Franco, Essous & OK Jazz:
1006   Etali yo/ Colette
       Bemi, Rossignol, Vicky & OK Jazz
1007   Que sorpresa Bemi / Mayela-Sanza
       Dewayon & Franco, Essous, Vicky, Rossignol
1008   Tango se elangisa / Alliance mode succes
       Fataki Camille & OK Jazz
1009   Na mokili bakonzi mibale / Mokili oyo sala malamu
       Malapet, Edo & OK Jazz
1010   Aime wa bolingo / Zozo kobanga te
       Vicky, Edo & OK Jazz
1011   Ozalaki ya motema / Mboka etumba
1012   Grand mbongo lawu / Kolanda te o
       OK Jazz (Dewayon)
1013   Imana champion 1956 / Ofele
       Vicky, Edo, Franco, De la Lune, Willy
1014   La rumba negritta / Moziki ya Daring
       Diderot & OK Jazz
1015   Namipesi se na yo / Zonga mama
       OK Jazz (Vicky)
1016   Toka bwani mwana te / Naboyi libala bombanda
       Franco, Vicky, De la Lune
1017   * Botika Tembe / Merengue
       Bowane Chantuers & Bana Loningisa
1018   Moko Mibale / Sukurumba
       Ebengo Paul (Dewayon) & Bana Loningisa

1019	Bikunda / Groupe Watam

Kalafayi Jean & Bana Loningisa

1020	Kitoko na yo ekosaki nga / Baloba na pimbwa

Ebengo Paul (Wayo) & Bana Loningisa

1021	Nainu ngai (Nakufa te) / Bana Bosenge

Lwambu Francois & Watam na Bana Loningisa

1022	* Kombo ya Loningisa / Lilima dit cherie wa ngai

Franco (François Lwambu)

1023	* Bayini ngai mpo na yo / Marie Catho

Pholidor, Vicky, Franco, Roitelet

1024	Oyo elingi motema / Rumbamba

Edo, Franco, Vicky

1025	Ejoni banganga / Marie nde kolimwa

Celestin, Edo, Vicky, Franco, Willys

1026	Mawa ya hotelet / Ezali se bofela (by OK Jazz)

Brazzos & OK Jazz

1027	Na banzaki anzelu / Nde okobanza

Paul Ebengo (Wayo) & Bana Loningisa

1031	Esengo ya Mokili / Tuba mbote

Bowane na Bana Loningisa

1032	Liwa/ Wa ngai moko
1033	Caroline/ Banza na ngai na banza yo
1034	Libala ya mbangu/ Lopadi ya sika
1035	Achiko/ Sebene Marie-Louise

Paul Ebengo (Wayon) & Bana Loningisa

1036	Yembele Yembele/ Tango ya Mpokwa

Franco & OK Jazz

1037	* Mousica tellama / Bolingo ekoma niongo?

Vicky & OK Jazz

1038	Nakobanza Cherie / Nalingi nabina

Edo & OK Jazz

1039	Naloti Eugenie / Kumavula tubakueto

Vicky & OK Jazz

1040	Obanzi sika oyo / Ah, nabanzi zozo

Franco & OK Jazz

1041	* Rumba de Ondo Ondo / Obungi ngai

Kouka Celestin & OK Jazz

1042	Georgina wa bolingo / Kosenzela bolingo mabe

Franco, Rossignol, De la Lune

1043	* Elo Tnama (mama) / Naboyi yo te

OK Jazz

1044	Tcha tcha tcha Modeiro / Ndima ngai

Brazzos & OK Jazz
1045 Tcha tcha tcha de mi amor / Yaka nakoti te
Franco & OK Jazz
1046 * Elaka nzakomba / Batela mwana ya Moninga
Vicky, OK Jazz & Franco
1047 Bobina na esengo / Tomeseni zonga coco
Edo & OK Jazz
1048 Germaine yebaka ngai / Taxi Avalon
Willys & OK Jazz
1049 Elingi yo elingi ngai / Luka ya yo moko
Franco
1050 * Motindo na yo te / Aya la mode
Essous & OK Jazz
1051 Seraphie / Annee 1958
Brazzos
1052 Biguina el mambe / Kendo naino
Franco & OK Jazz
1053 * Franco de mi amor / Mwasi ya mboka
Vicky & OK Jazz
1054 Ah bolingo pasi / Nakolela mama azonga
Franco & OK Jazz
1055 * Agnes-Majos / Linga ngai tolinga ye
Edo & OK Jazz
1057 Tondimi la mode / Azali mwasi baponeli ngai
Brazzos & OK Jazz
1058 Tcha tcha tcha del Zombo / Mokili mobongwani
Celestin Kouka
1059 Oboyi ngai likamo te / Tika na bala ye
Vicky, Rossignol (& Franco, De la Lune)
1066 Alice / Cherie atiki ngai
Franco (& Brazzos, De la Lune, Vicky, Edo)
1083 * Oye-Oye-Oye / Micorasson
Franco & OK Jazz
1087 * Mosala ekomi mpasi embonga/ Tango ekoki nabatela
  mwana
Edo & OK Jazz
1091 Me bu nibanza mama / Sois sage amour

OK Jazz 45 rpm singles

CEFA label (some of which were later released in Europe by
Decca on the Surboum OK Jazz label)

201		Nalibala oyo ata kisi / Kondima balobi te mama
202		Ngai responsable na yo / Mbanda na memeli yo kuruse
203		Canalo / Soki ayei tokosamba
204		Y que se passa / Monzemba mpasi na elanga
205		Nakobanga mangungu te / Tolobi
206		Oyo nde zoba / Yaka Lisusu
207	*	Botika mindondo / Bazuzi batunaki ngai
208		Finga kasi okopesa ngai makasi / Nakopesa yo etumbu
209		Ya luna umbazila / Ata ndele nde oleli
210		Bokilo batela mimi / Ayi que par gosar
211		Yo prefiero / Monzemba mpasi
212		Boue na nkusa / Ezali oyo elingi tembe
213	*	Awa nazui likambo oyaki? / Libongi lizongi
214	*	Bolingo mpe ekosaka? / Pardon nabungaki ekila ya libala
215	*	Telegramme maloba mokuse / Nani apedalaki te?
216		Eboka carra ya nini? / Mboka oyo tapale
217	*	Accident ya cherie / Mbongo zi ya voni
218		Athenee muziki ya OK / Tata otika ngai na mawa
219		Likasa bango olingi ngai / Affaire ya moto
220		Bayini bakotela biso / Banguna
221	*	Bamboko awuti na New York / Boseka ngai te
222		Kolekaka mado / Muntsambu kadingu
223		Oyo libaku mabe?
224		Congo-Nigeria 'One' / Meet the OK Jazz
225		Mwana ntsana / Charlotte wa Simon
226		Ngali Henriette merci / Yo nde nzete ya mbongo?
227		Lilonge aliciana / Amelia banzaka ngai
228		Nakeyi, namoni yo te? / Elongwe bolingo ekomi mbongo
229		Bakomi kobanga concours / Kwela na bomwana obota
230		Lobela ngai nyosno oyokaki/ OK Yasolo okatisi ebale?
231		Ngai se mwana ya OK / Una bella muchacha

Epanza Makita label

EM 34	*	Mauvais temoins / Jose-Maria
EM 40		Desholey toko di mfunu / Kama mitamo ekomi pata
EM 42	*	Oyo mobali tapale / Timothee abangi makambo
EM 43	*	Quatre boutons / Savon Reward chez Marsavco
EM 44		El sa brosso / Omonaki Jean-Jean na Billy
EM 45		Mama ngai mwana nazongi / Monoko na ngai nganga
EM 46		Dit Malou nakanisaki te!/ Louise aboyi frigo
EM 47		Ngai natuni Annie / Suzie tuna Kester
EM 48	*	Chaleco / Chicotte-Chaleco
EM 49 (58)		El paso de Incarnation / Samba tokosamba
EM 50		Ma iwasso / Bolingo nzo etumbu?
EM 58		[see 49]
EM 60		Paraque Linda / Mokonzi ya likolo
EM 61		Kifi ofaontana / Nsua biesi - kuna makala
EM 62		Wapi OK Jazz? / Yango niongo to zuwa?
EM 63		Naboyi yo okomi niongo? / Oyeba ngai liboso ya
EM 64		Baciame / Katukela ngai kuna?
EM 65		Mokolo se mokolo / Palado Palado!
EM 66		Kadioka / Ya mbala Sima
EM 67		Baka yawu! / La temperana
EM 69		Opusi / Permission
EM 70		Maria / Mbala moko ca va, mibale te
EM 71	*	Botika kosomba 'Ambi' / Lisaso ya Kronenbourg
EM 72	*	Reno bakongo sika / Mino ya Luambo diamant
EM 73		Nakosala nyonso mpo ! / Omemi ngambo mama !
EM 74		Heureusement kisi ya mabe te ! / Nazali koluka na likambo
EM 75		Naboyi ba provocation / Nalingaka ye ndenge nyonso
EM 76	*	Gare a toi Marie / Natali nyonso mpamba
EM 77		Ah, ne croyez jamais a ces belles paroles/ Ce palmier
EM 78		Dis Laurence / G.G. Yoka
EM 79	*	Bonne année ya bana Vea / Ah, Senor!
EM 80	*	Puis tala mode preferee / Ah nazangi tata
EM 81		Tomeseni zonga Coco / Nakolela mama azonga
EM 82		Naboyi libala ya bombanda / Nakobala oyo motema alinji

EM 83	Natali nayei zoba? / Ata osali ngai se na yo
EM 84	Azali mwasi baponeli ngai / Tokeyi kobina calypso
EM 85	Rithmo de nostro amor / Tika na bala ye
EM 86	* Kenge okeyi elaka te? / Oye-Oye-Oye
EM 87	* Aya la mode / Bana Ages
EM 88	* Alice atiki biso na elembo / Oh Katherina
EM 89	Nalingaka ta balobisa ye/ Youyou
EM 90	Santa Guy Guyna / Ti toboyana nakoma ndoki?
EM 91	Mpungu ya bolingo / Nakoluka ye Banzila nyonso
EM 95	Amour sans souci / Trop bon trop couyon
EM 96	Nago nionso bambanda / Nayboyi publicité
EM 97	Niongo na ngai souza / Nalembi ba promesses
EM 98	Pasi ezali / Lunda Maguy
EM 99	Decision eleki makasi 1 & 2
EM 100	Zozo mama na Tina / Likweyi
EM 101	Nazali kitoko mingi / Emilie na Gabon
EM 105	Papi zali reconnaissant / Catho ya poupee
EM 110	Songi-songi eboka mabala / Eugenie la blonde
EM 111	Nabanzi tele / Nganda Penda Bika
EM 112	Bolingo Marie-Angel / Nawela Tina nini
EM 113	Simon temoin ya libala / Fololo ya bolingo
EM 114	Ta Noel / Bana bakufelaka ngai Tina nimi
EM 115	Kwela kempazoko / Akei Mbandaka
EM 117	Mathieu Togangana / Hisenga senga

OK Jazz label

OK 1	* La mode ya plus epiki de la po / Ngai mwana na weyi
OK 2	* Amida asuki mulato / Mboka mosika mawa
OK 3	* Mibali bakomi mpasi na Leo / Pa Roger na Doli
OK 4	* Cha cha cha Erique / Soki ngai na bandaki yo
OK 5	* Liwa ya Wechi / Na likuanga na seli
OK 6	* Baiser na litama / Bana mpoto
OK 7	* Franco cantar / Tika toloba lelo
OK 8	* Lopanga ya bana na ngai / Mbanda muasi alingi ngai
OK 9	* Amida muziki ya OK / Motema ya fa fa
OK 10	* Muana moko mawa / Ye bo
OK 11	Comme guere / Jalousie ya mini na ngai
OK 12	Elena el Mujos Cara / Soki ye te nani carra
OK 13	Ele wa bolingo / Miguel canta

OK 14	Motema na M. J. /Ngombele mama
OK 15	Bana OK babomi mboka / Linda-Linda
OK 16	Maria de mi vida / na banzi zozo
OK 17	Bolingo ya mbongo mabe / La mulata Congolaisa
OK 18	Liwa ya Champagne / Na koyiba mpo na Matinda
OK 19	Catho musai ya libala / Godo Pauline
OK 20	Okaka ngai te / Omelisi ngai nini
OK 21	Nayebisi yo Valentina / Wanda ya nde
OK 22	Basekele ya muasi na ngai / Molinard danser cha cha cha
OK 23	Florinne bolingo / Yo soy prilonniero
OK 24	* Bomboko Justine/ Florette modele
OK 25	Isaac don't be so funny / Isaac Ombele
OK 26	Mama moke / Na kondi mingi
OK 32	* Club de sept / alliance de sept
OK 34	Cuidado / Victoire de Bruxelles
OK 36	* Bo bongisa Congo / Ngele ya bato
OK 37	OK Jazz Kisangani / Maria mama na mulamba
OK 38	Mbanda na ngai / Ngai na kati saka
OK 39	Gueno cha-cha / Yamba ngai na Leo
OK 40	Nous deux moziki ya OK / Bebe ngai nazongi
OK 41	Licencie / Tete abli Simon
OK 42	Brigitta mwasi ya makwela / Tele-Mujos
OK 43	* Ya mbala / Yokela ngai mawa
OK 44	* Bulundue na zongwe / Liw ya Emery
OK 45	Mwasi nalingaki / Rendezvous chez Cassien
OK 46	* La vida del un negro / Lipopo oyo mboka
OK 47	* Botika bana / Fungola ngola
OK 48	* Prosabel Roi des disques 3em Avenue / Zongela nzela na ngai
OK 49	Kimuene Limbisa ngai / Paracletto Lolinga
OK 50	Mikebo ya mama / Sabina el Kwamy
OK 51	Teben Matiba / Baninga babesi yo?
OK 52	Nakobanga mama na mwana / Sakina Jacky
OK 53	* Mpata ezangi mokolengi / Ndale Miquerida
OK 54	Conge nde mabe boye? / Sentiment poto-poto
OK 55	* Ba Katanga balingi toyo kana / Bato ya mabe batondi mboka
OK 56	* Kaka ayo keja ngai / Kingotolo mbota ngani mbote
OK 57	* Mboka ya bato / OK akeyi sango

OK 58   *   Barumba ekeseni/ Ma nkewa
OK 59   Mwasi mabe / Pesa nagi nzela naloba
OK 60   Kanisa ngai Annie / Lelo na echouer
OK 61   Mboka nini ekende? / Nani akunsimdila muana
OK 62   Mado aboyi Simaro / Guitar de l' Enfer
OK 63   Cherie Maite / Muasi ya Zoba
OK 64   Muana na ngai mawa / Muasi ya motema mabe
OK 65   Onze Teuna / Bolingo ya Bozoba
OK 66   Kitoko ezali mayele te / Mabanzo makeyi mosika
OK 67   Nono bolingo na Mujos / Olongi yo mayi ya bwatu
OK 68   *   Mobembo mabe boye/ Ona reseignement na bana OK

Boma-Bango

BB 1   *   Bondoki na boniama / Mwaku elombe ya kwango
BB 2   Quand le film est triste / Tonton
BB 3   Ata na yebi/ OK asuanaka te mpo na mwasi
BB 4   El cuini / Oh ! Madame de la maison
BB 5   Finga mama munu? / Revolver
BB 6   Annie obosani ngai? /Na kosalaka ndenge yo okolingaka
BB 7   Sala omona passi ya mbongo / Tuna mageda
BB 8   *   Na seki mingi / Yo soy Guajiro
BB 9   *   Akomi ya ngai / Baila charanga
BB 10   Oyangani ngai mpo na kimbundi? / Tete ngelele ebaki ngai
BB 11   Boni ochanger ? / Mpo tokabuana
BB 12   Aquela mas / Komikosaka te na basi
BB 13   *   Balingaka ngai te / Solo Monique oboyi ngai?
BB 15   Cherie ochanger? / Gina simba nga
BB 18   *   Tango ngai nazalaki somele / Course au pouvoir
BB 19   Ce n'est pas possible chou chou/ Zuani nawelikitayele
BB 20   Tango ya ba Wendo / Mindondo ya kosuana na mobali
BB 21   Cheri Lovy / Cuenta nama
BB 22   *   Cesar aboya yo / Matinda
BB 23   Jeannine abimi mbwe / OK Jazz elombe nganga te
BB 24   Baila mi carabine / Frantail akosa
BB 25   *   Cafe / Est-ce que oyebi?
BB 26   Ekongo ya Bolobo
BB 27   Okomi na nzemba? / Ven y ven y ven

BB 28		Bombanda nakoka te /A si gozar
BB 29		Cherie Vicky / Yo sey que soy
BB 30		Nzela ya engamba / Celine
BB 31		Elongo yo jalousie / Mbanda mbanda
BB 32		Kundi / Porque mi amada
BB 33	*	Lumumba heros national/ Regime etikali 4 ans
BB 34		Coco babengi ngai poison / Kathy modude
BB 35		Alexandre mon Dieu! / Emile ngai mobali natelemi
BB 37		Ya liboso yamba mbote / Ndoto
BB 38		Carabinero / Mobemba ya cherie
BB 40		Libala ya Kinshasa / Ami pachanga
BB 41		Babotoli ngai te / Obimi mbwe?
BB 42	*	Tozonga na nganga wana / Yayi
BB 43		Mbanda akamwi / El Pinazo
BB 44	*	Naboyi libala na moko / Si vous passez par la
BB 45	*	Nalingaka balobela ngai te / Que no muera el son

Tcheza

T 260	Semba M'Boua Semba Dibou / Tsia koi bou tchele
T 261	Kosoka bazoba ngai te / Ngala nabino ekosila
T 262	Fungola ngai pardon mama / Yeba nameki komeka
T 286	Balingi naboya yo / Kotuna Banco te

Likembe

LIK 1	*	La verité de Franco / Mona opuasi
LIK 2	*	Mouvement populaire de la révolution / Mobali na ngai
LIK 3		Annie ngai nalinga / * Nayebaki likambo
LIk 4	*	Dede kabola mikolo / Nganda maboke naboyi
LIK 5	*	Biso nysonso basi na yo / Likambo ekosua na motema

Viclong

VC 1		Nakosala nakolata / J'ai trompe mon amour
VC 2		Numero ya Kinshasa / Dodo tuna motema
VC 3	*	Mwasi ya ba patrons / Regina- Regina
VC 4		Henriette / ngai muana ya dihonga
VC 5		Maria- Maria / Anto ozali se wa ngai
VC 6		Zimbombo / Ineza
VC 7		Josetta Palado / Ye songi-songi azalaka na galons?
VC 8		Ayokaki na bimaki? / Nalingi nde kauka
VC 9		Nakolela epayi na nani?/ Batindeli ngai telegramme

VC 10	Monoko oyo ezali na ngai / Maria na ye
VC 11	Mama ya bilamba / Roger okosi, ngai kaka
VC 12	Nazui te papa / Cherie ondage
VC 15	Mandona Yifuidi / Boya Vicky okende na mpoto
VC 16	Liwa yo nde mabe boyei / Josetta Palado
VC 20	A moins que namikosa / Natiyi nainu raison pembeni
VC 22	Votre Renault / Nzela ya poto esili

Editions Populaires (1970s)

EP 1	* Lokolo / Ku kisanto kikuonda ko
EP 2	* Luvumbu ndoki / Beyos
EP 3	* Mabuidi / Congo mibale
EP 4	* Marie Cecile / Tel pere tel fils
EP 5	* Balobi mbanda / Naboyi kokaba
EP 6	* Josephine naboyi ye / Thomas
EP 7	* Catherine moziki / Ngai naboya naboya te
EP 8	Club 53 / Dix makuta
EP 9	Mbanda na ngai / Marie Elena
EP 10	* Mado / Socomeubles
EP 11	* Nzorba / Kiwita kumunani
EP 12	* Ya zefu nsola / Marie tika Eugenie
EP 13	* Obwa oshu nzeme / Nsontin
EP 14	* Nazangi mwana / President Eyadema
EP 77	* Belela Authenticité na congres ya MPR
EP 80	Bolingo na ngai mwana Shaba 1 & 2
EP 142	* Nakobala mbwa 1 & 2
EP 143	Inousa/ * Ezui voisin
EP 146	* Zenaba 1 & 2
EP 205	* Tata na Bebe 1 & 2

Ngoma - Succès Africaine

J 1055	Maboudi/ Naboyi kokaba
J 1056	* Beyos / Ngai naboya naboya te
J 1057	Michelle bolingo / Mbanda na ngai
J 1058	* Marie Cecile / Marie Elena
J 1059	* Congo mibale / Thomas
J 1060	Dix makuta / Club 53
J 1061	Balobi mbanda ho / Mobembo
DJN 1062	Mado / Bolingo mpasi mawa
DJN 1063	Ah ngai na weyi / Bakubuana ka boye te

DJN 1064   Ikuwa ndinga / Na kobala muasi na lingi
DJN 1065   Alingi la paix / Na yokali lisolo na yo
DJN 1066   Yazefu / Biloko ya niekese

Pathé singles (originally released on **Surboum OK Jazz**)
            Orchestre Franco
PF 11501 * Katherine / Zuani nabala mbonso
PF 11502 * Dodo oublie le passé / Docteur Moise Tshombe
PF 11503 * Gouvernement ya Katanga Oriental / Masua emani
PF 11504 * Mauvais temoin / Na Congo nazali refugie te
PF 11505 * Vincent / Nzambe
PF 11506 * Matinda / Colonel Bangala
            Franco & OK Jazz
PF 11507 * Course au pouvoir / Tango ngai nazaleki somele
PF 11508 * Cesar aboya yo / Est-ce que oyeba
PF 11509   Cherie Lovy / Zwani naweli kitayele
PF 11510   Ce n'est pas possible chou chou / * Cafe
PF 11511   OK Jazz elombe nganga te /Jeannine abimi mbwe
PF 11512   Okomi na mbemba? / Ven y ven y ven
PF 11513   Poussons les manches / Tango na Wendo
PF 11514   Mindondo ya kosuana na mobali / Baila ma carabine
PF 11515   Ekingo ya bolobo / Cuento mama
PF 11516   Frantail akosa ngai / Ce palmier
PF 11521 * Lumumba heros national / Regime etikali 4 ans
PF 11522   Heureusement nkisi ya mabe te / Nazali koluka ye
            na likambo
PF 11523   Tozonga na nganga wana / El Pinazo
PF 11524 * Gare a toi Marie / G.G. Yoka
PF 11525   Dit Laurance / Ah ne croyez jamais a ces belles
            paroles
PF 11526 * Obimi boue / Cigarette Leopard
PF 11532   Yayi / Ntali yonso pamba
PF 11540   Babotoli ngai ye / Cigarette filtre Leopard
PF 11541   Si vous passez par la / Mbanda akamue
PF 11547 * Polo / Na ndimi kosasa
PF 11548   Nalingaka balobela ngai te / Que ne muera el son
PF 11549   FNMA Congo / Naboli libala na noko
PF 11559   Annie nainu bandima ngai te / Youyou
PF 11560   Eva na Kampala / Santa Guy Guyna
PF 11561   Omana wapi / Nokoluka ye banzela nionso
PF 11562   Badzilaka ngai na yo taboyana / Mpungu ya bolingo

PF 11563   Litongi elekaka te / To tokobuana nakoma ndoki
PF 11564   Tembe ezali mabe / Nalingaka te balobisa ye
PF 11586   Lokolo / Tel pere et tel fils
PF 11587   Josephine naboyi ye / Ngai tembe eleka ngai
PF 11588   Nandimi koboma / Louvoumbou ndiki
PF 11589   * Catherine moziki / Kukisantu Kikuendaku
PF 11590   * (side 2 only) Bilombe ya mindule /

2C 006 series
15023   Ndalo ya mawa / Eva
15025   Bilombe ya sensation /Catho
15072   Motema ebouge / Marie tika Eugenie
15073   Nazangi muana / Nazangi muana

Fiesta label, reissues of **Editions Populaires** and **Epanza Makita**
51 010   * Nzorba / Kiwita Kumunami (Ed Pop 11)
51 024   * Marie tika Eugenie / Mbanda asikile (Ed Pop 12)
51 028   * Obwa oshu nzeme / N'sontin (Ed Pop 13)
51 040   * Mobali na ngai azali etudeint na m'poto / Edo aboya
             ngai   (Ed Pop 15)
51 041   Na bolingo conseil ezali te / Mosaka ya kilo
51 042   Owawa / Camp Luka   (1751 042)
51 051   * Bokassa na Mobutu / Makambo Maneno   (1951 051)
51 054   * Salongo alinga mosala / Cing ans ekoki   (Ed Pop 18)
51 060   * La loi bakajika / Le pouvoir noir   (2251 060)
51 083   Pension na Bandalungwa /   *Cardiaque
51 084   Ba soucis ya weekend / Zozo
51 086   Mokolo ya mpasi / Fifi nazali innocent
51 095   Accept que c'est vrai / Mecontentements
51 096   Kufa ntangu civilise / Argadja
51 105   Bon de livraison / Lolo sousir
51 109   Caro sex machine / Atakala nakobosano
51 111   Ma Hele / Infidelite Mado (Ed Pop 42)
51 112   Libala ya Bondongo / Lolango
51 122   Beya / Johnny Yuma (credited to Bavon Marie Marie)
51 123   Lola / Celita   (Ed Pop 48)
51 126   Georgette 1 & 2
51 129   Ba numero ya telephone / Na bale
51 130   Osabote ngai Jean-Jean / Nakweyi
51 131   Bakoka te fiance / Nzela Claude
51 133   * Aya la mode / Bana Ages

51 134		Sentence ya / Kamalandua (Ed Pop 45)
51 135	*	Kengi okei elaka te / Oye, Oye, Oye
51 136		Ata osali ngai se na yo / Nabali naye zoba
51 137	*	Ah, Signor / Bonne année ya bana Vea (Ed Pop 76)
51 138	*	Alice atiki biso na elembo / Oh, Katherina
51 140		Si vous passez par la / Yayi
51 141	*	Cafe / Mauvais Temoin
51 142		Santa Guy Guyna / Nakoluka ye banzela nionso
51 143		J'attends / Dodo oublie le passé
51 144		Misele / On a ose le dire
51 149		Likambo ya nganga / Casier judiciare
51 151		Mbanda nazali nini / Siluvangi wapi accordeon?
51 153		Celina / Aimee
51 154		Mwasi tata abali sika / Tout se pays ici bas
51 155		Nzoto na Makanisi / Abaza
51 156		Nzube oleka te / Motema na yo retroviseur
51 184		Ebale ya Zaïre / * Ba masta bonne année
51 192		Envoutement / Jo
51 198		B.S.K. / Cedou
51 211		Minuit eleki lezia 1 & 2
51 212		Lukika / Zando ya tipo tipo
51 214		Mohumbu ya Makanisi / Mele
51 220		Luka mobali moko / Sens interdit au kumbi 12
51 221		Monzo / * Kinsiona
51 229	*	Ye ! 1 & 2

African label, reissues of **Epanza Makita** and **Viclong**

90 301	Nabir libala Bombanda / Nakobala oyo motema
90 422	Papa azali reconnaissant / Catho ya Poupee
90 423	Ba conseil ya Cherie / Bolingo esuki na maloba
90 428	Kozala mopayi / Ozali coupable ya ba soucis
90 442	Songo-songi eboma mabala / Eugenie la blonde
90 452	A moins que namikosa / Natiyi nainu raison pembeni
90 731	Kebana / Nzuzi
90 919	Masi 1 & 2

African label, re-pressings of **Editions Populaires** and **Zebi**

91 016	Cheri Bondowe 1 & 2 (Zebi 001)
91 080	Balenge 1 & 2
91 081	Presence na ngai ebangisaka 1 & 2
91 082	O ko regretter ngai mama 1 & 2

91 230 * Camarade nini akobomba ngai sango 1 & 2
91 231 * Bokolo bana ya mbanda na yo malamu 1 & 2
91 237   Melou 1 & 2
91 238   Nzete esololaka na motote 1 & 2 (Ed Pop 14)
91 263   Nioka abangaka nipe moto 1 & 2
91 452   Lifoka 1 & 2
91 448   Ibrahim 1 & 2 (Ed Pop 27)
91 449   Lutandila 1 & 2 (Ed Pop 28)
91 450   Vicky na 1 & 2 (Ed Pop 29)
91 451   Moleka 1 & 2 (Ed Pop 30)
91 452   Lifoka 1 & 2 (Ed Pop 32)
91 462   Moseka 1 & 2
91 463   Mobali amesana na ngai 1 & 2
91 487   Nakomi muselman 1 & 2 (028 BIS)
91 488   Radio trottoir 1 & 2 (029 BIS)
91 489   Faria 1 & 2 (030 BIS)
91 490   Efonge 1 & 2 (031 BIS)
91 509   Sekele 1 & 2 (Ed Pop 27)
91 510   Comprendre ngai 1 & 2 (Ed Pop 038)
91 511   Ba chance ya kobotama 1 & 2   (Ed Pop 040)
91 512   Zaïna mopaya 1 & 2 (Ed Pop 043)
91 513   Basala la vie 1 &2   (Ed Pop 045)
91 525   Napekisi ya kobima 1 & 2 (Ed Pop 036)
91 526   Tala ye na miso 1 & 2 (Ed Pop 042)
91 527   Malunzi 1 &2   (Ed Pop 046)
91 528   Semeki bakali 1 &2   (Ed Pop 051)
91 555   Appartement 1 & 2   (Ed Pop 035)
91 556 * Ba beaux frères 1 & 2 (Ed Pop 037)
91 557   Ba pensées 1 & 2 (Ed Pop 055)
91 558   Makambo 1 & 2   (Ed Pop 068)
91 570   Voyage na Bandundu 1 & 2 (Ed Pop 070)
91 571 * Tosambi bapesi yo raison na quartier 1 &2 (Ed Pop73)
91 594   Itschiofo 1 & 2   (Ed Pop 058)
91 595   Boni nkaka 1 & 2
91 596   Makaya 1 & 2   (Ed Pop 067)
91 597   Rena 1 & 2

Decca EPs (extended play), re-releases of **Surboum African Jazz**
451 081 * Bomboko Justin / Florette Modele
           Isaac ombele / Isaac don' t be so funny
451 163 * Mpata ezangi mokengeli / Ndale Miquerida

       *   Ona reseignment na bana OK / Mo Bembe Maby boya
460 863 *OK 40-50*
            Nous deux moziki ya OK / Bebe ngai nazongi
            Sabina el Kwamy / Mibeko ya mama

HMV EP 'Music of the World' series
7EN 101   Musica Tellama / Bolingo ekoma niongo
            Ah bolingo passi / Nokolela mama azonga
7EN 102   Tongo se elangisa / Alliance mode succes
            Hellena el Mujos / Dzioke Kwamy
7EN 103   Aimee wa bolingo / Cha cha cha Modeiro
            Micorasson/ Cha cha cha de Mivida
7EN 104   Nakobanza Cherie / Nalingi nabina
            Ndima na ngai / Maumbuku
7EN 105   On Entre OK, On Sort KO / Yaka nakoti te
            Lina / Se pamba
7EN 106   Cha cha cha del Zombo / Mokili mobongwani
            Cuidado cono mallo / Ata yo ozui
7EN 107   Nziel Kuami koe mama / Yo tellema mucho
            Sois sage amour / Me bu nibanza mama

Editions Populaires (EPs)
EMF 185   Nakobala Mimim / Calypso de nostra amor
           * Franco akeyi / Rhythmo de l'OK Jazz
EMF 218   * La Fiesta tcha tcha tcha / Tcha tcha de mi amor
            Taxi Avalon / * Aya la mode
EMF 278   Bolingo ekona nyongo / La mousica tellama
            Rumba de Ondo Ondo / Zozo kobanga te
EMF 302   * On entre OK, On sort KO / Yaka nakoke te
            Lina / Se pamba

Pathe-Marconi EPs
EG 812 *OK Jazz 1964 No 4*
            Lola / Niongo na yo nakokufa te/
            Bolingo na Bougie / Yamba Carolina
EG 840 *OK Jazz 1964 No 5*
            Si tu bois beaucoup / Alphonso /
            Le temps passe /   Ngai nde rideau ya nadako
EG 879 *Orchestre Franco*
            * Katherine / La complicite de Bulundue /
            * Ngele ya bato

EG 926   * Quatre boutons/ Didi / Jean -Jean
EG 1020   * Colonel Bangala / Ven y ven y ven /
            Zuani naweli kitayele / Baila ma carabine

Production Tchika (12-in maxi 45, 1985)
010 85   Momy & OK Jazz
            Lela ngai na mosila / Likingo li mboka

Albums

Albums which include sessions from the 1950s and 1960s were invariably collections of singles originally made for the home market. They are listed here if possible in chronological order of original recording. Compilation albums which combine material from different bands are listed separately. From the 1970s onwards the albums are listed in order of release. The list stops at the end of Franco's career. Tributes by OK Jazz and posthumous compilations released after October, 1989 are not included. All albums are by Franco & TP OK Jazz unless stated otherwise. Titles marked * are attributed to Franco.

RETRO2 *Originalité*
            Side 1 *On entre OK, On sort KO/ *La Fiesta/ Passi
            ya boloko/ Nini cherie / Na bosani yo te / Mado yo
            sango / Lina / Se pamba
            Side 2 *Merengue / *Botika tembe / Marie nde
            kolima / Ejoni banganga / Tondimi la mode / Azali
            mwasi baponeli na ngai/ *Tango ekoki nabatela
            mwana/ *Mosala ekomi mpasi-embonga
            RetroAfric, London, 1987(Recorded 1956-59)

360 158 *Les Merveilles du Passé (1957-58)*
            Side 1 *Motema ya lokoso / *Oyangani ngai? /Oleka
            tukamani/ Ngai oyo nazongi / *Bana Ages / *Oh!
            *Katharina
            Side 2 *La mulata rumber / *Malambo zela/ *Mami
            Majos / *OK Jazz makila mabe / *Grupo OK Jazz/
            *Baboni mboka
            Sonodisc, Paris, 1987
360 167 *Les Merveilles du Passé (1961)* Vicky, Kwamy, Edo & OK
            Jazz
            Side 1 Lobela ngai nyonso oyokaki / OK yasolo

okatisi ebale / Ngai se mwana ya OK / Una bella
muchacha / Mbongo ezali suka te / Prosabel 2eme Ave
Kabondo
Side 2 Gina garde tout pour moi / Tika kobebisa
muana/ Kapakola ngai boniama te / Yo Tellama /
Matinda kolemba ngai te / Nagi na yo pantalon na
mokamba
Sonodisc, 1987

360 168 *Les Merveilles du Passé (1962)* Franco, Vicky & OK Jazz
Side 1 Qu'est-ce que c'est Suzie? / Bulumbu obatala
Longomba/ *Nakobombela cherie/ *Nazongi lelo/
*Muasi azali kaka muasi na yo / Ngai oyo lia ngai
Side 2 *Kombe na mbokela / *Tika nainu zuwa /
*Dada de tu amor / *Linzanza ebongi na langi /
Kende libala kolangua te / *Sansi fingomo ngoma
Sonodisc, 1987

360 144 *Les Merveilles du Passé*
Side 1 *Oye, Oye, Oye / Tomesani zonga Coco /
Tokeyi kobina calypso / *Kenge okeyi elaka te /
nakolela mama azonga
Side 2 *Aya la mode / *Bana Ages / *Oh! Katharina
/ Naboyi libala bambando / Nako bala oyo motema
alingi
African/Sonodisc, 1984

360 156 *Les Merveilles du Passé 1963*
Side 1 *Mbanda ozui kizungu-zungu / *Ngai Marie
nzoto ebeba /Somba mbwa semba Dibou / Tsia koi
bou tchele
Side 2 Ngala na bino ekosita / Kosaka bazoba ngai te
/ Fungola ngai pardon, mama / Yeba namoki konoko
Sonodisc, African

DS 7950 *Le Bon Vieux Temps de l'OKJazz*
Side 1 *Malambo zela ngai / Del prison / Mboka yo
okeyi mosika / Linga ye to olingi ngai / Lobi na tongo
/ *Rhythmo de l'OKJazz
Side 2 Mama Elo / Yo te mususo / *Franco akeyi / *Ah
Signor / Mbongo ya lokoso
Discostock, Abidjan

360 070 *Authenticité Vol 1* (1961-62-64)
Side 1 *Liwa ya Wechi / *Na likuanga na seli / *Motema ya Fa Fa / *Amida muziki ya OK / *Bomboko Justin / Isaac Ombele /
Side 2 *Florette modele / Mpata ezangi mokengeli / *Ona reseignment na bana OK / *Ba Katanga balingi toyo kana / Mboka nini okende / Nani akunsimdila muana
African/Sonodisc

360 072 *Authenticité Vol 3* (1964-66)
Side 1 Ata ndele nde oleli / Ya Luna umbazila / Linda-Linda / Motema na M J / Bana OK babomi mboka
Side 2 Ngombele mama / *Bolingo mpe ekosaka? / *Telegramme maloba mokuse / *Nani apedalaki te / Oh Madame de la maison
African/Sonodisc

360 078 *Authenticité Vol 4*
Side 1 Ele wa bolingo / Miguel canta / Jalousie ya Mimi na ngai / Como quere / Guitars de l'Enfer
Side 2 Mado obeyi / Tele Mujos / Licencie / Balundue na zongwee / *La vida del un negro
African/Sonodisc

360 125 *Authenticité (1960-1962)*
Side 1 Yamba Leo / Gueno cha cha / Mibeko ya mama / Sabina el Kwamy / Kitoko ezali Mayelle te / Mabanzo makeyi mosika
Side 2 Kouende mabe boye / Tebba Matida / Mwasi na lingaki / * Kaya oyokela ngai / *Bato ya mabe batondi mboka / Nous deux moziki ya OK
African/Sonodisc

360 124 *Authenticité (1962-1964)*
Side 1 Na banzi Zozo / Maria de ma vida / Bolingo ya mbongo mabe / La mulata Congolaise / Olongi yo mayi ye bwata / Nono bolingo na Mujos
Side 2 Nakobanza mama na mwana / Sakiwa Jacky / Sentiment Poto Poto / *Mobembo mabe / *Ndale mi querida? / Bebe ngai nazongi
African / Sonodisc

150- 15973/74 *OK Jazz Vol 1 & 2*

Side 1 *Masumbuku (with De la Lune) * Nakobanza cherie (with Vicky) / * Matinda / *Course au pouvoir Obimi M'Bwe /*Vincent /*Na Congo nazali refugie te
Side 2 *Cesar aboya yo / *Est-ce que oyebaka *Mauvais temoin / *Tango nazalaki somele / Alliance mode succès / Tango se elangisa
Side 3 Cherie Lovy / *Gare a toi Marie / Nakozela mama azonga / Ah Bolingo passi / *N'dima ngai (with De la Lune) / *Nalingi na bina (with Vicky)/ *Masua emani
Side 4 Zuani naweli kitayele / *Katherine / *Zuana na bala na mbonso / Dit Laurance / Fantail akossi ngai
Pathé Marconi/EMI (1965, reissued 1977)

STX 229 *A Paris*

Side 1 Mindondo ya kosuama na mobali / Baila mi Carabine / *Colonel Bangala / Ven y ven y ven
Side 2 *Tango ngai nazalaki somele / Retroussons les manches/ *Matinda / OK Jazz elombe nganga te / *Course au pouvoir
Pathé Marconi

360 006 *L'Afrique Danse No 6*

Side 1 *Nganda maboke naboyi / *Dede kabola mikolo / *La verité de Franco / *Matinda / *Cesar aboya yo
Side 2 *Gare à tois Marie / *Chaleco-Chicotte/ *Lisaso ya Kronenbourg / *Timothee abangi makambo / *Oyo mobali tapale
African/Sonodisc, 1966

360 010 *Les Merveilles de Passé*

Side 1 *Nani apedalaki te / *Accident ya cherie / *Bomboko awuti na New York / *Mbongo ziya voni / *Nazongi lelo /
Side 2 *Ngai Marie nzoto ebeba / *Linzanza ebongua langi/ *Mbanda ozui tuzungu-zungu / *Fwala mongu ngula Kadia / *Nakobombela cherie
African/Sonodisc

062 15574 *Les Grandes Succès Africaines Vol 4*

Side 1 *Marceline / Na mokili na mibale / *Celina laissez moi voir Franco
Side 2 Mado / Je ne peux pas fave autrement / Aimée
Pathé Marconi, 1972

360 053 *Editions Populaires*
    Side 1 *AZDA 1 & 2 / *Assitu 1 & 2
    Side 2 Minuit eleki lezi 1 & 2 / Zando ya tipo-tipo /
    Lukika
    African/Sonodisc, 1974 (Pathé-EMI 2C 054 15711)

360 056 *Editions Populaires*
    Side 1 Mabele / *Kinsiona / Luka mobali moko
    Side 2 Monzo / *Kinzonzi kitata Mbemba / *Muana
    Oyo/ *Mambu miondo
    African/Sonodisc, 1974 (Pathé-EMI 2C062 15734)

360 081 *10ème Anniversaire 1965-1975*, Luambo & OK Jazz
    Side 1 *Cinq ans ekoki/ *Salongo alingi mosala /
    *Votez vert / *Republique du Zaïre
    Side 2 *Tolanda nzela moko/ *Ba deputé mbilinga-
    mbilinga toboyi/*Belela authenticité naCongres 1& 2
    African/Sonodisc, 1975

360 103 *Grands Succès*, Franco & le TP OK Jazz
    Side 1 *Matata ya muasi na mobali ekoki kosila te 1
    & 2 / Oko regretter ngai mama 1 & 2
    Side 2 Mace 1 & 2/ *Bandeko na ngai ya mibali 1 &
    2/ Basundoli ngai 1 & 2 / Moleka 1 & 2
    African/Sonodisc, 1975

360 082/3 *20ème Anniversaire*
    Side 1 *Liberte/ *Matata ya muasi na mobali ekoki
    kosila te / Melou
    Side 2 Voyage na Bandundu / Kamikaze / Nzete
    esololako na moto te
    Side 3 Baninga tokola balingaka ngai te / Seli-Ja /
    Salima
    Side 4 *Tosambi bapeji ya raison na quartier /
    *Bokolo bana ya mbanda na yo malamu
    African/Sonodisc, 1976

360 096 *African Party*
> **Side 1** *Fwala nbombu ngulu Kadia / *Yaka nalongolo yo botutu / *Daɗa de tu amor / *Linzanza ebongi na langi / Anny sukisa ngai bandoto / Ata mosika yoka mongongo na ngai
> **Side 2** *Telegramme maloba mokuse / *Nani apedelaki te/ *Awa na zui likambo oyaki/*Libongi lizongi/ *Accident ya cherie / *Mbongo ziya voni
> African/ Sonodisc, 1977

360 104 *Naloba Loba Pamba te (Vol 1)*
> **Side 1** *Naloba loba pamba te 1 & 2/Tolinganaki 1 &2
> **Side 2** Kamusengele 1 & 2 / Monzo 1 & 2
> African / Sonodisc, 1977

360 105 *Ba Beaux Frères (Vol 2)*
> **Side 1** *Ba beaux frères 1 & 2 / Ba pensées 1 & 2
> **Side 2** Fariya 1 & 2 / Tala ye na miso 1 & 2
> African/ Sonodisc, 1977

360 108 *Mbongo (Vol 3)*
> **Side1** Mbongo / Lisolo ya Adamo na Nzambe / Lotambe
> **Side2** Badjekate / Tambwe luntadila / Moleka okoniokolo ngai ntina?
> African/ Sonodisc, 1977

360 116 *Live Chez 1-2-3 à Kinshasa*
> **Side 1** *Mama na Kyky / *Azwaka te azwilelo
> **Side 2** *Falaswa / Ibrahim
> African/ Sonodisc, 1977

360 114/15 *Live Recording of the Afro-European Tour*
> **Side 1** *Oh! Miguel/ Sala lokola luntadila / Malou-O Bijou /
> **Side 2** *Bomba, bomba, mabe / Na vanda bombanda / Libala ya bana na bana
> **Side 3** Lisolo ya Adamo na Nzambe / Mama na Bebe / Meta Mama na bana
> **Side 4** Mbongo / Amour Viole / Lotambe
> African/ Sonodisc, 1978

360 129 *Mobali Aboye na ye Kaka*
>**Side 1** *Mobali aboye na ye kaka / *Nakomi pesa na nani / *Yoma mayenge ngai na kabalo
>**Side 2** Leki na ngai abalukeli ngai / Obwabeli ngai bisaka
>African (Ghana pressing)

360 132 *L'Afrique Danse*
>**Side 1** On ne vit qu'une seule fois / Bisengambi
>**Side 2** Momi / Oyangani ngai na moto
>African/ Sonodisc, 1979

FRAN 001 *Vraiment en Colère Vol 1*
>**Side 1** *Tokoma ba camarade pamba / *Arzoni
>**Side 2** Tokabola sentiment / *Loboko
>Visa, 1980 (Also Makossa M2376, USA)

FRAN 002 *Vraiment en Colère Vol 2*
>**Side 1** Peuch del sol / Na bali misere
>**Side 2** Mbawu na ko recouperer yo / Bolingo ya Moitie Moitie
>Visa, 1980

FRAN 003 *A Paris*
>**Side 1** Liyanzi ekoti ngai na motema / Youyou
>**Side 2** *Nakomi pesa na nani/ Kadima
>Visa, 1980 (Also Makossa M2377,USA)

FRAN 004/5 *Le 24ème Anniversaire*
>**Side 1** Proprietaire / *Locataire
>**Side 2** Heretier / Ayant droit
>**Side 3** Kufua ntangu / Meka okangama
>**Side 4** Likambo ya moto / Banza
>Visa, 1980 (LPM 2379/80, USA. FRAN002, Kenya)

FRAN 009 *A Bruxelles*
>**Side 1** *Nalingaka yo yo te
>**Side 2** Pamelo / Mindondo esila
>Visa, 1980

POP 01 *Le Quart de Siècle, Vol 1, Respect*
    Side 1 Bina na ngai na respect
    Side 2 Mobali malamu / *Mujinga
    Edipop, 1981

POP 02 *Le Quart de Siècle, Vol 2, Bimansha*
    Side 1 Bimansha
    Side 2 *Ilousse / Mbamba
    Edipop, 1981

POP 03 *Le Quart de Siècle, Vol 3, Tailleur*
    Side 1 *Tailleur / Kalebo
    Side 2 Belle mere / Tuti
    Edipop, 1981

POP 04 *Le Quart de Siècle, Vol 4, Mandola*
    Side 1 Mandola/ Loloaka
    Side 2 *Sandoka / Ambozi ya pambu
    Edipop, 1981

POP 06 *Coupe du Monde*
    Side 1 Coupe du monde / *Fabrice
    Side 2 Wallo / Ngaliene
    Edipop, 1982

POP 017 *Coopération* , Franco & Sam Mangwana
    Side 1 Coopération/ *Loboko nalitama
    Side 2 Faute ya commercante / Zala sportif
    Edipop, 1982

POP 018 *Se Déchaînement*
    Side 1 Nostalgie / *Princesse Kiku
    Side 2 Tantine / Mawe
    Edipop, 1982

MICH 01 *Bénédiction*, Franco & Michelino
    Side 1 Mutabula mpimpa / Prince D' XL
    Side 2 Point Carre / Va et vient
    Michelino/ Sonodisc, 1983

POP 012 *Special Mix '83*
    Side 1 Mukadi rendezvous wapi / Na ndimi bapasi /

Mandola
Side 2 Tantine / La vie etumba / Kaya lisusu te
Visa/Edipop, 1983

POP 021/2 *Disque d' Or et Maracas d'Or*
Side 1 *Tres faché/ Soeto
Side 2 Coup de foudre/ *Farceur
Side 3 Tangawusi/ Nganda
Side 4 Na yebi ndenye bokelela
Edipop, 1983

POP 020 *A O Heure Chez 1-2-3*
Side 1 *Tikaka kosenga / Tambou luntadila
Side 2 Kabongo / Sema ya Kinalo
Edipop, 1983

POP 023 *Franco Presente Simaro Masiya*
Side 1 Mbongo-money-l'argent / Nganga lopanga
batekisa
Side 2 Faute ya commercante / Mandola
Edipop, 1983 (Polygram, Kenya)

POP 025 *Franco Presente Josky*
Side 1 Mehida / Alita
Side 2 Massini / Limbisa ngai
Edipop, 1983

POP 027 *Chez Fabrice a Bruxelles*
Side 1 *Frein a main / *5 ans ya Fabrice
Side 2 *Non
Edipop, 1983

JJLP 008 *Greatest Hits*
Side 1 Toyobana kaka / Bodutaka / Ledi
Side 2 *Assitu / Zanda ya tipo-tipo / Bana breke te/
Lukika
Jumbo Jet/ Polygram, Kenya

GEN 103 *L'Evénement*, Franco & Rochereau
Side 1 Ngungi / Omani wapi
Side 2 Lisanga ya banganga / Kabesele in memorium
Genidia, 1983

CHOC 000/1*Choc Choc Choc 1983*, Franco & Rochereau
    Side 1 *Lettre a M. le Directeur General
    Side 2 *Suite Lettre No 1
    Side 3 *Suite Lettre No 2
    Side 4 *Suite Lettre No 3
    CHOC, 1983

CHOC 002/3 *Franco & Josky Kiambukuta du TP OK Jazz*
    Side 1 Missile/ Chacun pour soi
    Side 2 *Partagez
    Side 3 Adieu je m'en vas / Tu es mechante
    Side 4 Laissez passer/ Ngai te
    CHOC, 1983

POP 026 *Chez Safari Club de Bruxelles*
    Side 1 Mbazi ya kamundele / Okundji
    Side 2 Serment / Amour perdue
    Edipop, 1984

POP 028 *Très Impoli*
    Side 1 *Très impoli
    Side 2 *Tu vois? / *Temps mort
    Edipop, 1984

POP 030 *Candidat Na Biso Mobutu*, Luambo Makiadi & TP OK Jazz
    Side 1 *Candidat na biso Mobutu
    Side 2 *Candidat na biso Mobutu
    Mopap, 1984

POP 031 *A l'Ancienne Belgique*
    Side 1 K.S.K. / Nda-ya
    Side 2 Pesa position na yo / Mukungu
    Edipop, 1984

POP 032 *Chez Rythmes et Musique*
    Side 1 *Makambo ezali bourreau / *Kimpa kisangameni
    Side 2 *12,600 lettres a Franco / *Débat
    Edipop, 1984

MD 9091 *US Tour (Vol 2)*
      Side 1 *12, 600 lettres à Franco
      Side 2 Missile
      Makossa, USA, 1984

POP 029 *Le FC 105 de Libreville*
      Side 1 *FC 105 du Gabon
      Side 2 Bourreau des couers / Aimer sans amour
      Edipop, 1985

CHOC 004 *Mario*
      Side 1 *Mario
      Side 2 Je m'en fou de tu passé/ Esuke
      CHOC, 1985

CHOC 005 *Mario*
      Side 1 *Mario (part 2)
      Side 2 Likambo na moto te / Ekoki ya nzube
      CHOC, 1985

ASLP 996 *Camarade Nini Akobomba Ngai Sango*
      Side 1 *Camarade nini akobomba ngai sango/
      Salima
      Side 2 *Matata ya mwasi na mobali ekosila te/ Mace
      ASL/Polygram, Kenya, 1985 (Material from 1970s)

ASLP 999 *10 Years Ago*
      Side 1 Bamasta bonne année / Ebale ya Zaïre / Ce Dou
      Side 2 Mosala etindi / Lilian / Yoka Meje
      ASL/Edipop/Polygram, Kenya 1984 (1970s material)

ASLP 1001 *Fifteen Years Ago*
      Side 1 *Minoko / *Edo / *Mokili macaramba
      Side 2 *President Leon Mba / *Basi ya makango /
      *Nakosala nakolota / Mwasi ya bapatrons
      ASL/Polygram, Kenya, 1985 (Origin Eds Pop, 1970)

CHOC 006 *La Vie des Hommes*
      Side 1 *La Vie des Hommes
      Side 2 *Ida / *Celio
      CHOC, 1986

ESO 8427 *Massu, Franco & Jolie Detta*
    Side 1 *Massu / Cherie okamuis ngai
    Side 2 *Layile / Likamba ya somo lumbe
    Esperance, 1986

POP 033 *A Nairobi*, Franco & Ses Stars du TPOK Jazz
    Side 1 Boma ngai, ngai naboma yo / Kuma okeyi bongisa
    Side 2 Eperdument / Massikini
    Edipop, 1986

REM 570 *Bois Noir*
    Side 1 Bois noir / Clemance
    Side 2 Bomba pema / Ma zamba
    Rythmes et Musique, 1986

CHOC 007 *Special 30 Ans*, Franco, Simaro & OK Jazz
    Side 1 *Testament ya Bowule / *Vaccination ya ba soucis
    Side 2 *Tala merci bapesaka na mbua / *Aminata ya zangi Visa (* all songs credited jointly)
    CHOC, 1986

ASM 01 *Attention na Sida*
    Side 1 *Attention na Sida (with Victoria et al)
    Side 2 Mp no nini kaka ngai?/Na poni kaka yo mayi zo (with OK Jazz)
    African Sun Music, 1987

9508 *Ekaba Kaba*
    Side 1 *Ekaba kaba
    Side 2 Mobembo ekosila Titi / Cherie A
    Celluloid, 1987

87.011 *Live en Hollande*
    Side 1 *Mono muntu/ *Miguel / Mandola / Testament ya Bowule
    Side 2 Cherie obesi musi / Papa Yeye / Boya ngai
    Sango, Africa Mama, 1987

KOCH 122 411*Franco Still Alive*
     Side 1 *Likambo/ Bolingo ya ngai na tata / Pesa ngai position nayo/ *Tres faché
     Side 2 *Mario / *Mono muntu naleki amo ta ndile / *Etumba / Mawe/ *Tokoma ba camarade pamba
     Koch Int/Africa Mama (Live in Holland part 2)

ASM 02 *Mamie Zou*, Franco, Dalienst & OK Jazz
     Side 1 Mamie Zou / Batandeli ngai mitambo
     Side 2 Dodo / Nalobi ngai rien
     African Sun Music, 1987-88

CHOC 008 *Mata, Kita, Bloqué*, Franco, Josky & OK Jazz
     Side 1 Kita, mata, bloqué (*sic*)
     Side 2 Minzata / Osilisi ngai mayele
     CHOC, 1988

CHOC 009 *Les on Dit*, Franco, Baniel, Nana & OK Jazz
     Side1 *Les on dit / *C'est la vie d'une femme celibetaire
     Side 2 Je vis avec le PDG / *Flora une femme dificile
     CHOC, 1988

POP 034 *L'Animation No-Stop*
     Side 1 *Mario 3 / 7 ans de marriage / Iran-Irak / Merci bapesa na chien / In memorium
     Side 2 *Mamou 2 / Decision echange maloba / Bolingo etondi na souvenirs / Nganda parcel ba yanda
     Edipop, 1988

ASM 03 *Coeur Artificiel*, Lutumba Simaro & OK Jazz
     Side 1 Coeur artificiel / Mangassa
     Side 2 Sindo na Bruxelles / Maclebert
     African Sun Music, 1988

CHOC 010 *La Réponse de Mario*
     Side 1 *La Réponse de Mario / *Sadou
     Side 2 *La Bralima et Brasserie 2000 / *Mon rival cherche à m'avoir
     CHOC/ASM/Sonodisc, 1988

CHOC 011 *Cherche une Maison à Louer Pour Moi, Cherie*, Franco,
Nana, Baniel & OK Jazz
Side 1 *Cherche une maison à louer pour moi,
Cherie / Detruis moi ce dossier la
Side 2 *J'ai peur / Trahison
CHOC/ASM/Sonodisc, 1988

CHOC 012 *Anjela*, Franco, Pepe Ndombe & OK Jazz
Side 1 Anjela
Side 2 Tawaba
CHOC/ASM/Sonodisc, 1989

38775 (SYL 8396) *For Ever*, Sam Mangwana, Franco & OK Jazz
Side 1 Toujours OK / Cherie B.B.
Side 2 Bowane choc / Process
Syllart/Melodie, 1989

REM 850 *Franco Joue Avec Sam Mangwana*
Side 1 *Lukoki / Awela-Awela
Side 2 *Aziza / Decca
Rythmes et Musique, 1989 (Also POP 043, Kenya)

Compilation albums (Only OK Jazz titles listed)

360 001 *L'Afrique Danse*
Side 1 *Quatre boutons/* Savon Reward chez
Marsavco/ Finga mama munu/ Revolver
Side 2 Tonton/ Quand le filme est triste/ *Timothee
abangimakambo / *Oyo mobali tapale
African/ Sonodisc, 1966

360 050 *L'Afrique Danse*
Side 2 Ou est le serieux?

360 090 *L'Afrique Danse*
Side 2 Regina Regina

360 164 *Stars of the 1950s*, Victor, Roger, Franco
Side 2 Josephine

PTX 40654 *Pont Sur Le Congo* (*Bridge over the Congo* CPMC 25)
Side 1 Misele / On a ose la dire / *Polo/ Bolingo ya Bougie / Si tu bois beaucoup/ Le temps passe
Pathé Marconi, 1965

HNLX 5211 *From Congo with Love*
Side 1 *Celina
Side 2 *Marcelina / Lulika / *Infidelite
EMI, Nigeria

SAF 50043 *Les Grands Succès Zaïrois Vol 2*
Side 1 Dix makuta
Side 2 Club 53
Sonafric/ Sonodisc, 1977

SAF 50044 *Les Grands Succès Zaïrois Vol 3*
Side 1 *Ngai na boya na boya te
Side 2 *Beyos
Sonafric/ Sonodisc, 1977

MC 005 *Musique du Zaïre Vol 2*
Side 1 *Mouvement Populaire de la Révolution / *Mona opuasi / Amour sans souci
Side 2 Mado/ Bolingo mpasi mawa/ Trop bon couyon
Mwana Congo, Nigeria 1979

BSPOT 007 *Stars of Zaïre, Verse 1*
Side 1 *AZDA (part 1 & 2 transposed)
Black Spot/ Decca, Nigeria, 1980

OMA 102 *The Sound of Kinshasa*
Side 1*Bomboko awuti na New York / Finga mama manu
Side 2 Kokokosaka te na basi
Original Music, 1980

PAN 1001 *Africa For Africa* (Franco, Abeti, Bibi Dens, Pamelo et al, playing together)
Side 1 Africa For Africa
Side 2 Africa For Africa
Discostock/ Makossa / Polygram, 1986

Compact Discs

CRAW 4   *Roots of Rumba Rock* (Franco as session player for Loningisa, pre-OK Jazz playing with Dewayon, Bowane et al)
　　　　　Crammed Discs, 1991

CRAW 7   *Roots of OK Jazz* (Various artistes, as above)
　　　　　*La rumba OK / Anduku Lutshuma / Bolole ya mwasi oyo / Vis-a-vis / Oyo elengi motema / Wa bolingo/ Houlala mopanze /Mabele yo okanisaka / Viclong Julie / Mwana pause / Maria Antonia/ Nabosani ndako / Banzanza / Wapi Yo?/ Osili obebi /Tika bizeti / *Makambo mayiza mazono / *Tika kondima na Zolo / *Meya te, kaka elamba
　　　　　Crammed Discs, 1993

RETRO2CD *Originalité* (See album entry)

Sonodisc series: (Re-packaged material released posthumously including some tracks not previously issued outside Zaïre)

'Merveilles du Passe' series

CD 36501   *1957/1975* Various artistes
　　　　　　Groupo OK Jazz, etc
CD 36502   *Franco et l'OK Jazz*
　　　　　　OK Jazz makila mabe, etc
CD 36505   *Franco et l'OK Jazz*
　　　　　　Ah senor, etc
CD 36508   *Franco et l'OK Jazz*
　　　　　　Na likwanga na seli, etc
CD 36511   *Franco et l'OK Jazz avec Mujos, Simaro & Kwamy*
　　　　　　Linda Linda, etc
CD 36514   *Franco et l'OK Jazz (1970, 71, 72)*
　　　　　　Boma l'heure, etc
CD 36518   *Franco et l'OK Jazz*
　　　　　　Est-ce que oyebi?, etc
CD 36519   *Franco, Simaro et l'OK Jazz (1974-75)*
　　　　　　Alimatou, etc
CD 36520   *Franco, Simaro, Sam Mangwana et l'OK Jazz*

	Ebali ya Zaire, etc
CD 36521	*Franco, Vicky et l'OK Jazz*
	Ngai Marie nzoto ebeba, etc
CD 36522	*Franco et l'OK Jazz (1966-68)*
	Gare a toi Marie, etc
CD 36529	*Franco & OK Jazz (68-71)*
	Koun koue Edo aboyi ngai, etc
CD 36533	*Franco, Vicky & OK Jazz*
	Valenta yoka, etc
CD 36538	*Franco et le TP OK Jazz (72-74)*
	Azda, etc

Franco & le TP OK Jazz

CD 50382	*20ème Anniversaire Vol1*
	Liberté. etc
CD 50383	*20ème Anniversaire Vol2*
	Baninga tokola balingaka ngai te, etc
CD 8461	*Mario*, etc
CD 8462	*Mario Non Stop*
	Réponse de Mario, etc
CD 8473	*Le Grand Maître Franco*
	Testament ya Bowule, etc
CD 8474	*C'est dur la vie d'une femme celibetaire*, etc
CD 8475	*J ai peur*, etc
CD 8476	*Eperduement*, etc
CD 8477	*Live en Europe*
	Cherie oyebisi musi, etc
CD 8482	*Mario*, etc
CD 8489	*Nalingaka yo yo te*, etc
CD 8490	*Princesse Kikou*, etc
CDS 6851	*3 Anniversaire de la Mort du Grand Maître*
	Très impoli, etc
CDS 6852	*Tokoma ba camarade pamba*, etc
CDS 6853	*Tu Vois?*, etc
CDS 6854	*Faut ya comercante*, etc
CDS 6858	*Makambo ezali burreau*, etc

Franco & Rochereau

CDS 6857	*Lettre a M. le Directeur General*, etc
GENCD1003	*L'Evenement*
	Ngungi, etc

'Bana OK' Playing members of OK Jazz, 1956-89

Vocalists:
'Franco', Lokanga La Ndju Pene Luambo Makiadi,
'Le Grand Maître' (1956-89)*
'Rossignol', Landot Philipe (1956-57)*
Vicky Longomba, Besenge Lukuli (1957-70)
Edo Nganga (1957-60)
Celestin Kouka (1957-60)
'Mujos' Mulamba Joseph (1960-66)
Kwamy Munsi, Jean Mossi (1960-66 & 1970-72)
'Djeskin' (1960-66)
'Jojo' (1960-66)
'Flujos' (1960-66)
Lola Checain, Djangi (1963-92)
Boyibanda Baba, Michel 'Michaux' (1964-75)
Youlou Mabiala, Gilbert (1965-72)
Sam Mangwana, Mwana Ndjoku (1972-75)
Josky Kiambukuta, Londa (1973-)
'Wuta Mayi' Blaise Mayanda (1974-82)
Ndombe Opetum, 'Pepe' (1975-)
Ntesa Dalienst, Zitani (1976-89)
Diatho Lukoko, Dialu Antoine (1977-)
Mayukuta, Alex (1978-79)
Djo Mpoyi, Kaninda (1978-)
Nguashi Timbo (1979-81)
Madilu Bialu 'System' (1980-)
Kiwakana Kiala, 'Aime' (1980-92)
Lokombe Ntal (1980-)
Kikame (1982-83)
Siathis (1983)
'Djo Djo' (1984-)
Bonyeme, Denis (1984)
Momy, Momene Mikengo (1985)
Kiesse Diambu 'Wanted' (1985-87)
Malage de Lugendo (1985-89)
Jolie Detta (1986)
Baniel Bambo (1986-89)
Nana Akumu (1986-89)
Lomingo Alida (1988-)
Carlito Lassa, Essou-Doue (1989-)

Guitarists:
Franco*
'De la Lune' Daniel Lubelo (1956-60)*
'Brazzos' Armando Antoine (1957-66 & 1972-)
Leon Bolhen, Bombolo (1960-63)
'Bemi' (1960-61)
'Simaro' Lutumba Ndomamueno 'Masiya',
(1961 & 1963-)
'Fan Fan', Mose Se Sengo (1967-72)
Thierry Mantuika, Kobi (1974-)
'Gege' Yoka Mangaya (1974-88)
Mayaula Mayoni, Freddy (1974-87)
'Michelino', Mavatiku Visi (1975-78)
Gerry Dialungana, Kasia (1976-)
Makonko Kindudi, 'Makos' (1976-)
Monogi Mopia, 'Petit Pierre' (1976-78 & 1984-89)
'Papa Noel' Nono Nedule (1978-88)
'Dizzy' Mandjeku, Lengo (1982-)
Jerry Malekani (1983)
Pela Simba (1983)

Bass:
Roitelet Munganya (1956-60)*
Alphons Epayo (1959-69)
Piccolo Tshiamala (1960-66)
Celi 'Bitchou', Bitchoumanou, Francis (1965-72)
Decca Mpudi, Mpasi Zinza (1970-)
Flavien Makabi Mingini (1976-)
Thoms Toroma Sika (1983)

Drums/percussion:
'Dessouin', Bosuma Bakili (1956-90)*
Pandy Saturnin (1956-58)*
Li Berlin (1956)*
La Monta (1956)*
'Amigo' (1958-59)
Simon Moke (1960-66)
Ntoya Fwala, Pajos Na Ndjili (1969-89)
Ceskin Molenga (1979-83)
Didier Boluwe (1983-84)
'Armando' (1983)

Boffi Banengola (1983)
Kakoma Nado (1984-89)

Saxophones and woodwind:
Jean-Serge Essous (1956-57)*
Lievre (1956)
Edo Lutula (1957)
Nino Malapet (1957)
Isaac Musikewa Siki (1957-90)
'Verckys' Kiamuangana Mateta (1962-69)
Albino Kalombo (1960-)
Dele Pedro (1964-84)
Lunama Mbemba (1965-)
'Rondot' Kawaka, Kasongo wa Kasongo (1969-)
Emompo Loway, 'Deyesse' (1975-77)
'Matalanza Sax' (1979-83)
'Rubens' Kunsita Madiata Ngo (1982-92)

Trumpets:
Willy Mbembe, 'Willys' (1957-59)
Barami-Miranda, Nkuta-a-Zowa (1971-89)
'Vieux' Kalloux (1971-)
Kapitena Kasongo (1971-84)
Adamo Seye Kadimoke (1971-)
Chandala Kosuana (1976-80)
Zinga Ngole (1980-)
Fwamba Musanga (1984-86)
Mukula-Muindila-Muki (1984-89)
Bilolo-Mutshipayi (1984-89)

(* denotes orginal members)

Chronology

1938 François Luambo Makiadi born July 6, Sona Bata, near Mbanza Ngungu in Bas-Zaïre. First son of Emongo Joseph and Mbonga Makiesse. Family move to Leopoldville.

1948 Father died. Mother trading at Wenze ya Bayaka market, François attracts customers with home-made guitar.

1949 Joins folk group Watam, led by Paul Ebengo 'Dewayon'.

1950 Loningisa and Opika studios both started by Greek proprietors, following Ngoma.

1953 Belgian Bill Alexandre imports electric guitars. Recruits singer Vicky Longomba, guitarist Brazzos and bassist Roitelet. First recordings of African Jazz for Opika. 'Luambo François' makes debut recording for Loningisa. House bandleader Bowane nicknames him 'Franco'.

1954 Franco makes debut at dance with studio equipment.

1955 Band play Omer Kashama's OK Bar. Franco, Essous(s), De la Lune(g), Roitelet(b), Pandy, LiBerlin, La Monta, Dessouin(d/p), Lievre(f), Rossignol(v)

1956 June 6. Inauguration of OK Jazz at Sunday matinee.

1957 First OK Jazz recordings with Vicky. Essous and Rossignol leave. New line up: Edo Nganga, Celestin Kouka (voc), Brazzos(rg), Isaac Musekiwa(s), Edo Lutula(cl), Willy (tr).

1958 Franco jailed for motoring offence. Returns home to hero's welcome. Proclaimed Sorcerer of the Guitar.

1960 Congo independence year. Vicky and Brazzos leave for Europe with African Jazz. The singer replaced by Mujos. Franco pioneered slow rock beat to counteract cha cha cha.

1961 Political problems with Congo-Brazzaville. Some musicians return home. Civil War. Lumumba assassinated. OK Jazz recording in Belgium. Simaro Lutumba joins for the sessions and one year later returns as a permanent member.

1962 Singer Kwamy and saxophonist Verckys join.

1964 OK Jazz revival as Edo, De la Lune and Vicky return with Boyibanda. Now about 20 strong, band makes first foreign tour to Nigeria. Sax player Dele Pedro joins.

1965 Mobutu takes control of country. Franco and band define the mature OK Jazz style. Youlou Mabiala joins front line.

1966 Leopoldville renamed Kinshasa. TV station opens. OK Jazz play Festival of African Arts, Senegal. Kwamy forms Orchèstre Révolution. Franco and Kwamy do battle in song.

1968 Fan Fan joins from Orchèstre Révolution. Verckys leaves.

1969 James Brown plays Kinshasa. Copyright agency set up.

1970 Franco's brother Bavon Marie-Marie killed in car crash: Franco devastated. Rochereau plays at Paris Olympia.

1971 Four trumpets and dance troupe added to OK Jazz. Kwamy and Mujos return. Franco marries Annie Mbule. Name of country changes from Congo-Kinshasa to Zaïre.

1972 Mobutu decrees Authenticité programme after returning from China. Franco takes full name L'Okanga La Ndju Pene Luambo Makiadi. Vicky leaves to form Orchèstre Lovy. Guitarist Gege Mangaya joins. Sam Mangwana joins.

1973 Josky joins. Tour of Zambia, Tanzania, Guinea, Congo, etc

1974 Wuta Mayi joins. Franco building Un-Deux-Trois, entertainment complex. Ali-Foreman heavyweight fight. Masekela, Dibango, James Brown, BB King, play festival.

1975 Sam Mangwana goes solo. Michelino, Ndombe defect from Afrisa. Empompo Loway and others join OK Jazz.

1976 Franco decorated as Officer of National Order of Leopard.

1977 OK Jazz play at Lagos Festac.

1978 First European Tour. Dalienst, Djo Mpoyi join. Franco and several of the band jailed for singing obscene songs.

1979 Tour Gabon, Cameroon, West Africa and Europe.

1980 Franco consecrated as Grand Maître. Moved to Europe, set up labels, Visa 80, Edipop, Choc. Madilu System joins.

1981 In Kinshasa band run by Simaro. Lokombe joins. Franco converted to Islam, taking name Aboubakar Sidiki.

1982 Made up feud with Tabu Ley and recorded together. Dizzy Mandjeku (ex-Afrisa) and Papa Noel join.

1984 Toured USA. British debut, and only show, London. Play Uganda

1985 *Mario* brings another revival. Malage joins. Tour of Europe.

1986 30th anniversary in Kenya and Zambia. Introduced female singers Jolie Detta, Nana and Baniel. Second visit to USA.

1987 *Attention Na Sida* recorded in Brussels without OK Jazz.

1988 Franco ailing in Kinshasa. Problems with band. Final recording sessions with Mangwana.

1989 Attempts to play Europe. Malage, Lokombe, Dalienst leave. Carlito joins. Franco plays last gig in Holland. OK Jazz play London without him.

October 12, died in hospital at Namur, Belgium. Body flown home accompanied by Musekiwa and Dessouin. Four days of national mourning. After lying in state at the Palais du Peuple, Franco buried in Gombe cemetery on October 17.

Bibliography

Single issue publications on Franco & OK Jazz

Franco & TP OK Jazz in the USA, American tour programme, 1983.

Franco, Kiswahili tour souvenir, Linguaphone Publications, Nairobi, 1986

Ewens, Graeme. *Luambo Franco and 30 Years of OK Jazz*, Off The Record Press, London, 1986

L'As des As, special anniversary issue, Kinshasa, October, 1990,

Mbamba Toko W. *Autopsie de la chanson de Luambo Makiadi Franco*, Uhuru, Paris, 1991

Articles on Franco & OK Jazz

Anon. 'La vedette du mois -- Luambo Makiadi' *Afro Music*, Oct 1976

Andrianirado, Sennen. 'Franco: Le Chanteur qui Derengeait', *Afrique Magazine*, Dec. 1989

Badi, Nzunga. 'Franco et l'OK Jazz', *Antilles Afrique*, June 1983

Essomba, Pilippe. 'Franco, le roi de la musique zaïroise' *Bingo*, June 1978

Ewens, Graeme. 'King of the Congo Sound', *Africa Music*, Sept. 1983

—— 'Keeping up the Congo Beat', *New African*, Dec. 1983

—— 'Franco - a True Giant', *Africa Music*, Sept. 1984

—— 'The Sorcerer of the Guitar', *Africa Beat*, Spring 1985

—— 'Thirty Years of OK Jazz', *West Africa*, 30 June 1986

—— 'Franco sings AIDS message' *The Daily Nation*, Kenya, 27 June 1987

—— 'Franco's no-show', *West Africa*, 20 March, 1989

—— 'Zaïre in mourning for musical giant Franco', *The Guardian*, London, 14 Oct. 1989

—— 'Passing of the Sorcerer', *West Africa*, 23 Oct. 1989

—— 'Le Grand Maître est Mort, Vive le Grand Maître', *Straight No Chaser*, Winter, 1989

—— 'The Guide is Gone', *New African*, Nov. 1990

—— 'The Franco Files' *World Beat*, Nov. 1990

Glass, Randall F. 'Not Quite Congo Heaven', *Village Voice*, New York, 13 Dec. 1983

Iyolela, Oissa-Fumnkany. 'Franco a Coeur Ouvert', *Zaïre Digest*, No5, Jan/Feb. 1986

Jumba, Allan. 'A Dream Come True', *African World*, April 1984

Kaba, Ousmane. 'Franco Superstar', *Africa International*, 1986

—— 'Franco Je n'ai pas le Sida', *Africa International*, Oct. 1989

Kelaka, Luya Laye. 'Le torchon brule entre Luambo et Tabu Ley', *Stars* No2, Kinshasa, July 1988

Mbemba, Lusende. 'Luambo Makiadi et le TP OK Jazz: 30 Ans de Complicite',*Zaïre Digest* No5, Jan/Feb. 1987

Misser, Francois. 'People: Franco', *New African*, Dec. 1989

Ngoy, Tonton. 'Franco, Vive les Femmes !',*Afrique Elite*, Sept. 1986

Opanga, Kwendo & Kariuki, John, 'Franco Fever'. *The Weekly Review*, Kenya, June 6, 1986

Pareless, Jon. 'Franco Makes New York Debut Friday',*New York Times*, 30 Nov. 1983

—— 'The Influential and Joyous Legacy of Zaïre's Franco', *New York Times*, 29 Oct. 1989

Prince, Rob. 'Le Grand Maître', *Folk Roots*, Jan/Feb. 1990

Sobo, Elizabeth. 'Luambo Makiadi, 1938-89; A Remembrance', *The Beat*, Vol 8, No 6, 1989

Stapleton, Chris. 'Heavyweight Champion of the World' *Black Music and Jazz Review*, June, 1984

Stewart, Gary. 'Toujours OK', *The Beat*, Vol 8, No 6, 1989

Books with reference to Congo-Zaïrean music

Bemba, Sylvain.*50 Ans de Musique du Congo-Zaïre*, Presence Africaine, Paris, 1984

Bender, Wolfgang. *Sweet Mother: Modern African Music*, Chicago, 1991

Dibango, Manu. *Trois Kilos du Café*, Lieu Commune, Paris, 1989

Dzokanga, Mwana Mboka.*Proverbes, chansons et contes Lingala*, Paris c. 1984

Ewens, Graeme. *Africa O-Ye! A Celebration of African Music*, Guinness, London, 1991. (Da Capo, USA, 1992)

Graham, Ronnie *Stern's Guide to Contemporary African Music*, Zwan/ Off The Record Press, London, 1988 (Da Capo, USA)

——*The World of African Music*, Pluto Press/Research Associates, 1992

Hommage à Grand Kalle, Editions Lokole, Kinshasa, 1985

Lonoh, Malange Bokelenge. *Essai de commentaire de la Musique Congolaise Moderne*, Kinshasa, 1963, 1969, 1970

——*Negritude, Africanité et Musique Africaine*. Centre de Recherches Pedagogiques, Kinshasa, 1990

Roberts, John Storm. *Black Music of Two Worlds*, Original Music, USA, 1982 (Morrow, 1974)

―――*The Latin Tinge,* Original Music, 1985
Stapleton, Chris & May, Chris,*African All Stars - The Pop Music of a Continent*, Quartet, London, 1987
Stewart, Gary.*Breakout*, Chicago, 1992

Articles and papers on Zaïrean music and culture

Bokanga, Ekanga Botombele.*Cultural Policy in the Republic of Zaïre*, UNESCO, 1976
Conseil Francophone de la Chanson. 'La Chanson au Zaïre', *Un Autre Chanson*, 29, Belgium,Dec/Mar 1990
Debhonvapi, Olema. 'Societé Zaïrois dans le Mirroir de la Chanson Populaire',*Canadian Journal of African Studies* Vol 18/1, 1984
Jacquemin, Jean-Pierre. 'Ils ont tout de même le sens des mots!', *Un Autre Chanson*, No29, Dec/Mar. 1990
Kazadi, Pierre. 'Trends of 19th Century and 20th Century Music in Congo-Zaïre,*African Music*, 1970
―――'Congo Music- Africa's favourite Beat',*Africa Report*, 1971
Kazadi wa Mukuna. 'The Origins of Zaïrean Urban Music: A Socioeconomic Aspect'*African Urban Studies*, No 6, 1979-80
――― The Genesis of Urban Music in Zaïre, *African Music*, 1992
――― L'Evolution de la musique urbaine au Zaïre durant les dix premiers années de la Deuxième République (1965-1975), *Aquarium*, Paris, 1993
Putman, John. 'Yesterday's Congo, Today's Zaïre',*National Geographic Magazine*, March, 1973
Stapleton, Chris. 'Soukous Without Tears', *The Wire*, 1985
Tshonga-Onyumbe. 'Les problemes socio-economiques dans la chanson Zaïroise moderne',*Zaïre-Afrique*, No 205, May, 1986

Historical background and general reading

Gide, André, *Travels in the Congo*, Alfred A. Knopf, 1929
Gunter, John.*Inside Africa*, Harper, New York, 1955
Kanza, Thomas.*Conflict in the Congo*, Penguin, 1972
Legum, Colin.*Congo Disaster*, Penguin, 1961
Lumumba, Patrice.*Congo, My Country*, London, 1962
Morel, E.D.*Red Rubber, The Story of the Rubber Slave Trade on the Congo,* Fisher Unwin, London, 1906
Payne, John.*Universal Geography*, Dublin, 1794
Stanley, H.M.*The Congo and the Founding of its Free State*, Samson Low, London, 1885

INDEX

Picture credits:
G. Ewens: pp 12, 15, 26,
146, 191, 205, 225
Chris Stapleton: 21. Bill
Alexandre: 63. L'As des

As: 46, 245. Crammed
Discs/Vincent Kenis: 91.
Pathé-EMI:108, 132.
Ernest Potters: 35,159.

Zaïre Digest: 182, 198.
The Nation, Kenya: 194.
Francois Misser: 217.
ASM:220. African: 82, 123